Planning Appeals:
Practice and Materials

Planning Appeals:
Practice and Materials

Richard Kimblin QC

Bloomsbury Professional
LONDON · DUBLIN · EDINBURGH · NEW YORK · NEW DELHI · SYDNEY

BLOOMSBURY PROFESSIONAL
Bloomsbury Publishing Plc
41–43 Boltro Road, Haywards Heath, RH16 1BJ, UK

BLOOMSBURY and the Diana logo are trademarks of Bloomsbury Publishing Plc

Copyright © Bloomsbury Professional, 2020

All rights reserved. No part of this publication may be reproduced or transmitted in any form or by any means, electronic or mechanical, including photocopying, recording, or any information storage or retrieval system, without prior permission in writing from the publishers.

While every care has been taken to ensure the accuracy of this work, no responsibility for loss or damage occasioned to any person acting or refraining from action as a result of any statement in it can be accepted by the authors, editors or publishers.

All UK Government legislation and other public sector information used in the work is Crown Copyright ©. All House of Lords and House of Commons information used in the work is Parliamentary Copyright ©. This information is reused under the terms of the Open Government Licence v3.0 (http://www.nationalarchives.gov.uk/doc/open-government-licence/version/3) except where otherwise stated.

All Eur-lex material used in the work is © European Union, http://eur-lex.europa.eu/, 1998-2020.

British Library Cataloguing-in-Publication Data

A catalogue record for this book is available from the British Library.

ISBN:	PB:	978-1-52651-529-2
	ePDF:	978-1-52651-531-5
	ePub:	978-1-52651-530-8

Typeset by Evolution Design and Digital Ltd (Kent)
Printed and bound by CPI Group (UK) Ltd, Croydon, CR0 4YY

To find out more about our authors and books visit www.bloomsburyprofessional.com. Here you will find extracts, author information, details of forthcoming events and the option to sign up for our newsletters

Preface

Participation in a public inquiry or a hearing is a privilege. It is one means by which all may see the rule of law in action, before an independent tribunal, applying a fair and transparent system. It offers an opportunity to persuade, to challenge and to resolve disputes. This book seeks to navigate the practical implementation of those ideals for the busy practitioner and decision-maker.

Turning to the practical, the front cover includes a constraints plan, wonderfully prepared by Clive Self at CSA. It captures the range of issues which a substantial appeal may have to grapple with: heritage in the form of a World Heritage Site and a cathedral, a SSSI, flood risk, and minerals impacts. This richness of the attributes of England and Wales combined with the needs of its thriving population, make the appeals system a guiding force in the implementation of whatever planning legislation the government of the day may prefer.

I have only been able to draw together the chapters of this book because of the opportunities so generously provided by numerous participants in the planning system. I record my thanks to them all. The front cover includes a decision bearing the name of Ben Linscott, who was Group Manager at the Planning Inspectorate during much of my time appearing frequently as counsel for the Secretary of State. He often 'marked my homework' via the Treasury Solicitor's emails announcing that *'The GM comments ...'*. He provided a terrific insight into the complex framework which makes up the appeals system: a statutory scheme, procedural rules, case law in planning and environmental law and in public law more generally, policy, guidance and professional practice and codes of conduct.

James Corbet Burcher contributes enormously to the profession, particularly through PEBA, and in similar fashion, gave freely of his time in commenting on the chapters on remote events and *Rosewell*. Nina Pindham does likewise through UKELA, with equal lack of fanfare. I thank both of them for their help.

I am particularly grateful to Lord Justice Lindblom for taking the time and care to read and engage with the themes of the book, then to illuminate them, as he has, in his Foreword.

Richard Kimblin QC
August 2020

Foreword

This is an excellent and timely book. Unlike others on planning law, it concentrates on appeals from local planning authorities to the Secretary of State: how they are made, how they are managed, and how they are won and lost.

Such appeals are a fundamental part of the statutory scheme of planning control in this country. Most are determined by Inspectors, only a small number by the Secretary of State himself. Of those decided by Inspectors, the written representations procedure accounts for all but a tiny fraction. But as Richard Kimblin QC demonstrates well, whether the decision is an Inspector's or the Secretary of State's, and whether it is made after a public inquiry or hearing or on written representations, the value of the statutory right of appeal and the quality of the decision itself depend not only on the procedures set in place by the legislative framework but also on principles of fairness, consistency and transparency carried forward from the report of the Franks Committee in 1957 and refined in modern practice.

The book explains how good practice, government guidance and codes of professional conduct can maintain an efficient system of appeals. Contesting a planning appeal, as we are shown, requires – on both sides – realism and good sense. Decision-making is improved by the ability of professional teams to present a case crisply, and the willingness of expert witnesses to give solid evidence on which the decision-maker can rely. Like a judge dealing with advocates' submissions on the law, Inspectors in planning appeals can expect participants to help them in reaching the right decision.

Another powerful theme is the need for economy in the drafting and testing of evidence, and in composing submissions. In Chapter 3 – on 'Written evidence and representations' – we find a section headed 'Drafting – spending longer producing less text'. Succinctness and clarity are welcomed by Inspectors, and do not prevent a proper treatment of the subject matter. To underline the point, the book cites Winston Churchill's one-page memorandum on 'Brevity'. Its lucid explanation of the purpose and utility of oral evidence – in Chapter 5, 'Inquiries' – will assist both witnesses and Inspectors, and lawyers too. So will its discussion of the role and responsibilities of the advocate. As it emphasises, carefully prepared and well directed cross-examination serves to sharpen the matters in dispute. This is a benefit of an adversarial process, an advantage over the merely inquisitorial.

There is a great deal more to commend in 'Planning Appeals'. Richard Kimblin has brought together the relevant rules and practice, and has provided much insight into the system of appeals as it operates today. His book will strengthen the literature of planning. I wish it success.

The Rt Hon Lord Justice Lindblom
August 2020

Contents

Preface		*v*
Foreword		*vii*
List of Abbreviations		*xiii*
Table of Statutes		*xv*
Table of Statutory Instruments		*xvii*
Table of Cases		*xxi*
Chapter 1	**The scope of appeals**	**1**
	Why appeal?	1
	What is an appeal?	1
	Appealing against what?	3
	By whom?	5
	Recovery and call-in by a Secretary of State	6
	Recovery	6
	Call-in	7
Chapter 2	**Commencement**	**10**
	Making the appeal	10
	DMPO requirements	14
	Validity	15
	The procedure rules	17
	Commencement in practice: mode of appeal, statement of case and statement of common ground	20
	Tables of timescales (as at April 2020)	21
	Testing	24
	Complexity	24
	Local interest	24
	Statements of common ground	25
	Statements of case and hearing statements	28
	Enforcement – grounds of appeal	30
	Practical pointers	30
Chapter 3	**Written evidence and representations**	**32**
	What are you trying to show?	32
	Main issues	32
	The positive case	33
	Other issues	34
	A case example	34
	How are you going to show it?	36
	Audiences	37
	Professional duties and declarations by experts	38
	Codes of Professional Conduct	38
	Fee agreements	40
	Drafting – spending longer producing less text	41

Contents

Brevity		41
Structure		41
A specialist's proof – facts, assessments and opinions		43
Issues within issues		45
Format and practicality		46
Core documents		47
Summary proofs		47

Chapter 4 Managing appeals and Rosewell — 49

Appeal timetables	49
Summary of deadlines	50
Written representations	50
Hearings	51
Rosewell Review	51
Scope	51
Focus and recommendations	52
Case management conferences	53
An effective and efficient Rosewell inquiry	56

Chapter 5 Inquiries — 58

The structure and purpose of the inquiry	58
Types of inquiry and running orders	58
Section 78 appeals and call-in inquiries	58
Enforcement	59
CPO, highways, Transport and Works Act	59
Appearances	61
From opening remarks to closing submissions	62
Oral evidence	64
Effective evidence in chief	66
Objectives of cross examination and its conduct	69
A right to cross examine?	69
Purpose	70
Practice	71
Parameters	73
Inspector's questions and third parties	74
Re-examination	75
Conditions, obligations and site visits	76
Procedural fairness	78
Practical matters	81
Interested persons	81
Inquiry rooms	81
Welsh language	82
Adjournment	82

Chapter 6 Hearings — 84

Overview	84
Rules	84
Notification of hearing	84
Appearances	85
Inquisitorial proceedings	85
The Inspector's duty at a hearing	86
Late evidence	88

		Format, roles and being effective	90
		Conditions and site visit	91
Chapter 7		**Remote events and electronic documents**	**92**
		The issues	92
		Digital documents	95
		Virtual events	99
		Site visits	101
Chapter 8		**Costs**	**102**
		Legal basis	102
		Aims, objectives and purpose	103
		Scope and nature of the costs jurisdiction	105
		Two different regimes – planning appeals and CPO etc	105
		Compulsory purchase and other objections based on property rights	107
		Unreasonable behaviour	109
		Procedure	110
		Current guidance	110
		Examples of costs decisions	115
		Call-in	118
		Interested parties	118
		Amount of the award	118
Chapter 9		**Applications and appeals against Secretary of State decisions**	**120**
		Rights	120
		Venue and timescales	121
		Parties	122
		Costs	123
Chapter 10		**Where next?**	**125**
		Full use of digital documentation	125
		Proportionate and careful use of telephone and video	126
		Integration and transparency	127
		Professional teams	130

APPENDICES

	1	Town and Country Planning Act 1990, ss 70, 77 and 78 (as amended)	131
	2	Town and Country Planning (Development Management Procedure) (England) Order 2015 (SI 2015/595)	137
	3	Town and Country Planning Appeals (Determination by Inspectors) (Inquiries Procedure) (England) Rules 2000 (SI 2000/1625) (as amended)	141
	4	Town and Country Planning (Hearings Procedure) (England) Rules 2000 (SI 2000/1626) (as amended)	162
	5	Town and Country Planning (Enforcement) (Determination by Inspectors) (Inquiries Procedure) (England) Rules 2002 (SI 2002/2685) (as amended)	179
	6	Town and Country Planning (Referred Applications and Appeals Procedure) (Wales) Regulations 2017 (SI 2017/544)	197

Contents

7	Timescales – Rosewell	238
8	Plan of an inquiry room	239
9	Bar Council Code of Conduct – extracts	240
10	RTPI Code of Professional Conduct	247
11	RICS Rules of Conduct for Members	257

Index **260**

List of Abbreviations

BSB	Bar Standards Board
CMC	case management conference
CPO	compulsory purchase order
CPR	Civil Procedure Rules
DMPO 2015	Town and Country Planning (Development Management Procedure) (England) Order 2015, SI 2015/595
DMP(W)O 2012	Town and Country Planning (Development Management Procedure) (Wales) Order 2012, SI 2012/801
Hazardous Substances Act	Planning (Hazardous Substances) Act 1990
Listed Buildings Act	Planning (Listed Buildings and Conservation Areas) Act 1990
LPA	local planning authority
NPPG	National Planning Practice Guidance
PIM	Pre-Inquiry meeting
PINS	Planning Inspectorate
RICS	Royal Institution of Chartered Surveyors
RTPI	Royal Town Planning Institute
TCPA 1990	Town and Country Planning Act 1990

Table of Statutes

A

Acquisition of Land Act 1981
   s 13A(1) 8.17
Acquisition of Land (Authorisation
   Procedure) Act 1946 .... 5.91

B

Business and Planning Act 2020
   s 20 .... 2.35; 4.38

C

Criminal Justice and Courts Act 2015
   s 91 .... 9.05
   Sch 16 .... 9.05

G

Gas Act 1965 .... 1.07

H

Highways Act 1980
   s 26 .... 8.19
      118–119A 8.19
Housing Act 1957
   Pt III (ss 42–75) 5.91
Housing and Planning Act 1986
   s 43 .... 8.18

L

Local Government Act 1972
   s 125 .... 8.18
      250 .... 8.02
         (2), (3) 8.01, 8.28
         (4) 8.01
         (5) 8.01, 8.04, 8.11, 8.16

N

National Parks and Access to the Countryside Act 1949
   s 65 .... 8.19

P

Planning Act 2008 .... 2.34; 7.03
Planning and Compensation Act 1991
   s 22 .... 8.14
   Sch 2 .... 8.14

Planning and Compulsory Purchase Act 2004
   s 8 .... 9.05
      38(6) 1.06
Planning (Hazardous Substances) Act 1990
   s 14, 15 .... 8.14, 8.18
      17(1) 8.18
      20 .... 2.24; 8.14
      21 .... 2.05, 2.24; 8.14
      22 .... 9.05
      25 .... 8.14
Planning (Listed Buildings and Conservation Areas) Act 1990 .. 8.02; 9.04
   s 12 .... 2.24; 8.14
      19 .... 2.24
      20 .... 1.09; 2.05, 2.21, 2.24; 6.02; 8.14
      23, 24 .... 8.14, 8.18
      26K 2.22
      29 .... 6.04
      33, 34 .... 8.14
      39 .... 1.09; 2.05, 2.22, 2.24; 8.14
         (2) 2.05
      62, 63 .... 9.05
      74(2)(a) 8.14
         (3) 2.24; 8.14

T

Town and Country Planning Act 1990 .... 1.15; 2.09, 2.34; 5.43; 7.03
   s 62(4A) 2.13
      62A 2.26
      62ZB 2.12
         (6) 2.12
      70 .... 1.08; 2.15
      70A 2.02
      70B, 70C 2.02
      72(1) 2.15
      77 .... 1.15, 1.19; 2.02, 2.21, 2.24; 8.14, 8.37
         (1), (2) 1.23
         (5) 1.23

Table of Statutes

Town and Country Planning Act 1990 – *contd*
s 78 .... 1.05, 1.08, 1.14; 2.02, 2.05, 2.14, 2.21, 2.24, 2.41, 2.65, 2.67; 4.02, 4.21; 5.03, 5.07, 5.11; 6.02, 6.04, 6.11; 8.14
   (1), (2).................................... 2.05
   (3A), (4A), (4BA), (4BB)...... 2.03
79(1) 1.05; 2.02, 2.14, 2.17
   (2) 6.11
   (3) 2.02
   (6) 2.15, 2.17
90(2A) 1.12
95 .... 8.14
97, 98...................................... 8.14, 8.18
102, 103.................................. 8.14, 8.18
106........................ 5.23, 5.84; 6.19, 6.27
139, 140.. 8.14
174..................... 1.09; 2.02, 2.06, 2.22, 2.24, 2.65; 8.14
   (1) 1.16
   (6) 1.16
177 .... 2.02
195 .... 1.09; 2.09, 2.10, 2.22, 2.24; 8.14
198(3)(c).. 2.24
   (4) 2.24
   (b)....................................... 8.14
208 .... 2.05, 2.23, 2.24; 8.14
   (2) 2.05
217... 2.24
220............................... 2.24; 8.14, 8.18
Pt X (ss 247–261)........................ 8.14
s 253(2)(c)..................................... 2.02
266(1)(b)....................................... 2.02

Town and Country Planning Act 1990 – *contd*
s 284 .... 9.05
286 .... 1.15
287 .... 9.05
288 .... 9.03, 9.05
   (1), (1A)............................... 9.13
   (2) 9.13
   (10)(b).................................... 2.02
289 .... 9.03, 9.10
319A 2.34
   (2) 2.35; 4.38; 10.15
   (4) 2.35
   (7)(b)....................................... 2.02
319B 2.34
   (4).. 2.35
   (7).. 1.23
   (b)....................................... 2.02
323 .... 2.08
327A 2.15
333(5) 2.02
Sch 5... 8.14
Sch 6... 8.02
   para 4..................................... 8.01
Sch 9.. 8.14, 8.18
Transport and Works Act 1992......... 1.13; 8.19; 9.04
s 1–5... 1.12
11 .... 5.08
22 .... 9.04, 9.05
Tribunals and Inquiries Act 1992..... 2.08, 2.09; 9.04
s 9 .... 2.08

W

Wildlife and Countryside Act 1981
s 29... 8.19

Table of Statutory Instruments

C

Civil Procedure Rules 1998, SI 1998/
   3132.. 9.06
   r 44.2 .... 9.15
   45.43 .... 9.15
   Pt 54 .... 9.09
   PD 54E 9.09
Compulsory Purchase by Local Authorities (Inquiries Procedure) Rules 1962, SI 1962/1424   5.91
   r 4(4) 5.91
   7(5) 5.91
Compulsory Purchase (Inquiries Procedure) Rules 2007, SI 2007/
   3617 .... 5.10
Compulsory Purchase (Inquiries Procedure) (Wales) Rules 2010, SI 2010/3015 .... 5.10
Conservation of Habitats and Species Regulations 2010, SI 2010/490.   2.39

E

Electricity Generating Stations and Overhead Lines (Inquiries Procedure) (England and Wales) Rules 2007, SI 2007/841 .... 5.10

N

Network Rail (Ordsall Chord) Order 2015, SI 2015/780 .... 1.12

P

Planning (Hazardous Substances) Regulations 2015, SI 2015/627
   reg 13(1) 2.05
Planning (Hazardous Substances) (Wales) Regulations 2015, SI 2015/1597
   reg 13(1) 2.05
Planning (Listed Buildings and Conservation Areas) Regulations 1990, SI 1990/1519
   reg 8 .... 2.05
Planning (Listed Buildings and Conservation Areas) (Wales) Regulations 2012, SI 2012/793
   reg 8 .... 2.05

T

Town and Country Planning Appeals (Determination by Inspectors) (Inquiries Procedure) (England) Rules 2000, SI 2000/1625 .... 2.20; 5.03
   r 4 .... 3.24
   6 .... 6.19
   (8) 2.61; 3.05
   7 .... 3.18
   10 .... 5.19
   (6) 5.19
   11 .... 5.23; 6.19
   12(1), (2), (4) 6.30
   14 .... 5.37
   16 .... 4.36, 4.38
   (1) 4.37
   (2) 5.20, 5.21
   (4) 5.03, 5.24
   (5) 4.37; 5.41
   (6) 5.36, 5.41, 5.53
   (9) 5.41
   (11) 5.14
   17(1) 5.87
   (2)(b) 5.87
   (3) 5.83
   (4) 5.87
Town and Country Planning (Appeals) (Written Representations Procedure and Advertisements) (England) (Amendment) Regulations 2013, SI 2013/2114 .... 2.20
Town and Country Planning (Appeals) (Written Representations Procedure) (England) Regulations 2009, SI 2009/452 .... 2.20
   Pt 2 (regs 11–16) 4.10
Town and Country Planning (Control of Advertisements) (England) Regulations 2007, SI 2007/783 .... 8.14, 8.18
   reg 15 .... 1.23; 2.05
   17 .... 2.05
   Sch 4 .... 2.05

Table of Statutory Instruments

Town and Country Planning (Determination of Appeal Procedure) (Prescribed Period) (England) Regulations 2009, SI 2009/454	2.34
Town and Country Planning (Determination of Procedure) (Wales) Order 2014, SI 2014/2773	
art 2	1.23
Town and Country Planning (Development Management Procedure) (England) Order 2015, SI 2015/595	2.19, 2.25
art 12	2.13
13, 14	2.07
35(1)(b)	3.05
37	1.14; 2.03
(2)(b)–(d)	2.05
(8)	2.41
Town and Country Planning (Development Management Procedure) (Wales) Order 2012, SI 2012/801	2.03, 2.10
art 24(1)(b)	3.05
26	2.05
26B	2.09
Town and Country Planning (Enforcement) (Determination by Inspectors) (Inquiries Procedure) (England) Rules 2002, SI 2002/2685	2.20; 5.06, 5.08
r 17(6)	5.36
(11)	5.14
18	5.83
Town and Country Planning (Enforcement) (Hearings Procedure) (England) Rules 2002, SI 2002/2684	2.20; 6.02
r 2	2.55
6(1)	6.05
(5), (6)	6.06
11(1), (2)	6.08
Town and Country Planning (Enforcement) (Inquiries Procedure) (England) Rules 2002, SI 2002/2686	2.20
Town and Country Planning (Enforcement) (Written Representations Procedure) (England) Regulations 2002, SI 2002/2683	2.20
Town and Country Planning (General Permitted Development) (England) Order 2015, SI 2015/596	
Schedule	2.16
Town and Country Planning General Regulations 1992, SI 1992/1492	
reg 3	1.15
5(1)(a)	1.15
Town and Country Planning (Hearings Procedure) (England) Rules 2000, SI 2000/1626	2.20, 2.23; 6.02
r 2	2.56
7(1)	6.05
(2), (5), (6)	6.06
9	6.07
11(1), (2)	6.08
Town and Country Planning (Inquiries Procedure) (England) Rules 2000, SI 2000/1624	2.20, 2.23
r 14(3)	5.41
15(4)	5.03
Town and Country Planning (Inquiries Procedures) Rules 1974, SI 1974/419	5.91
Town and Country Planning (Major Infrastructure Project Inquiries Procedure) (England) Rules 2005, SI 2005/2115	2.27
Town and Country Planning (Referred Applications and Appeals Procedure) (Wales) Regulations 2017, SI 2017/544	2.10, 2.20, 2.41; 5.04; 6.04, 6.06, 6.17
reg 3(1)	6.05
12	6.17
24	4.14
Pt 5 (regs 26–34)	6.05
reg 29(1)	6.05
(3)–(5)	6.06
31	6.07
33(1)–(3)	6.08
39	5.14
44(1)	5.37
45	5.20
(6)	5.42
(7)	5.36
(8)(b)	5.53
(9)	5.36
(15)	5.24
Town and Country Planning (Section 62A Applications) (Written Representations and Miscellaneous Provisions) Regulations 2013, SI 2013/2142	2.26
Town and Country Planning (Validation Appeals Procedure) (Wales) Regulations 2016, SI 2016/60	2.12
reg 3, 4, 6	2.12

Table of Statutory Instruments

Transport and Works (Applications and Objections Procedure) (England and Wales) Rules 2006, SI 2006/1466.................. 1.12

Transport and Works (Inquiries Procedure) Rules 2004, SI 2004/2018............................ 1.12; 2.27; 5.08

Table of Cases

B

Bernard Wheatcroft Ltd v Secretary of State for the Environment [1982] 43 P & CR 233, (1981) 257 EG 934 .... 3.59
Bolton MDC v Secretary of State for the Environment (Costs) [1995] 1 WLR 1176, [1996] 1 All ER 184, [1995] 7 WLUK 63 .... 9.15
Bushell v Secretary of State for the Environment [1981] AC 75, [1980] 3 WLR 22, [1980] 2 All ER 608 .... 5.42, 5.100

C

Campaign to Protect Rural England – Kent Branch v Secretary of State for Communities & Local Government [2019] EWCA Civ 1230, [2020] 1 WLR 352 .... 9.15
Castleford Homes Ltd v Secretary of State for Environment, Transport & the Regions [2001] EWHC Admin 77, [2001] PLCR 29 .... 5.94

D

Dingley v Chief Constable of Strathclyde Police (No 1) 1998 SC 548, 1998 GWD 13-677 .... 3.26
Dyason v Secretary of State for the Environment, Transport & the Regions (No 1) (1998) 75 P & CR 506, [1998] 2 PLR 54 .... 6.11

E

Energy Solutions EU Ltd v Nuclear Decommissioning Authority [2016] EWHC 1988 (TCC), [2016] BLR 625 .... 5.28
Engbers v Secretary of State for Communities & Local Government [2016] EWCA Civ 1183, [2017] JPL 489 .... 3.15

F

Factortame Ltd v Secretary of State for the Environment, Transport & the Regions (Costs) (No 2) [2002] EWCA Civ 932, [2003] QB 381 .... 3.46
Fairmount Investments Ltd v Secretary of State for the Environment [1976] 1 WLR 1255, [1976] 2 All ER 865 .... 5.91, 5.92

G

Gardiner & Theobald LLP v Jackson (Valuation Officer) [2018] UKUT 253 (LC), [2018] 5 Costs LR 987 .... 3.43, 3.46
Geall v Secretary of State for the Environment, Transport & the Regions (1999) 78 P & CR 264, [1999] 2 PLR 1 .... 2.11

H

Hopkins Developments Ltd v Secretary of State for Communities & Local Governmnet [2014] EWCA Civ 470, [2014] PTSR 1145 .... 5.98

K

Kennedy v Cordia (Services) LLP [2016] UKSC 6, [2016] 1 WLR 597, 2016 SC (UKSC) 59 .... 3.43

Table of Cases

M

Manchester City Council v Secretary of State for the Environment [1988] JPL 774.... 8.20, 8.21

Maximus Networks Ltd v Secretary of State for Communities & Local Government [2018] EWHC 1933 (Admin), [2019] PTSR 312 .... 2.16, 2.17

Moore v Secretary of State for Communities & Local Government [2015] EWHC 44 (Admin), [2015] JPL 762 .... 1.22

N

National Justice Compania Naviera SA v Prudential Assurance Co Ltd (The Ikarian Reefer) (No 1) [1993] 2 Lloyd's Rep 68, [1993] FSR 563 .... 3.43

P

Parker v Secretary of State for Communities and Local Government [2009] EWHC 2330 (Admin) 2.19

R

R v Secretary of State for the Environment, ex p Westminster City Council [1989] 1 PLR 23 .... 8.04

R v Secretary of State for the Environment, Transport & the Regions, ex p Bath & North East Somerset DC [1999] 1 WLR 1759, [1999] 4 All ER 418 .... 2.11

R (on the application of Bedford Land Investments Ltd) v Secretary of State for Transport & Bedford Borough Council) [2015] EWHC 3159 (Admin), [2016] PTSR 31 .... 8.17

R (on the application of ClientEarth) v Secretary of State for the Environment, Food & Rural Affairs [2017] EWHC 1618 (Admin) 5.75

R (on the application of Poole) v Secretary of State for Communities & Local Government [2008] EWHC 676 (Admin), [2008] JPL 1774 .... 2.47; 5.96

R (on the application of Tatham Homes Ltd) v First Secretary of Sate [2005] EWHC 3538 (Admin), [2008] JPL 185 .... 5.95

R (on the application of Taylor) v Maidstone BC [2004] EWHC 257 (Admin) 1.04

W

Walton v Scottish Ministers [2012] UKSC 44, [2013] PTSR 51, 2013 SC (UKSC) 67 .... 9.14

Whitby v Secretary of State for Transport [2016] EWCA Civ 444, [2016] JPL 980 .... 1.11

Chapter 1

The scope of appeals

WHY APPEAL?

1.01 Planning appeals are better suited to conscripts than to volunteers. Appeal is neither the only nor the first option to resolve a difference with a planning decision-maker. Rather, the first option is to consider whether the concern may be overcome by further and better information, amendment of the application, re-submission, planning condition or planning obligation. Any or all of these points will have to be considered in any event on appeal. The National Planning Practice Guidance (NPPG) advises that:

> 'Before making any appeal the party seeking permission should first consider re-engaging with the local planning authority to discuss whether any changes to the proposal would make it more acceptable and likely to gain permission. It is possible that a further planning application may be submitted without charge.'[1]

Of itself, this may become relevant in the course of an appeal because:

> 'applicants should give consideration to the merits of the case, and whether there are strong grounds to contest the reasons for refusal of permission, or the conditions attached to a permission, before submitting an appeal. Parties who pursue an appeal unreasonably without sound grounds for appeal may have an award of costs made against them.'[2]

WHAT IS AN APPEAL?

1.02 It would be a tedious title for this chapter, and indeed the book, to refer to appeals against refusals, non-determination appeals, applications called-in by a minister for his own determination, inquiries into objections against compulsory purchase, highways and various infrastructure orders etc. But this chapter is concerned with all of those means by which an independent decision or report is produced which is concerned with a development or closely related activity. What is lost in terms of accuracy in using the term 'appeals' is made up for by what is gained in brevity. So, in this chapter, and in this book, a reference to an appeal may or may not in fact be a reference to a means of overturning an adverse decision. In most cases it will be exactly that, because the bulk of the work of Inspectors appointed by the Secretaries of State is the adjudication on disputes between planning authorities and applicants.

---

[1] NPPG, Paragraph 001 Reference ID: 16-001-20140306.
[2] NPPG, Paragraph 001, ibid.

1.03 *The scope of appeals*

1.03 Neither this chapter, nor this book, are concerned with adjudication on disputes between planning authorities and those who complain about decisions to grant consent or decisions not to enforce planning controls. Those who simply disagree with the judgment reached by a planning authority have no avenue of complaint available to them. There is no right of appeal against a decision to grant planning permission. There is no mechanism for the merits of the decision to be re-ventilated before an independent person or body. Rather, the disappointed objector may only challenge such a decision as being wrong in law. Being wrong in law and being a bad decision with which one may profoundly disagree are very far from being the same thing. Rather, they are fundamentally different questions in all but the most extreme cases. It would be for such a person to make an application for judicial review. Such an application would be heard in the specialist list within the Queen's Bench Division of the High Court, namely the Planning Court. The available grounds for such an application are public law errors which are not the subject of this book.

1.04 Conversely, there is no effective access to the court by a disappointed applicant. Rather, the applicant should make use of the right of appeal to the Secretary of State. There is a theoretical route to apply for judicial review of an adverse planning decision, but it will inevitably be met with the response that there is an alternative remedy on the merits, and permission to apply for judicial review would be refused in all but wholly exceptional circumstances of plain unlawfulness.[3]

1.05 Appeals are about the merits. They are concerned with the question, should the application be approved, or not? Appeals often take reasons for refusal as their starting point and their guide to considering the merits of the appeal, but in large measure, appeals are not answering a question of whether the planning authority was wrong. The statutory basis for this summary of the position is s 79(1) of the Town and Country Planning Act 1990 (TCPA 1990):

> 'On an appeal under section 78 the Secretary of State may—
>
> (a) allow or dismiss the appeal, or
>
> (b) reverse or vary any part of the decision of the local planning authority (whether the appeal relates to that part of it or not),
>
> and may deal with the application as if it had been made to him in the first instance.'

1.06 The Inspector has a very wide discretion as to how to approach the appeal. In practice, regard is had to the decision of the local planning authority (LPA), but the Inspector may deal with the application as if it were made to him. That is the approach which is taken – the focus derives from the LPA's decision, but the decision is taken afresh. This must be so because the decision is made in accordance with s 38(6) of the Planning and Compulsory Purchase Act 2004. The development plan and the weight to be given to the relevant parts of it will very frequently be different at the time of an appeal decision, compared to the time of the LPA's decision. The same applies to other material considerations. Those development plan and other material considerations may have changed in ways which tend to point in different directions: some changes may assist an appellant while other changes may strengthen the reasons for refusal. So, the Inspector is obliged to treat the appeal proposal as she or he finds it, at the time of the decision. The same applies to a Secretary of State who

---

[3] *R (on the application of Taylor) v Maidstone BC* [2004] EWHC 257.

is to consider an Inspector's report in a recovered or called-in appeal. There may have been, and often are, material changes in planning circumstances between the date of the report to the Secretary of State and the date of the decision letter. The Secretary of State therefore makes the decision on the basis of the law, policy and facts which are to be applied at the time of the decision, not some earlier time.

APPEALING AGAINST WHAT?

1.07 There are independent determinations of appeals against a very wide variety of refusals, failure to determine and objections to proposed orders. The source of the principal workload of the Planning Inspectorate is highlighted here, but it is not comprehensive. Research shows that there have been inquiries into objections to a storage authorisation order under the Gas Act 1965. But there have only been two such inquiries. They were no doubt important but are nevertheless rare. Moreover, they would now be decided under the development consent order procedure under the Planning Act 2008. There are other examples of important but rarely used provisions. Though the scope of 'planning appeals' is very broad and the routes to a determination or report from an Inspector are numerous, the themes are common to many of them.

1.08 TCPA 1990, s 78 provides a right of appeal against planning decisions and against the failure to take such decisions. The right of appeal is in play where an LPA:

- refuse an application for planning permission;
- grant planning permission subject to conditions and the applicant is aggrieved by a condition or conditions;
- refuse permission in principle;
- refuse to discharge a planning condition;
- refuse an application under a development order, such as a prior approval;
- fail to determine an application within the relevant time limit;
- decline to determine an application for the reasons in TCPA 1990, s 70 (subsequent, overlapping and retrospective applications); or
- give notice that the Secretary of State has called-in the application for his own determination.

1.09 The scheme of the Planning Acts contains the following further rights of appeal:

- appeal against an enforcement notice pursuant to TCPA 1990, s 174;
- appeal against refusal of a lawful development certificate pursuant to TCPA 1990, s 195;
- appeal against a listed building enforcement notice pursuant to s 39 of the Planning (Listed Buildings and Conservation Areas) Act 1990;
- appeal against a listed building consent decisions pursuant to s 20 of the Planning (Listed Buildings and Conservation Areas) Act 1990 (the Listed Buildings Act);
- Tree Preservation Order appeals; and
- advertisement consent appeals.

1.10 *The scope of appeals*

1.10 A local inquiry into planning issues may also be triggered by the publication of draft orders to which objections are received and not withdrawn. The range of orders to which similar provisions apply is broad, but the more frequently used provisions include:

- highway diversion orders;
- Transport and Works Act orders;
- harbour orders;
- compulsory purchase orders; and
- railway crossing closure orders.

1.11 To illustrate the interactions between promoters, local authorities, statutory consultees and order making authorities, it is worthwhile to consider the Ordsall Chord.[4] This was a scheme to provide a new direct rail link between the three main railway stations in Manchester, namely Victoria, Oxford Road and Piccadilly. A new rail chord was required to join the Bolton line to the Chat Moss line, crossing the River Irwell. This required the demolition and replacement of existing railway bridges and would be within the setting of heritage assets of great significance.

1.12 The parameters of the inquiry can be gauged from the following:

- hearing the case for and objections to:
    - the Network Rail (Ordsall Chord) Order 2015[5] under ss 1–5 of the Transport and Works Act 1992;
    - a request for a direction for deemed planning permission under TCPA 1990, s 90(2A); and
    - applications for listed building consent, made to the City Council and transferred to the Secretary of State for Communities and Local Government for his decision; and
- a three-week inquiry conducted under the:
    - Transport and Works (Inquiries Procedure) Rules 2004;[6] and
    - Transport and Works (Applications and Objections Procedure) (England and Wales) Rules 2006.[7]

1.13 Though this was evidently an inquiry of some complexity, under provisions which are not the day-to-day material for Inspectors, the essential approach is common to the determination of such issues by Inspectors. There is a party which is asking the Inspector to do something. Here it is in fact three things arising from a Transport and Works Act order, a deemed planning permission and consent to carry out works to listed buildings. Those three things give rise to easily identifiable issues which in this inquiry included, for example, heritage impacts, alternative schemes, and the need and justification for compulsory acquisition. Those issues were determined by

---

[4] For a description of the scheme, the issues and the legal argument on the assessment of heritage impacts see *Whitby v Secretary of State for Transport* [2016] EWCA Civ 444, [2016] JPL 980.
[5] SI 2015/780.
[6] SI 2004/2018.
[7] SI 2006/1466.

applying the relevant procedure rules. The general pattern of preparing for such an inquiry is quite similar to that which is encountered in the bulk of planning appeals:

- commencing the process of appeal;

- stating the case to be advanced and the material which will be relied upon to make out that case;

- engaging with the other parties to manage the issues and the logistics of the hearing or inquiry;

- exchanging written evidence which addresses the issues;

- hearing the cases opened, the evidence called and submissions which marshal the case as it stands at the end of the inquiry; and

- awaiting a decision.

BY WHOM?

1.14 Take the common example of the right of appeal being granted to the applicant: TCPA 1990, s 78 and art 37 of the Town and Country Planning (Development Management Procedure) (England) Order 2015.[8] That right of appeal is not conferred on those with an interest in the land, though such persons will frequently be the same as the applicant.

1.15 Applications in which a planning authority has an interest in the application land are a special case. Planning authorities may grant planning permission to the Council of the area in which they have administrative responsibility where the land is in the Council's ownership, ie it is interested in the application: reg 3 of the Town and Country Planning General Regulations 1992 (the 1992 Regulations).[9] This part of the statutory code is subject to a number of modifications which make both the process and the outcome different from applications and permissions in respect of which the Council has no interest, namely: (1) by reg 5(1)(a) of the 1992 Regulations there is no right of appeal, and (2) TCPA 1990 provides an ouster clause which prevents legal challenges to the grant of planning permission on the ground that the wrong planning authority made the decision (s 286).

1.16 An interest in land is, however, a feature of appeals against an enforcement notice. A person having an interest in the land to which an enforcement notice relates may appeal to the Secretary of State, as may a relevant occupier.[10] It is irrelevant whether the appellant has been served with a copy of the enforcement notice.

---

[8] SI 2015/595.
[9] SI 1992/1492. Regulation 3 of the 1992 Regulations provides: 'Subject to regulations 4 and 4A, an application for planning permission by an interested planning authority to develop any land of that authority, or for development of any land by an interested planning authority or by an interested planning authority jointly with any other person, shall be determined by the authority concerned, unless the application is referred to the Secretary of State under section 77 of the 1990 Act for determination by him.'
[10] TCPA 1990, s 174(1); a relevant occupier is 'a person who on the date on which the enforcement notice is issued occupies the land to which the notice relates by virtue of a licence ...; and continues so to occupy the land when the appeal is brought': see s 174(6).

1.17 *The scope of appeals*

1.17 Those statutory and non-statutory objectors who have not withdrawn their objections to the making of a relevant order, as discussed above, will have an opportunity to be heard before an Inspector appointed by the relevant Secretary of State.

RECOVERY AND CALL-IN BY A SECRETARY OF STATE

1.18 Call-in and recovery are not the same, though the result is similar. In both situations, the decision is not transferred to and made by an Inspector. Rather an Inspector prepares a report and recommendations. The report is to the Secretary of State. The Secretary of State considers the report, but makes his own decision which is recorded in his decision letter.

1.19 A call-in is pursuant to TCPA 1990, s 77. The power is in respect of planning applications, not planning appeals. The Secretary of State calls-in the decision for his own determination.

Recovery

1.20 Recovery is in respect of planning appeals, not planning applications. The default position is that the power to determine planning appeals is transferred to an Inspector who will decide the appeal. The Secretary of State will not, himself, have any direct involvement in the decision. Rather, it is a decision which is handled wholly by the Planning Inspectorate. However, in certain cases the Secretary of State decides that he will determine the appeal. The criteria (not an exclusive list) which the Secretary of State applies are:[11]

- Proposals for development of major importance having more than local significance.
- Proposals giving rise to substantial regional or national controversy.
- Proposals which raise important or novel issues of development control, and/or legal difficulties.
- Proposals against which another government department has raised major objections or has a major interest.
- Proposals of major significance for the delivery of the Government's climate change programme and energy policies.
- Proposals for residential development of over 150 units or on sites of over 5 hectares, which would significantly impact on the Government's objective to secure a better balance between housing demand and supply and create high quality, sustainable, mixed and inclusive communities.
- Proposals which involve any main town centre use or uses where that use or uses comprise(s) over 9,000 square metres gross floorspace (either as a single proposal or as part of or in combination with other current proposals) and

---

[11] Parliamentary Statement dated 30 June 2008 https://publications.parliament.uk/pa/cm200708/cmhansrd/cm080630/wmstext/80630m0001.htm.

which are proposed on a site in an edge of centre or out of centre location that is not in accordance with an up-to-date development plan document.

- Proposals for significant development in the Green Belt.
- Major proposals involving the winning and working of minerals.
- Proposals which would have an adverse impact on the outstanding universal value, integrity, authenticity and significance of a World Heritage Site.
- Proposals involving traveller sites in the Green Belt.[12]
- Proposals for residential development of over 25 units in areas where a qualifying body has submitted a neighbourhood plan proposal to the local planning authority, but where the relevant plan has not been made.[13]
- Proposals for exploring and developing shale gas.[14]

1.21 The recovery criteria reflect the particular policy imperatives of the government of the time. Traveller sites in the Green Belt were controversial when the Secretary of State for Communities and Local Government was the Rt Hon (now Baron) Eric Pickles. Other types of development have also been likely to be recovered, and dismissed, such as onshore wind proposals which were often recovered and dismissed against the recommendations of Inspectors during 2014 and 2015. This merely reflects the role of politics in planning.

1.22 In *Moore*,[15] the evidence showed that there was a considerable disparity between recovery in non-traveller residential Green Belt cases and recovery of traveller residential Green Belt cases and it was common ground that it was taking longer to deal with the cases than if they been determined by Inspectors. The effect was discriminatory and not shown to be justified or proportionate.

Call-in

1.23 The Secretary of State may direct that a wide range of planning decisions be referred to him instead of being dealt with by the local planning authorities.[16] The power is most commonly used in respect of applications for planning permission, but the power exists in respect of reserved matters, prior approvals under development order and advertisement consent.[17] Further, the call-in may be broader than in respect of a particular application and apply to a class of applications in one, more or all local planning authorities.[18] In England, the applicant and the planning authority have the

---

[12] See statement to Parliament, 17 January 2014: https://hansard.parliament.uk/Commons/2014-01-17/debates/14011787000011/GreenBelt?highlight=traveller%20sites#contribution-14011787000034.

[13] See statement to Parliament, 17 January 2014: https://hansard.parliament.uk/Commons/2016-07-07/debates/16070737000016/NeighbourhoodPlanning?highlight=residential%20development#contribution-BA1F322D-6DB1-4F45-A74E-F97108E938C8.

[14] See statement to Parliament, 16 September 2015: https://hansard.parliament.uk/Commons/2015-09-16/debates/15091631000013/ShaleGasOilPolicy?highlight=shale%20gas#contribution-15091631000037.

[15] *Moore v Secretary of State for Communities and Local Government* [2015] EWHC 44; [2015] JPL 762.

[16] TCPA 1990, s 77(1).

[17] See Town and Country Planning (Control of Advertisement) (England) Regulations 2007, SI 2007/783, reg 15.

[18] TCPA 1990, s 77(2).

1.24 *The scope of appeals*

right to be heard on the application, before an Inspector.[19] In Wales, it is for the Welsh Ministers to decide what procedure to adopt on call-in.[20]

1.24 There are call-in criteria in both England and Wales. When asked a question in Parliament on the Government's policy on calling-in applications, the Minister at the time, Mr Caborn, replied:

> 'My right hon. Friend's general approach, like that of previous Secretaries of State, is not to interfere with the jurisdiction of local planning authorities unless it is necessary to do so. Parliament has entrusted them with responsibility for day-to-day planning control in their areas. It is right that, in general, they should be free to carry out their duties responsibly, with the minimum of interference.
>
> There will be occasions, however, when my right hon. Friend may consider it necessary to call in the planning application to determine himself, instead of leaving the decision to the local planning authority.
>
> His policy is to be very selective about calling in planning applications. He will, in general, only take this step if planning issues of more than local importance are involved. Such cases may include, for example, those which, in his opinion:
>
> - may conflict with national policies on important matters;
> - could have significant effects beyond their immediate locality;
> - give rise to substantial regional or national controversy;
> - raise significant architectural and urban design issues; or
> - may involve the interests of national security or of foreign Governments
>
> However, each case will continue to be considered on its individual merits.'

1.25 These are the 'Caborn criteria'.[21] Their terms were expressed differently (differences highlighted) in the Written Ministerial Statement of Nick Boles, Under-Secretary of State of 26 October 2012, namely:

- may conflict with national policies on important matters;
- *may have significant long-term impact on economic growth and meeting housing needs across a wider area than a single local authority*;
- could have significant effects beyond their immediate locality;
- give rise to substantial *cross-boundary* or national controversy;
- raise significant architectural and urban design issues; or
- may involve the interests of national security or of foreign Governments.

These criteria are applied in Wales by the Welsh Ministers.[22]

1.26 Decisions to call-in are relatively rare. There were six call-in decisions during 2019. There were 12 call-in decisions during 2018. The decision to call-in or

---

[19] TCPA 1990, 77(5).
[20] See TCPA 1990, s 319B(7), as inserted by the Town and Country Planning (Determination of Procedure) (Wales) Order 2014, SI 2014/2773, art 2.
[21] https://publications.parliament.uk/pa/cm199899/cmhansrd/vo990616/text/90616w02.htm#90616w02.htm_sbhd5.
[22] Planning Policy Wales (10th edn) at para 1.35.

not to call-in is sometimes challenged by way of judicial review of the decision. It is necessary to show that the decision is Wednesbury unreasonable and to persuade the court to exercise its discretion to provide relief. The decided cases show both to be substantial hurdles for a claimant.

Chapter 2

Commencement

MAKING THE APPEAL

2.01 This is about getting started. It is about the first and most strategic of procedural decisions (mode of appeal), the most important step in making a case (the statement of case) and navigating the legal requirements. Each type of appeal against a decision of a planning authority has its own foundation in the substantive and procedural law. Taken together, these provisions prescribe what the appellant has to do in order to make a valid appeal, and how the planning authority must respond. Getting started therefore involves procedural hurdles and the framing of the issues and merits of the case.

2.02 The large majority of appeals in England and Wales are under s 78 of the Town and Country Planning Act 1990 (TCPA 1990). Given the central nature of the section to so many appeals it is worthwhile to set it out, as currently in force in England and in Wales. The words in italics have been repealed in Wales.

'(1) Where a local planning authority—

(a) refuse an application for planning permission or grant it subject to conditions;

(aa) refuse an application for permission in principle;

(b) refuse an application for any consent, agreement or approval of that authority required by a condition imposed on a grant of planning permission or grant it subject to conditions; or

(c) refuse an application for any approval of that authority required under a development order, a local development order, a Mayoral development order or a neighbourhood development order or grant it subject to conditions, the applicant may by notice appeal to the Secretary of State.

(2) A person who has made such an application to the local planning authority may also appeal to the Secretary of State if the local planning authority have done none of the following—

(a) given notice to the applicant of their decision on the application;

(aa) given notice to the applicant that they have exercised their power under section 70A or 70B or 70C to decline to determine the application;

(b) given notice to him that the application has been referred to the Secretary of State in accordance with directions given under section 77, within such period as may be prescribed by the development order or within such extended period as may at any time be agreed upon in writing between the applicant and the authority.

(3) Any appeal under this section shall be made by notice served within such time and in such manner as may be prescribed by a development order.

(4) The time prescribed for the service of such a notice must not be less than—

(a) 28 days from the date of notification of the decision; or

(b) in the case of an appeal under subsection (2), 28 days from the end of the period prescribed as mentioned in subsection (2) or, as the case may be, the extended period mentioned in that subsection.

(4A) A notice of appeal under this section must be accompanied by such information as may be prescribed by a development order.

(4AA) An appeal under this section may not be brought or continued against the refusal of an application for planning permission if—

(a) the land to which the application relates is in Wales,

(b) granting the application would involve granting planning permission in respect of matters specified in an enforcement notice as constituting a breach of planning control, and

(c) on the determination of an appeal against that notice under section 174, planning permission for those matters was not granted under section 177.

(4AB) An appeal under this section may not be brought or continued against the grant of an application for planning permission subject to a condition, if—

(a) the land to which the application relates is in Wales,

(b) an appeal against an enforcement notice has been brought under section 174 on the ground that the condition ought to be discharged, and

(c) on the determination of that appeal, the condition was not discharged under section 177.

(4B) *The power to make a development order under subsection (4A) is exercisable by—*

(a) the Secretary of State, in relation to England;

(b) the Welsh Ministers, in relation to Wales.

(4BA) Once notice of an appeal under this section to the Welsh Ministers has been served, the application to which it relates may not be varied, except in such circumstances as may be prescribed by a development order.

(4BB) A development order which makes provision under subsection (4BA) must provide for an application which is varied to be subject to such further consultation as the Welsh Ministers consider appropriate.

(4C) *Section 333(5) does not apply in relation to a development order under subsection (4A) made by the Welsh Ministers.*

(4D) *A development order under subsection (4A) made by the Welsh Ministers is subject to annulment in pursuance of a resolution of the National Assembly for Wales.*

(5) For the purposes of the application of sections 79(1) and (3), 253(2)(c), 266(1)(b), 288(10)(b), 319A(7)(b) and 319B(7)(b) in relation to an appeal under subsection (2), it shall be assumed that the authority decided to refuse the application in question.'

2.03 The time limits and procedural requirements referred to in subsections (3), (4A), (4BA) and (4BB) are contained in art 37 of the Town and Country Planning (Development Management Procedure) (England) Order 2015 (DMPO 2015)[1] in England. In Wales, the equivalent provisions are in the Town and Country Planning (Development Management Procedure) (Wales) Order 2012 (DMP(W)O 2012).[2]

---

[1] SI 2015/595 (see Appendix 2).
[2] SI 2012/801.

2.04 *Commencement*

2.04 The provisions in respect of time limits are more detailed in England, with, for example, short time limits for those cases in which the local planning authority (LPA) have given notice that the application is in respect of development which is substantially similar to an application which has previously been considered. The time limits also differ as between types of appeal: six months for an appeal against refusal of planning permission but 28 days if, for example, an appellant wishes to advance a ground 'a' appeal against an enforcement notice, ie that planning permission should be granted. Both appeals ask an Inspector to grant planning permission but the route to a valid appeal is much shorter for one than the other.

2.05 Some time limits are set out in Table 1. It is important to check the current provision carefully against the particular circumstances appealed against.

Table 1 Some time limits

Type of appeal	Right of appeal	Procedural provision	Time limit
Refusal of/ to: planning permission, grant reserved matters consent, discharge a planning condition	TCPA 1990, s 78	England: DMPO 2015, art 37(2)(d) Wales: DMP(W)O 2012, art 26	6 months from the date on the decision notice, except for: householder and minor commercial 12 weeks;
Refusal of planning permission for development which is substantially the same as that which is the subject of an enforcement notice	TCPA 1990, s78(1) or (2)	England: DMPO 2015, art 37(2)(b) and (c) Wales: DMP(W)O 2012, art 26	England: 28 days from the date that the enforcement notice is served, or the decision notice for the same development; *or* before the expiry of the specified period. Wales: 6 months
Refusal of advertisement consent	TCPA 1990, s 78, as modified by the Town and Country Planning (Control of Advertisements) (England) Regulations 2007[3]	England: Town and Country Planning (Control of Advertisements) (England) Regulations 2007, reg 17 and Sch 4 Wales: Town and Country Planning (Control of Advertisements) Regulations 1992,[4] reg 15 and Sch 4	Within 8 weeks from the date of receipt of the decision notice, or within 8 weeks of the date on which the planning authority should have given its decision.

---

[3] SI 2007/783.
[4] SI 1992/666.

Making the appeal **2.06**

Type of appeal	Right of appeal	Procedural provision	Time limit
Refusal of hazardous substances consent	Planning (Hazardous Substances) Act 1990, s 21	England: Planning (Hazardous Substances) Regulations 2015,[5] reg 13(1) Wales: Planning (Hazardous Substances)(Wales) Regulations 2015,[6] reg 13(1)	Within 6 months of the decision or, if no decision has been made, within 6 months from when a decision should have been given.
Refusal of listed building consent	Planning (Listed Buildings and Conservation Areas) Act 1990 (the Listed Buildings Act), s 20	England: Planning (Listed Buildings and Conservation Areas) Regulations 1990,[7] reg 8 Wales: Planning (Listed Buildings and Conservation Areas) (Wales) Regulations 2012,[8] reg 8	Within 6 months of the decision or, if no decision has been made, within 6 months from when a decision should have been given.
Listed building enforcement notice	Listed Buildings Act, s 39	See Listed Buildings Act, s 39(2)	Before the date on which the enforcement notice comes into effect.
Refusal or non-determination of a prior approval under the DMPO 2015	TCPA 1990, s 78	Householder appeal process	12 weeks
Refusal of consent for work/felling of a tree subject to a preservation order	TCPA 1990, s 208	See TCPA 1990, s 208(2)	Within 28 days of the date of notification of the authority's decision, within 28 days from when a decision should have been given.

2.06 In such an appeal, the parties' cases will first be identified from: (1) the decision notice which contains the reasons for refusal; and (2) the statements of case. In contrast, an enforcement appeal against an enforcement notice will also require the grounds of appeal to be identified by specific reference to the statutory grounds of appeal in TCPA 1990, s 174.

---

[5] SI 2015/627.
[6] SI 2015/1597.
[7] SI 1990/1519.
[8] SI 2012/793.

2.07 *Commencement*

DMPO requirements

2.07   The DMPO requirements are:

- Serve completed appeal form on the Secretary of State (ie submit to the Planning Inspectorate (PINS)).
- Copy the completed appeal form to the LPA.
- For all appeals, send the following to the Planning Inspectorate:
  - a copy of the application;
  - other plans and documents relating to the application;
  - the decision notice or determination.
- For cases other than householder and minor commercial appeals, also send:
  - all correspondence with the LPA;
  - article 14 certificate confirming compliance with notice requirements for the application (DMPO 2015, art 13);
  - full statement of case;
  - statement as to which procedure should be used for the appeal;
  - draft statement of common ground.

2.08   Once a Minister is seized of an appeal of a first instance decision then the procedural framework switches from, say, the Planning Acts, to the procedural rules. It does not matter whether, as in the vast majority of cases, the Minister is performing an appellate function such as hearing and determining an appeal against an enforcement notice or whether the Minister's function is that of first-instance decision-maker, having decided to call-in a planning decision and make the decision him- or herself, or being seized of a decision whether to make an order affecting land. Either way, the Minister is exercising powers under a statutory scheme which is enabled by the Tribunals and Inquiries Act 1992. Section 9 of that Act provides a power to make rules. Moreover, TCPA 1990, s 323 provides a specific power to make regulations which govern the procedure in appeals determined by inquiry or hearing, or by written representations.

2.09   In this way, almost all planning appeals are started under one piece of legislation and are then managed and determined under a second piece of legislation, namely the rules made under the Tribunals and Inquiries Act 1992 and, often, TCPA 1990. An example would be an appeal against a Welsh planning authority's refusal of a certificate of lawfulness, started under TCPA 1990, s 195, for which notice of appeal would be given under DMP(W)O 2012, reg 26B. The appellant would provide:

- the application made to the LPA which occasioned the appeal;
- all plans, drawings and documents sent to the authority in connection with the application;
- all correspondence with the authority relating to the application;
- any other plans, documents or drawings relating to the application which were not sent to the authority;

- the notice of the decision or determination, if any; and
- a full statement of case.

2.10 In this example, if the appeal is validly made and is in time, then the 2012 Order has no further bearing on the appeal. The future conduct of the appeal is governed by the Town and Country Planning (Referred Applications and Appeals Procedure) (Wales) Regulations 2017.[9] Thus:

- TCPA 1990, s 195 provides the right of appeal;
- DMP(W)O 2012 sets out the requirements to make a valid appeal, and;
- the Town and Country Planning (Referred Applications and Appeals Procedure) (Wales) Regulations 2017 govern the appeal process.

VALIDITY

2.11 The question of validity first arises when a planning authority receives an application. So far as appeals are concerned, the issue of validity may arise in two ways. First, there may be a validation dispute in which the applicant appeals to the Secretary of State against the refusal by a planning authority to validate and register a planning application. This is a form of appeal which the Secretary of State may properly entertain.[10] If the Secretary of State takes the view that the application is invalid, then he does not have jurisdiction.[11]

2.12 In Wales, validation appeals are governed by the Town and Country Planning (Validation Appeals Procedure) (Wales) Regulations 2016.[12] These set out the procedure for the determination of validation appeals made to the Welsh Minsters under TCPA 1990, s 62ZB. In accordance with s 62ZB(6) validation appeals are considered on the basis of written representations. The procedure includes the following steps:

(a) the Welsh Ministers must give notice that they have received the appeal (reg 3);

(b) the appellant and LPA are not given an opportunity to comment on each other's representations (reg 4); and

(c) the Welsh Ministers must notify the appellant and the LPA of their decision and their reasons for reaching that decision (reg 6).

2.13 The process in England is contrived. Article 12 of the DMPO 2015 permits a dissatisfied applicant to submit a notice explaining why further information requested by a planning authority does not meet the statutory tests in TCPA 1990, s 62(4A), namely it must be reasonable having regard, in particular, to the nature and scale of the proposed development; and about a matter which it is reasonable to think will be a material consideration in the determination of the application. If the planning authority counters with a non-validation notice, then the applicant may appeal.

---

[9] SI 2017/544.
[10] *R v Secretary of State for the Environment, Transport and the Regions Ex p Bath and North East Somerset DC* [1999] 1 WLR 1759 (CA).
[11] *Geall v Secretary of State for the Environment, Transport and the Regions* [1999] LSGaz., 10 February, p 31 at [1766] per Schiemann LJ, followed with approval in *Bath and North East Somerset DC*.
[12] SI 2016/60.

2.14 *Commencement*

2.14 Secondly, on receipt of an appeal, the Secretary of State will consider whether the appeal is valid. For a s 78 appeal, the Secretary of State may deal with the application as if it had been made to him in the first instance.[13] He may allow or dismiss the appeal or may reverse or vary any part of the decision whether the appeal relates to that part or not. The Secretary of State has a free hand on appeal, not to simply review what the planning authority has done but to consider the application afresh. It follows that the Secretary of State may take a different view on the validity of an application to that taken by the planning authority.

2.15 However, if a planning authority finds that an application is invalid, the extent of the discretion to consider the appeal further is limited by the effect of TCPA 1990, s 327A which is in mandatory terms so far as it constrains a planning authority from determining an application which does not meet the relevant requirements. However, the Secretary of State is in a somewhat different position by reason of TCPA 1990, s 79(6) which provides:

> 'If, before or during the determination of such an appeal in respect of an application for planning permission to develop land, the Secretary of State forms the opinion that, having regard to the provisions of sections 70 and 72(1), the development order and any directions given under that order, planning permission for that development—
>
> (a) could not have been granted by the local planning authority; or
>
> (b) could not have been granted otherwise than subject to the conditions imposed,
>
> he may decline to determine the appeal or to proceed with the determination.'

2.16 The scope for considering an invalid application was considered in *Maximus Networks Ltd v Secretary of State for Communities and Local Government*.[14] Maximus applied to install telephone kiosks using the prior notification procedure under Part 16 of and the Schedule to the Town and Country Planning (General Permitted Development) (England) Order 2015[15] which included a number of restrictions and conditions. One of those was the requirement to provide evidence of notification of the relevant land owner. Many such applications had been rejected as invalid because the application did not include such evidence. The Planning Inspectorate took the same view and refused to validate the appeals. Maximus challenged those decisions. The issue was the nature and extent of the Planning Inspectorate's discretion to allow an appeal to proceed even though there was a failure to comply with a procedural requirement.

2.17 *Maximus* is a case which decides that the Secretary of State may proceed with an appeal which does not comply with a procedural requirement, or may decide at any stage not to proceed further with the appeal. In other words, the Secretary of State has a discretion which arises under TCPA 1990, ss 79(1) and 79(6).

2.18 In practical terms, the Secretary of State, via the Planning Inspectorate, is likely to expect strict adherence to procedural requirements. The development management and the appeals systems are a coherent statutory scheme for which all of the elements serve a purpose, which is often to protect the public interest or at least the interests of some section of the public. It is likely that a procedural requirement

---

[13] TCPA 1990, s 79(1).
[14] [2018] EWHC 1933 (Admin), [2019] PTSR 312.
[15] SI 2015/596.

which is omitted will result in the Planning Inspectorate refusing to validate an appeal unless there is some good reason and an absence of prejudice to others.

2.19 One example of the sort of situation in which the Secretary of State may exercise his discretion in favour of an appellant is *Parker v Secretary of State for Communities and Local Government*[16] in which the requirements for details of scale for an outline application for planning permission changed between the date of the application and the date of the appeal. The Inspector considered that he could determine the appeal despite the fact that the application would have to be different if made under the requirements of the General Development Procedure Order then in force. The court agreed that there was no impediment to this course. This case shows that there is flexibility within the statutory scheme which governs the appeals process, in an appropriate case, to deal with unusual circumstances in a pragmatic manner.

THE PROCEDURE RULES

2.20 Rules have been made by way of statutory instrument. In England they are generally specific to a particular task. They are specific to either Wales or to England. So, for example, there is a specific set of rules which applies to an enforcement appeal determined by way of hearing in England.

Table 2 Principal procedure rules

Type of appeal	Applicable rules in England	Applicable rules in Wales
Planning – by written representations	Town and Country Planning (Appeals) (Written Representations Procedure) (England) Regulations 2009,[17] including advertisement appeals	Town and Country Planning (Referred Applications and Appeals Procedure) (Wales) Regulations 2017[18]
Planning – by hearing	Town and Country Planning (Hearings Procedure) (England) Rules 2000[19]	Town and Country Planning (Referred Applications and Appeals Procedure) (Wales) Regulations 2017
Planning – by inquiry	Town and Country Planning Appeals (Determination by Inspectors) (Inquiries Procedure) (England) Rules 2000[20] Or for Secretary of State determinations: Town and Country Planning (Inquiries Procedure) (England) Rules 2000[21]	Town and Country Planning (Referred Applications and Appeals Procedure) (Wales) Regulations 2017

---

[16] [2009] EWHC 2330 (Admin).
[17] SI 2009/452, as amended by Town and Country Planning (Appeals) (Written Representations Procedure and Advertisements) (England) (Amendment) Regulations 2013, SI 2013/2114.
[18] SI 2017/544.
[19] SI 2000/1626.
[20] SI 2000/1625.
[21] SI 2000/1624.

2.21 *Commencement*

Type of appeal	Applicable rules in England	Applicable rules in Wales
Enforcement – by written representations	The Town and Country Planning (Enforcement) (Written Representations Procedure) (England) Regulations 2002[22]	Town and Country Planning (Referred Applications and Appeals Procedure) (Wales) Regulations 2017
Enforcement – by hearing	Town and Country Planning (Enforcement) (Hearings Procedure) (England) Rules 2002[23]	Town and Country Planning (Referred Applications and Appeals Procedure) (Wales) Regulations 2017
Enforcement – by inquiry	Town and Country Planning (Enforcement) (Determination by Inspectors) (Inquiries Procedure) (England) Rules 2002[24] Or for Secretary of State determinations: Town and Country Planning (Enforcement) (Inquiries Procedure) (England) Rules 2002[25]	Town and Country Planning (Referred Applications and Appeals Procedure) (Wales) Regulations 2017

2.21 'Planning' appeals (as indicated in Table 2, above) in England are in relation to an application for planning permission or permission in principle under TCPA 1990, ss 77 and 78 and in relation to listed building consent under s 20 of the Listed Buildings Act. They also relate to advertisement appeals which are determined by way of written representations.

2.22 'Enforcement' appeals (as indicated in Table 2.2, above) relate to appeals under:

- TCPA 1990, s 174 (appeal against enforcement notice);
- TCPA 1990, s 195 (appeal against refusal or non-determination of an application for a certificate of lawful use or development);
- Listed Buildings Act, s 26K (appeal against a refusal or failure to give a decision on an application for a Listed Buildings Act certificate of lawfulness); and
- Listed Buildings Act, s 39 (appeal against listed building enforcement notice).

2.23 For the large bulk of planning appeals, there is an identifiable and well-established set of procedural rules. However, there are many gaps and anomalies. The user of the appeals system should not necessarily assume that their inability to find the obviously relevant set of procedural rules is a failing on their part. For example, an advertisement appeal may be determined by the hearing procedure if a party requests it and the Planning Inspectorate agrees. However, there are no specific procedural rules which apply to such appeals, but rather there is a series of adaptions to be made to the Hearings Procedure Rules 2000, which are hardly transparent and accessible. There is also a long list of statutory appeals which are determined by the

---

[22] SI 2002/2683.
[23] SI 2002/2684.
[24] SI 2002/2685.
[25] SI 2002/2686.

Planning Inspectorate for which no rules have been made, such as in respect of tree replacement notices under TCPA 1990, s 208, in respect of hazardous substances, or the wide range of appeals in respect of environmental permits or licences. These are dealt with 'in the spirit' of the 2000 rules.[26] In other words, such appeals tend to be dealt with as if the inquiry or hearing rules did apply.

2.24 It is striking that all modes of appeal for both planning and enforcement cases are governed by a single set of regulations in Wales, whereas in England there remains a multiplicity of rules. Via a single statutory instrument, the Welsh regulations address all of:

- an application for planning permission referred to the Welsh Ministers under TCPA 1990, s 77 (reference of applications to the Secretary of State);

- an appeal under TCPA 1990, s 78 (right to appeal against planning decisions and failure to take such decisions) or under that section as applied by s 198(3)(c) and (4) of that Act (tree preservation orders); and as applied by regulations made under TCPA 1990, s 220 (regulations controlling display of advertisements);

- an appeal under TCPA 1990, s 174 (appeal against enforcement notice);

- an appeal under TCPA 1990, s 195 (appeals against refusal or failure to give decision on application for a certificate of lawfulness of existing or proposed use or development);

- an appeal under TCPA 1990, s 208 (appeals against tree replacement notices);

- an appeal under TCPA 1990, s 217 (appeal against a notice requiring the maintenance of land);

- an application for listed building consent referred to the Welsh Ministers under the Listed Buildings Act, s 12, or for variation or discharge of conditions referred to them under that section as applied by s 19, or an appeal to them under s 20, of that Act;

- an application for conservation area consent referred to the Welsh Ministers under the Listed Buildings Act, s 12 (including an application to which that section is applied by s 19), or an appeal to them under s 20, as those sections are applied by s 74(3) of that Act;

- an appeal under the Listed Buildings Act, s 39 (appeal against listed buildings enforcement notice) or under that section as applied by s 74(3) of that Act (appeal against conservation area enforcement notice);

- an application for hazardous substances consent referred to the Welsh Ministers under the Planning (Hazardous Substances) Act 1990 (the Hazardous Substances Act), s 20 (reference of applications to Secretary of State); and

- an appeal under the Hazardous Substances Act, s 21 (appeals against decisions or failure to take decisions relating to hazardous substances).

2.25 It is difficult to see why the English procedure rules will not, in due course, be amended and consolidated along similar lines to the Welsh model. It would also

---

[26] Town and Country Planning (Hearings Procedure) (England) Rules 2000 and Town and Country Planning (Inquiries Procedure) (England) Rules 2000.

2.26 *Commencement*

seem sensible to move the provisions for making an appeal from the DMPO 2015 so that the commencement of appeals is governed by one scheme of regulation rather than two (see further 10.10–10.20 below).

2.26 Table 2 is not complete in that it does not include some of the little used provisions such as the Town and Country Planning (Section 62A Applications) (Written Representations and Miscellaneous Provisions) Regulations 2013.[27] TCPA 1990, s 62A allows applications for planning permission and reserved matters consent to be made directly to the Secretary of State where they involve major development and the LPA for the area has been designated as a result of previous underperformance in handling major applications. Very few such applications are made, perhaps in part owing to the negative outcome of the first such application for construction of up to 220 new dwellings on land located to the North of Hospital Lane, to the South of Mill Lane and to the East of Bouskell Park, Blaby, Leicestershire which was submitted by Gladman Developments Ltd in April 2014.

2.27 The Planning Inspectorate also undertakes specialist decision-making and reporting on infrastructure consenting under the Town and Country Planning (Major Infrastructure Project Inquiries Procedure) (England) Rules 2005[28] and the Transport and Works (Inquiries Procedure) Rules 2004.[29]

COMMENCEMENT IN PRACTICE: MODE OF APPEAL; STATEMENT OF CASE AND STATEMENT OF COMMON GROUND

2.28 At the outset of any appeal, there are key decisions to be made by the appellant and the planning authority: what is the mode of appeal: written representations, a hearing or an inquiry? It is for the appellant to make its choice first, for the planning authority to either agree or provide reasons in support of a different mode of appeal, and ultimately for the Planning Inspectorate to decide.

2.29 First, these choices and the decision are key because the parties may well have different views about the appropriate procedural route to follow. Therefore, it is an early point in the appeal at which to map out how the appeal is to be presented and how the contrary evidence and argument are to be overcome. It is a strategic choice with important advantages and disadvantages attached to each option. There is potential to fail to secure the mode of determination which best suits the particular party.

2.30 Secondly, the nature and extent of material to be provided in commencing the appeal will differ, depending upon the mode of appeal. This is particularly significant if there is a change between hearing and inquiry procedures because a statement of case will be the primary vehicle for communicating a party's case in a hearing, whereas the proofs of evidence will be the dominant tool for presenting the evidence at an inquiry. If the mode of appeal changes, then the appeal materials are likely to have to change too. For present purposes, the rules are considered on the footing that the appeal proceeds as the appellant requests.

---

[27] SI 2013/2142.
[28] SI 2005/2115.
[29] SI 2004/2018.

2.31 Thirdly, the timescales which apply to the stages of the appeal and to obtain a decision will differ as between modes of appeal, and also types of appeal. The relative speed with which appeals are conducted and determined has been the subject of great variation from year to year. The Planning Inspectorate publishes its performance data for each type of appeal. If timing is important, then the current data should be inspected.[30]

TABLES OF TIMESCALES (AS AT APRIL 2020)

2.32

Written representations or a hearing

Planning Appeal	Receipt to Start	Start to Event	Event to Decision
Written Representations	7 weeks within which: Receipt to Validation is 2 weeks	10 weeks	7 weeks
Hearings	13 weeks within which: Receipt to Validation is 3 weeks	16 weeks	7 weeks

Inquiry

Planning Appeal	Receipt to Start	Start to Event	Event to Decision
Inquiry (Note Rosewell (see Chapter 4))	10 weeks	22 weeks	12 weeks
Inquiries (Rosewell)	6 weeks	16 weeks	8 weeks

Householder (including advertisement consent and other minor commercial) appeals

Householder Appeal	Receipt to Start	Start to Event	Event to Decision
Written Representations	9 weeks within which: Receipt to Validation is 1 week	6 weeks	4 weeks

Enforcement and lawful development certificate appeals

Enforcement Appeal	Receipt to Start	Start to Event	Event to Decision
Written Representations	16 weeks within which: Receipt to Validation is 3 weeks	13 weeks	5 weeks
Hearings	48 weeks within which: Receipt to Validation is 13 weeks	17 weeks	6 weeks
Inquiries	49 weeks within which: Receipt to Validation is 5 weeks	23 weeks	6 weeks

---

[30] https://www.gov.uk/guidance/appeals-average-timescales-for-arranging-inquiries-and-hearings. More recent data, such as the July 2020 Decisions Summary have not been included because they were so heavily affected by the Covid-19 emergency with only three inquiry decisions.

2.33 *Commencement*

2.33 In 2020, before the Covid-19 crisis, receipt to decision timescales indicate that:

- written representations appeals are quickest at around 24 weeks, but only six weeks ahead of a Rosewell Inquiry (see Chapter 4) (30 weeks);
- hearings (36 weeks) are two months quicker than a non-Rosewell Inquiry (44 weeks), but a month longer than a Rosewell Inquiry (30 weeks);
- save for enforcement work, which takes around 18 months unless dealt with by written representations.

2.34 Prior to the amendments made by the Planning Act 2008 to the 1990 Act, it was for the appellant to choose the mode of appeal. Sections 319A (in respect of England) and 319B (in respect of Wales) came into force in April 2009. They place a duty on the Secretary of State and on the Welsh Ministers to determine which mode of appeal appears to be most appropriate, and to do so within the prescribed period,[31] being seven working days from the date of receipt of a valid appeal. As a matter of practice, it often takes longer than seven days for the Planning Inspectorate to obtain the information which it needs and the representations of the parties before it makes a decision.

2.35 A determination of the mode of appeal may be varied at any time 'before the proceedings are determined'.[32] This provides complete flexibility, including changing the appeal procedure during a hearing or inquiry, or even, exceptionally, re-opening an appeal via a different mode. However, as also noted at para 4.38 below, the position is set to be amended in respect of planning appeals by reason of amendment to s 319A(2) of the 1990 Act so that the appeal procedure is determined as 'such one or more' of the ways of determining the appeal as appear appropriate (see s 20 of the Business and Planning Act 2020). This will provide still further flexibility in the combination of modes of appeal, though change to procedure rules will also be necessary.

2.36 The Secretary of State and the Welsh Ministers must publish criteria to be applied in making determinations of the mode of appeal. They have done so, and these are reproduced below (footnotes omitted).[33]

Mode of determination of appeals criteria

> **WRITTEN REPRESENTATIONS – WRITTEN REPRESENTATIONS WOULD BE APPROPRIATE IF:**
>
> - the planning issues raised or, in an enforcement appeal, the grounds of appeal, can be clearly understood from the appeal documents and a site inspection (if required); or

---

[31] See Town and Country Planning (Determination of Appeal Procedure) (Prescribed Period) (England) Regulations 2009, SI 2009/454.
[32] See TCPA 1990, s 319A(4) and s 319B(4).
[33] From Annex K of the Procedural Guide *Planning Appeals – England* July 2020 (https://assets.publishing.service.gov.uk/government/uploads/system/uploads/attachment_data/file/897145/Procedural_Guide_Planning_appeals_version_10.pdf); Appendix 1 to the Procedural Guide – Wales is in materially identical terms (https://gov.wales/sites/default/files/publications/2019-01/procedural-guide-wales.pdf).

- the issues are not complex and the Inspector is not likely to need to test the evidence by questioning or to clarify any other matters; or
- in an enforcement appeal the alleged breach, and the requirements of the notice, are clear.

Hearing – a hearing would be appropriate if:
- the Inspector is likely to need to test the evidence by questioning or to clarify matters; or
- the status or personal circumstances of the appellant are at issue; or
- there is no need for evidence to be tested through formal questioning by an advocate or given on oath; or
- the case has generated a level of local interest such as to warrant a hearing; or
- it can reasonably be expected that the parties will be able to present their own cases (supported by professional witnesses if required) without the need for an advocate to represent them; or
- in an enforcement appeal, the grounds of appeal, the alleged breach, and the requirements of the notice, are relatively straightforward.

Inquiry – an inquiry would be appropriate if:
- there is a clearly explained need for the evidence to be tested through formal questioning by an advocate; or
- the issues are complex; or
- the appeal has generated substantial local interest to warrant an inquiry as opposed to dealing with the case by a hearing; or
- in an enforcement appeal, evidence needs to be given on oath;
- in an enforcement appeal, the alleged breach, or the requirements of the notice, are unusual and particularly contentious.

Note – It is considered that the prospect of legal submissions being made is not, on its own, a reason why a case would need to be conducted by inquiry. Where a party considers that legal submissions will be required (and are considered to be complex such as to warrant being made orally), the Inspectorate requires that the matters on which submissions will be made are fully explained – including why they may require an inquiry – at the outset of the appeal or otherwise at the earliest opportunity.

2.37 In summary, the criteria focus on three features of an appeal: (1) whether there is a need to test the evidence; (2) complexity; and (3) the extent of local interest. So far as enforcement appeals are concerned, there is a fourth feature which is relevant, namely the need or otherwise for evidence to be given on oath. This will particularly be the case in respect of ground 'd' appeals in which there is an issue about immunity of the development from enforcement, but may also arise in respect of other legal grounds of appeal.

2.38 It will often be clear and obvious which mode of determination is most appropriate. The large majority of appeals are determined by written representations.

2.39 *Commencement*

Only 7% of s 78 and called-in applications are determined by hearings and inquiries, with the balance determined by written representations. Of the 91,000 appeals to be determined, there are some 5,000 in which the balance of considerations is between the hearing and inquiry procedure.

2.39 Taking the three main features of the criteria in turn, the reality plays out like this:

Testing

- Contested technical issues which are the subject of expert assessment and modelling are highly likely to require the inquiry procedure. Highways or acoustic evidence are good examples.

- But, assessments which are subjective or for which a site view will be an important part of the decision-making process are much less likely to be said to require the inquiry procedure. Landscape and visual impact assessments are a good example, subject to the further considerations below.

- Planning evidence which addresses the development plan and other material considerations to arrive at a planning balance is unlikely to be said to require an inquiry. However, where the decision-making framework is made more complex by reason of the development plan being said to be out of date or not up to date, then the inquiry procedure is often an effective means of hearing the planning evidence.

Complexity

- The overlap with the question of 'testing' is clear from the above – the more complex the topic area of the evidence, the more likely it is to benefit from the inquiry procedure and vice versa.

- Legally complex technical issues will often be said to be most appropriately addressed by the inquiry procedure. Good examples are ecological issues which are the subject of the Conservation of Habitats and Species Regulations 2010,[34] environmental impact assessment cases where adequacy of assessment is in issue or where matters of planning law arise, such as fallback.

Local interest

- It is unfair for an Inspector to be presented with a packed Council chamber and a procedure which gives everybody an opportunity to comment on everything, without notice. If there is substantial interest, then the appeal plainly needs the material points to be marshalled and coherently presented. That is an important function of Rule 6 status[35] which is only in play via the inquiry procedure.

2.40 Previously, the criteria have included reference to the length of a hearing. It was said that if a hearing would take more than two days, then that was an indicator in favour of the inquiry procedure. That part of the guidance has not been expressly

---

[34] SI 2010/490.
[35] See further para 2.64 below on the role of third parties and Rule 6 status.

carried forward. However, the reasonable time estimate for the appeal to be heard is nevertheless an indicator of complexity and ought to be considered by the parties.

STATEMENTS OF COMMON GROUND

2.41 A draft statement of common ground is to be submitted with a s 78 Appeal.[36] In England, art 37(8) of the 2015 Order explains that a 'draft statement of common ground' means:

> 'a written statement containing factual information about the proposal which is the subject of the appeal that the applicant reasonably considers will not be disputed by the local planning authority;'

2.42 PINS guidance on statements of common ground captures their purpose and importance in this way:

> '1. Statements of common/uncommon ground are essential to ensure that the evidence considered focuses on the material differences between the appellant and the local planning authority. They provide a commonly understood context to inform the subsequent production of proofs of evidence.
>
> 2. When the appeal is lodged, the appellant must submit a **draft** statement of common/uncommon ground comprising a written statement setting out factual information about the proposal that the appellant considers will/will not be disputed by the local planning authority.
>
> 3. An **agreed** statement is to be submitted within five weeks of the start date, signed off by the appellant and the local planning authority. This is to be prepared jointly by both parties and can be based on the appellant's earlier draft. Working together in agreeing a statement of common ground will assist the parties in providing relevant evidence, reduce the quantity of material which needs to be presented and considered, and help inform the early engagement process.
>
> 4. As well as identifying relevant areas of agreement, the statement is to focus on those areas where there is no consensus, ie where there is uncommon ground. This will help narrow the issues at the Inquiry and, importantly, will inform the evidence of the parties, allowing for concentration on the remaining areas of dispute.'

2.43 These are, perhaps, the most important paragraphs in any guidance concerned with planning appeals by way of hearing or inquiry. Assuming that an appellant has taken professional advice before appealing, there ought to be very much more material which is agreed than is disputed. The issues ought to be focused and clearly identified.

2.44 Within the scope of each issue there ought to be considerable areas of agreement. So, there may be a reasonable dispute about visual effects, but there should be little dispute about the location of the most important viewpoints. If an effect or impact has been quantified, it ought to be known whether there is agreement

---

[36] There is no reference to 'statement of common ground' in the 2017 Regulations, so in Wales there is no statutory requirement for one. The Welsh Procedural Guide deals with them at Annex 4 and defines one as 'Statements of Common Ground ("SoCG") are joint statements made by the appellant/applicant and other parties such as the local planning/relevant authority. The aim of the document is to agree factual information and to provide a commonly understood basis for the appellant/applicant; the local planning/relevant authority and/or other parties.'

2.45 *Commencement*

as to the baseline data, the method of assessment and the relevant criteria or standard against which to assess the effect. If this is done, then effect is given to what are perhaps the seven most important words in any guidance concerned with planning appeals by way of a hearing or inquiry: '… concentration on the remaining areas of dispute'.

2.45 A statement of common ground is not:

- a once-and-for-all document, but may improve and be refined as the issues refine;
- required to be wordy, repetitive or legalistic. Rather, it should communicate succinctly so that the user understands where to find evidence which is agreed and knows where and why the parties disagree;
- required to be contained within one document. There is no rule that nothing is agreed until everything is agreed. On the contrary, if, for example, the experts in assessing best and most versatile agricultural land have reached agreement then they should say so in their own signed document while discussion of other topic areas continues.

2.46 Statements of common ground are not new. They were established within the 2000 rules (see para 2.23 above). There was, however, a tendency for them to be side-lined in the preparation of evidence and their utility therefore much reduced. A statement of common ground which is produced on the opening of an inquiry with little more than agreement on the description of development, the application plans and the development plan policies cited in the reasons for refusal does not add very much to the process of deciding the appeal.

2.47 However, the statement of common ground was identified as an important tool in the modern appeal. In *R (on the application of Poole) v Secretary of State for Communities and Local Government*[37] it was stated:

> '40. However, it is most important when deciding whether the parties at an inquiry have had a fair opportunity to comment on an issue raised by an Inspector of his or her own motion, and whether they could reasonably have anticipated that an issue had to be addressed because it might be raised by an Inspector, to bear in mind the highly focused nature of the modern public inquiry where the whole emphasis of the Rules and procedural guidance contained in Circulars is to encourage the parties to focus their evidence and submissions on those matters that are in dispute.
>
> 41. Paragraph 40 of Circular 05/00 deals with statements of common ground. It refers the reader to Annex 3(ii) to the Circular as a guide to the function of statements of common ground. That Circular contains the following advice (so far as material):
>
>> "2. The statement of common ground is a written statement prepared jointly by the local planning authority and the applicant (or appellant). The purpose of the statement of common ground is to set out the agreed factual information about the proposal. The inclusion of agreed material in the statement of common ground should result in shorter proofs of evidence and shorter inquiries.
>>
>> 3. The statement of common ground should complement the proofs of evidence and both should be received by the Secretary of State no later than 4 weeks

---

[37] [2008] EWHC 676 (Admin), [2008] JPL 1774.

before the inquiry. The main parties will therefore need to meet before that date to try to narrow the areas of dispute and agree on what should go in the statement. It is the responsibility of the applicant (or appellant) to send the statement to the Secretary of State.

...

5. In all cases agreement can be reached on some matters: the precise nature of the proposal before the inquiry, the description of the site, its planning history and the relevant policies can all be agreed.

6. Evidence on technical matters and topics that rely on basic statistical data can often be fruitful areas for pre-inquiry agreement.

...

7. The statement of common ground, by clearly identifying the matters which are not in real dispute, may save time and cost at the inquiry. It may also be useful for the statement to identify areas where agreement is not possible.

8. Time can also be saved at the inquiry by seeking to agree beforehand the conditions that any permission granted should contain and any planning obligations being considered. The Rules reinforce the established presumption against taking into account material submitted after the inquiry is closed ..."'

2.48 This case, in which an Inspector refused an adjournment when the planning authority resiled from a statement of common ground, is instructive in two ways. First, it makes clear that the modern inquiry is a highly focused exercise (see [40], cited above). The statement of common ground is central to that objective of focusing the evidence. Secondly, the summary of the Secretary of State's advice in the (now cancelled) circular 05/00 captures the practicality of crafting a statement of common ground in a way which is presently absent in the National Planning Practice and the PINS Procedural Guide.

2.49 The statement of common ground is now required in draft with the appeal. The purposes of this earlier feature in the process are to give added emphasis to the identification of issues and to promote timely agreement, thus overcoming the tardiness which infected the usefulness of statements of common ground previously. Despite their long presence in the appeal system, Statements of Common Ground remain, on average, much less effective than they might be. As Bridget Rosewell observed:[38]

'the statement of common ground could be a powerful and effective tool for improving the efficiency and effectiveness of the process, but currently it is not.'

2.50 However, the statement of common ground can be a part of a structural imbalance in the appeal procedure. This derives from the way in which main issues are identified and resolved. In the large majority of hearings and inquiries, the reasons for refusal, the matters of disagreement in a statement of common ground and the Inspector's main issues for the decision will be very similar and consistent. In this way, the entire appeal process may become devoted to those matters which weigh against the proposal, leaving little or no space for those matters which weigh in favour, nor for consideration of the degree to which common harms may be

---

[38] Independent Review of Planning Appeal Inquiries (Main Report); Bridget Rosewell OBE (December 2018), para 5.26.

2.51 *Commencement*

absent from a particular scheme or proposal. There is a strong argument that there is a structural defect or bias in the appeal system in failing to address the merits as a whole and in the round. If a statement of common ground fails to fully explain the agreed benefits and the agreement on technical issues which would otherwise present a bar to development, then it merely serves to emphasise those elements of the scheme which have adverse effects. This feature of the appeal system can be navigated by careful attention to the content of a draft statement of common ground, taking the time to set out a balanced appreciation of the scheme, while remaining faithful to the guidance to identify what is disputed and why.

STATEMENTS OF CASE AND HEARING STATEMENTS

2.51 '*Statements of case*' and '*hearing statements*' are fundamental to any appeal. Bridget Rosewell described statements of case in this way:[39]

> 'These are critically important documents in identifying the main issues and the evidence to be called. The appellant's statement informs the Planning Inspectorate's decision on the appropriate mode of appeal and their initial assessment of the duration of any inquiry.'

2.52 Are statements of case and hearing statements the same thing and how do they fit into the progress and process of an appeal?

2.53 In practical terms, they are likely to be different things and fulfil different functions. This is because of the differences between the hearing and inquiry mode of appeal. A hearing statement will contain all of the evidence, comment, submissions and materials which a party wishes an Inspector to consider via the hearing route. There is a further opportunity to comment on the other side's hearing statement, but the primary written means of communicating a case to an Inspector is via a hearing statement.

2.54 In contrast, for an appeal determined by inquiry, the statement of case precedes and is distinct from the proofs of evidence. A statement of case will explain fully the case which is going to be advanced by a party and will refer to the evidence which will be relied upon. So, if landscape character is in issue, then a landscape and visual impact assessment which was submitted with the application may be referenced in the statement of case. The interaction between the statement of case and proofs of evidence is considered in Chapter 3.

2.55 Though the practical difference between a statement of case and a hearing statement is generally understood, the difference remains unclear in the rules. In the 2002 hearing procedure rules, a 'hearing statement':[40]

> 'means, and consists of, a written statement which contains full particulars of the case which a person proposes to put forward at a hearing and copies of any documents which that person intends to refer to or put in evidence'.

---

[39] Independent Review of Planning Appeal Inquiries (Main Report); Bridget Rosewell OBE (December 2018), para 4.17.
[40] Town and Country Planning (Enforcement) (Hearings Procedure) (England) Rules 2002, r 2.

2.56 Likewise 'full statement of case' in the Welsh and English rules means:[41]

'a written statement which contains full particulars of the case which a person proposes to put forward and copies of any documents which that person intends to refer to or put in evidence'.

2.57 So, they are defined in identical terms, but in practice are far from the same thing for the reasons just set out.

2.58 Turning to the statement of case which is required for an appeal submitted for the inquiry procedure, the Planning Inspectorate's short guidance note[42] makes it clear that the statement of case should:

- not contain the evidence – that is for the proof of evidence;
- identify the main issues, matters raised by interested parties, and the evidence to be called on those issues;
- explain the main arguments and policy justification for the conclusions contended for;
- identify issues which may be resolved or be resolvable;
- refer to the documents to be relied upon; and
- is not expected to exceed 3,000 words.

2.59 This guidance reflects earlier documents, now superseded, such as Circular 05/00 which at Annex 3 included this:

'This enables the parties to know as much as possible about each other's case at an early stage and will help the parties to focus on the matters which are in dispute. It can also help the parties assess whether there is scope for negotiation while there is still time for this to lead to a satisfactory outcome. Starting negotiations early can help avoid late cancellations of inquiries or requests for postponement.' (emphasis added)

2.60 While no longer extant guidance, it is nevertheless a useful statement of the purpose of the statement of case, namely to enable the other parties to know your case and to focus the appeal, aid negotiation, and avoid wasted costs.

2.61 There is provision in the procedure rules to require a party to give further information as to its case.[43] This may act as a remedy for a combined failure to provide clear, precise and full reasons for refusal and a failure to state a case in accordance with the rules.

2.62 The PINS guidance suggests that the parties should indicate and explain which issues should be dealt with by which procedure. The parties are invited to indicate how the evidence can be most effectively tested, with the options being cross-

---

[41] See r 2 of the Town and Country Planning (Hearings Procedure) (England) Rules 2000.
[42] https://assets.publishing.service.gov.uk/government/uploads/system/uploads/attachment_data/file/825596/statement_of_case.pdf
[43] For example, r 6(8) of the Town and Country Planning Appeals (Determination by Inspectors) (Inquiries Procedure) (England) Rules 2000 gives power to the Secretary of State to require any person who has submitted a statement of case to provide such further information as he may specify, and by when.

2.63 *Commencement*

examination or round table discussion. This forms no part of the rules, but is a means of obtaining the information which is necessary to organise the format of the inquiry and the split between more formal and less formal presentation of the evidence.

2.63 In many circumstances, a party's case will be clearer if it includes a separate section or a separate document which explains how the party sees the presentation of its case and what needs to be put to another party. It is unfortunate if the clarity of a party's case on a particular issue is fogged by submissions about the desirability of a particular procedure. They are quite separate questions.

2.64 A 'Rule 6 Party' is any party to the appeal by reason of sending a statement of case to the Secretary of State. In practice, the term 'Rule 6 Party' means an interested party; a person or organisation other than the local planning authority and the appellant who has provided a statement of case pursuant to r 6(6) of the Town and Country Planning Appeals (Determination by Inspectors) (Inquiries Procedure) (England) Rules 2000 and indicated that they wish to participate and appear as a party. This is an important step. It brings with it both the benefits and the burdens of providing evidence, calling evidence, questioning witnesses and making submissions. A Rule 6 Party may support or oppose the appeal and may be interested in all of the issues or only some of them. They may or may not be professionally represented.

Enforcement – grounds of appeal

2.65 In an appeal against an enforcement notice, the issues in any appeal derive from: (1) the terms of the enforcement notice, and; (2) the grounds of appeal. The differences between the way in which an enforcement notice appeal and a s 78 appeal are set up are quite marked. This is because:

(a) in a s 78 appeal, the primary source of the contentious issues in the appeal is the planning authority's reasons for refusal. These reasons are responding to an application. However, an enforcement notice raises legal, evidential and planning issues which may not have been presented and argued through an application;

(b) the only basis for an enforcement appeal is the grounds in TCPA 1990, s 174; and

(c) the appellant elects whether to pursue any or all grounds of appeal. In contrast, it is the planning authority which elects which reasons for refusal to pursue and defend.

It follows that the terms of the enforcement notice and the choice of grounds of appeal are determinative of the issues to be decided and, taken together, frame the entire case from the outset.

2.66 Ground (a) is that planning permission should be granted. This is the only ground which engages all of the planning merits. If ground (a) is not pursued then the planning merits are irrelevant to the appeal. The decision to appeal on ground (a) has a major bearing on the extent and content of the statement of case.

Practical pointers

2.67 For an appellant in a s 78 appeal, almost all of the material to support a statement of case will have been prepared and submitted as part of the application process. Drafting a statement of case is not an exercise in re-inventing the wheel. The wheel exists, needs to be described, and the spokes which hold it all together clearly identified.

2.68 The design and access statement and planning statements will provide the bulk of the material needed for most statements of case. From them it is necessary to extract the features of the scheme, development plan policy and other material considerations which bear upon the main issues. It is the case in respect of each of the main issues which should be explained. It is unnecessary and a distraction to rehearse anything other than points on which the case really turns. This does not mean that other matters will be ignored in the consideration of the appeal. On the contrary, those matters are incorporated by reference to documents which address those other matters. So, flood risk may not be a main issue and consequently does not need to be addressed expressly in a statement of case. However, a drainage report from the application stage may be before the inquiry and may be referred to when planning conditions are discussed.

2.69 A statement of case goes beyond identifying the appellant's positive case as presented to the planning authority. It explains the nature of the response to the opposing case, for example:

- the policy relied upon is inconsistent with current national policy, and explaining the consequences;
- the tilted balance applies to the decision and the planning authority was incorrect in failing to apply it;
- the highway authority is relying on a model which is incorrect;
- the sensitivity of visual receptors has been over-estimated, and explaining how that can be shown to be so; or
- the contributions to off-site infrastructure are not justified, or that they are now agreed to be justified and their costs will be met and so that issue falls away.

2.70 The usefulness of the time and thought which goes into drafting statements of case lies in the identification of the issues and the reasons for the parties' disagreement. Good statements of case resolve and narrow issues, shorten inquiries, reduce costs, free-up Inspector time and assist in obtaining more timely decisions.

2.71 However, the interaction with the draft statement of common ground should be clear and fully integrated. Taken together, the statement of case and statement of common ground ought to fully explain the merits of the proposal in the round and as a whole. To fail to do so risks a skewed approach to the issues with a bias, in terms of proper consideration, towards the reasons for refusal.

Chapter 3

Written evidence and representations

3.01 All three modes of determining appeals have written materials in their foundations. For the hearing and inquiry modes, those foundations are built upon through the oral evidence and submissions made directly to the Inspector. However, the marshalling of materials, thinking and careful expression of the evidence and conclusions is a process common to all procedures.

3.02 Therefore, this chapter addresses the written material for all appeals, in common, in six parts. The first three are concerned with the scope and objectives of written evidence: (1) what are you trying to show? (2) how are you going to show it? and (3) who are you addressing, ie who is your audience?

3.03 The last three are concerned with how to achieve those objectives in a manner which is: (1) permissible within an expert's code of conduct; (2) effective, in terms of drafting; and (3) practical, in terms of usability.

WHAT ARE YOU TRYING TO SHOW?

Main issues

3.04 First, there are the main issues which flow predominantly from the reasons for refusal.

3.05 The main issues will capture and include the planning authority's reasons for refusal. Article 35(1)(b) of the Town and Country Planning (Development Management Procedure) (England) Order 2015[1] provides:[2]

> 'where planning permission is refused, the notice must state clearly and precisely the local planning authority's full reasons for the refusal, specifying all policies and proposals in the development plan which are relevant to the decision'

---

[1] SI 2015/595.
[2] This is very clear. It is directive in that the notice *must* state the full reasons for refusal. It is also a requirement to be comprehensive in that the reasons must be clear, precise and full. This is a provision which was present in the now revoked General Development Procedure Order 1995, and so is long established. However, there is no provision within the Order to deal with a complaint that the reasons for refusal fail to meet the requirement. Likewise, there is no provision to deal with the circumstance where the local planning authority expands its case on appeal. However, r 6(8) of the Town and Country Planning Appeals (Determination by Inspectors) (Inquiries Procedure) (England) Rules 2000, SI 2000/1625 gives power to the Secretary of State to require any person who has submitted a statement of case to provide such further information as he may specify, and by when.

Article 24(1)(b) of the Town and Country Planning (Development Management Procedure) (Wales) Order 2012[3] is in like terms.

3.06 By reference to the reasons for refusal and the statements of case, it is essential that the parties accurately identify the main issues. This will determine the scope of the evidence. If the scope of the evidence is deficient, then one of the parties will be in real difficulty, as will the Inspector.

3.07 Opponents of the scheme seek to show that those reasons are well founded, both factually and by reference to relevant policy. The appellant seeks to show that the reasons for refusal are either factually incorrect, over-stated, or disagree with the policy weight to be attached.

The positive case

3.08 Secondly, there is the appellant's positive case. This comprises those factual and policy features of a proposal which weigh in favour of the grant of permission. They will very often be uncontentious as a matter of fact. The disagreement often lies in the weight to be given to the benefits. So, all parties need to address this element of the appeal so that the Inspector is properly informed about the planning balance. The planning balance must be one of the main issues, and so this second part of the scope takes us back to the first. However, within the appellant's positive case there will be facets and material considerations which need to be fully brought out and understood so that the planning balance may be accurately undertaken.

3.09 This second element of the written evidence is of primary importance to an appellant, but is nevertheless to be addressed head-on by those who oppose a proposal. It must be addressed by those who oppose a proposal because, for any appeal which is reasonably made, there is a planning balance to be struck. It is impossible to undertake that balance without a fair, accurate and complete understanding of the positive case. Evidence which fails in any of these respects risks amounting to little more than advocacy for one party, will lack credibility as a result and thus harm the overall case which that party seeks to advance. In other words, to avoid or minimise points which support a proposal may well have a counter-productive effect overall.

3.10 Rather, a planning authority or objector has to show where the balance of planning considerations require refusal, and the reasons for it. This may involve:

- responding to the appellant's positive factual case and testing it;

- explaining the relative strengths of the policies which support the proposal, in comparison to the protective or constraining policies which may be offended; and

- critically examining the means by which objections are said to be overcome by use of mitigation, planning conditions and planning obligations.

3.11 The appellant must seek to address the converse. The appellant must not assert anything about its proposal which is not fully supported or supportable by reference to the details of the scheme and the environment in which it would sit.

---

[3] SI 2012/801.

3.12 *Written evidence and representations*

This may be quite a substantial task. However, the more each positive aspect of the proposal is assessed and justified by reference to objective measures, the more convincing it becomes. One way in which to illustrate this is by reference to what can be said in respect of a full application for a residential scheme and what can be said in respect of an outline application.

Other issues

3.12 Lastly, there is everything else. The Inspector and, or, third parties may regard other matters as important, albeit that they do not figure in the planning authority's reasons for refusal. This is not uncommon and presents its own particular challenges for all parties, and for the Inspector. It is not objectionable at all because the Inspector is seized of the matter afresh and is bound to take account of all material considerations. The fact that the planning authority does not regard a matter as material, or to warrant refusal, does not alleviate the Inspector of the duty to come to an independent finding on it. If the point is raised, is material and is ignored, then the decision will be liable to be quashed as having been taken outside of the Inspector's powers.

3.13 In contrast, there are matters of disagreement (issues) which are not categorised as main issues. Interested persons and Rule 6 Parties (see para 2.64 above) are likely to have to take up the challenge of making out such points. The planning authority will largely confine its written evidence to those issues which arise from its reasons for refusal. This may or may not mean that the planning authority holds a contrary position to that relied upon by interested persons and third parties. It is often a question of degree. For example, the planning authority may agree that there would be a noticeable impact on traffic conditions at certain times arising from a proposal, but may disagree with third parties that the impact is one which is unacceptable by reference to relevant guidance and policy.

3.14 An appellant faced with such an issue has a judgement to make in the particular case. Is the objection and the objective evidence which might support it such that it requires evidence which specifically responds to the objection, albeit that no statutory consultee objects?

A case example

3.15 A developer sought outline planning permission to erect 110 dwellings on land near Lower Shiplake in South Oxfordshire on a site which fronts on to the A4155 Reading Road.[4] It was proposed that vehicular access to the site would be located at a point lying approximately in the middle of that frontage. One of two pedestrian routes was proposed as the main intended pedestrian route between the site and Lower Shiplake village. The A4155 follows a straight alignment alongside the eastern boundary of the appeal site and runs for a further 190m or thereabouts beyond the southern boundary of the site. It then bends to the west at the Shiplake War Memorial traffic island which is located at the junction with Station Road. Route A involved the creation of a new footway along the western side of the A4155 between the south eastern corner of the site and a new crossing point to the War

---

[4] *Engbers v Secretary of State for Communities and Local Government* [2016] EWCA Civ 1183, [2017] JPL 489.

What are you trying to show? **3.22**

Memorial traffic island at the junction with Station Road. The relevant lengths of the A4155 and Station Road are subject to a 30mph speed limit.

3.16 The planning authority refused the application for outline planning permission on seven grounds, none of which related to the proposed main pedestrian access.

3.17 The Council and the appellant prepared a statement of common ground which recorded the agreement that 'safe access can be provided into Shiplake for pedestrians with a new footpath along Reading Road'. Residents, however, did not agree. They made representations such as:

> 'It would cause serious traffic safety issues. It is near a double bend/chicane at the Shiplake War Memorial crossroads junction, this being the location of many road traffic accidents and a fatal road traffic accident in 2006.'

> 'The A4155 is already a busy road which is exceptionally difficult to cross safely even by the able bodied, let alone by anyone with a walking disability or visual impairment.'

> 'The A4155 Reading Road has a 30mph speed limit along the site's boundary, yet it exhibits the rural character of a road with a national speed limit of 60mph. Traffic is prone to speeding along its length and the presence of a sudden and sharp bend and hidden dips does nothing to improve its safety. The road is a known accident blackspot, it is difficult to cross due to traffic speed and volume and visibility, and there has been a fatality in recent years ... We are concerned that although an access solution is promoted that meets the technical requirements for a road limited to 30mph it does not take into account the true elements of this road ... Given the road's issues in terms of traffic speeds and safety, and the barrier the road creates between the village and the countryside to the west, the site at Thames Farm is wholly unsuitable for development.'

3.18 Having read the statement of common ground and the representations from third parties, the Inspector produced a pre-inquiry statement under r 7 of the Town and Country Planning Appeals (Determination by Inspectors) (Inquiries Procedure) (England) Rules 2000. The Inspector's statement outlined the main issues, based on the written evidence thus far, including:

> 'the safety and convenience of users of the highway and other public rights of way'.

> 'In considering the appeal the Inspector will take account of all written representations as well as the evidence heard at the Inquiry.'

3.19 At the opening of the inquiry, the Inspector said that the main issues included 'the safety and convenience of users of the highway and other public rights of way'. He had also referred to the fact that he had received a very large number of representations from interested parties and repeated that he would take them all into account.

3.20 The appellant's highways consultant was called to give evidence at the Inspector's request.

3.21 That in itself ought to have alerted the developer to the fact that the Inspector was taking the residents' concerns seriously.

3.22 The Inspector did indeed take into account the views of local residents and the Parish Council, even though there were no highway issues as between the developer and the authorities. He said:

3.23 *Written evidence and representations*

'Neither the Council nor the Highway Authority object to the scheme on the basis of its effect on the safety and convenience of highway users. Nonetheless, I have had regard to the concerns raised by other interested parties, including Shiplake Parish Council.'

3.23 The Court of Appeal upheld the Inspector's approach to the inquiry. If a third party raises an issue which is at variance with the agreed stance of the appellant and the local planning authority, the Inspector is duty bound to consider it. Fairness to third parties demands no less.

HOW ARE YOU GOING TO SHOW IT?

3.24 No party to an appeal is starting from scratch when it comes to drafting the written evidence in support of its position at appeal. Rather, the entire decision-making process has usually already happened, and may have happened more than once in cases where applications have been amended and re-submitted. Even call-in cases and inquiries into objections to order-schemes will have been the subject of detailed consultation. The application materials must contain full descriptions of the proposal within the plans, design and access statement, planning statement, supporting technical documents and possibly in an environmental statement. Similarly, there will be a questionnaire via which the local planning authority is required to send certain documents to the Planning Inspectorate (PINS).[5] It is likely to include:

- the application and plans;
- responses from statutory consultees;
- responses from the consultation and publicity of the application;
- the delegated report or report to committee;
- the decision notice;
- relevant development plan policies; and
- relevant emerging policies

3.25 In a case in which members and officers are of the same opinion, the delegated report or report to committee will include a reasoned explanation of the issues and the planning balance.

3.26 So, it may be that no more evidence is needed if all the work has already been done. All of the primary evidence exists, the policy context has been analysed, the views of statutory consultees and the public are known. The task, therefore, is to take the existing material, supplemented by additional evidence if required, and to set it out clearly and concisely. That is what sets out the process of reasoning which then leads to the conclusion: 'As with judicial or other opinions, what carries weight is the reasoning, not the conclusion'.[6]

---

[5] Eg, r 4 of the Town and Country Planning Appeals (Determination by Inspectors) (Inquiries Procedure) (England) Rules 2000.
[6] *Dingley v Chief Constable, Strathclyde Police* 1998 SC 548 at 604.

AUDIENCES

3.27 The evidence is addressed to the Inspector. The Inspector has both relevant qualifications and relevant experience, often in making planning decisions, before appointment as an Inspector. Inspectors' qualifications and experience will never extend to all of the technical or specialist topic areas which are relevant to the range of appeal work they do. It may be that an appeal with a main issue involving traffic impacts will be charted before an Inspector with relevant qualifications or experience. It may not. In either case, the written evidence is to be prepared for an audience which is adept at assimilating new technical information and who is experienced at considering the evidence critically.

3.28 Take, for example, a scheme which attracts the objection that it will impair the operation of a radio telescope.[7] No Inspector is an expert in measuring the electromagnetic radiation from pulsars, nor the measures which might be taken to deal with interference to such signals. However, even the most specialist material can be and sometimes must be addressed to an inquiry.

3.29 But the evidence is not solely addressed to the Inspector. It is addressed to the participants in the appeal. In order to inform the Inspector and also to advance the arguments beyond the point reached when the application was determined, the written evidence should address the contrary cases. In doing so, issues are narrowed or at least the competing arguments become more clear and focused. It is generally not in a party's overall interest to simply advance their own case without seeking to analyse and address the main points which go the other way.

3.30 Appeals are more inclusive of third parties than they once were. As a process of decision-making in the public interest, this change is as welcome as it is necessary. However, the public interest and the interests of the public are often not the same thing.

3.31 Some third parties will read the written evidence, whereas many will not. In either eventuality, it is highly desirable to identify third party concerns and to address them at a length which is proportionate to the nature of the issue. This alleviates the perception that third-party concerns are being ignored, provides the Inspector with the necessary evidence and provides a quick and simple answer to the point if it is raised orally at a hearing or inquiry.

3.32 The next stage in an appeal may be a hearing or inquiry. The written evidence is the starting point for questions, either from the Inspector as an inquisitor or from an advocate to advance that case or to test and put the contrary case. The written evidence is therefore also addressed to a process of examination.

3.33 Inspectors at inquiries will have had experience with written representations and hearings. But the reverse does not necessarily apply – an experienced Inspector may be charted to do a written representations appeal.

---

[7] Land off Main Road, Goostrey – APP/R0660/W/15/3129954.

3.34   *Written evidence and representations*

PROFESSIONAL DUTIES AND DECLARATIONS BY EXPERTS

Codes of Professional Conduct

3.34   Not all written evidence is prepared by experts. The evidence of third parties is not usually expert evidence, but that does not diminish its value at all.

3.35   The evidence of a planning witness will be a mixture of planning expertise and reliance on the expertise of specialists in other disciplines. However, it is clear that any planning statement of case or planning proof is expert evidence to which professional standards apply. Members of the Royal Town Planning Institute (RTPI) and the Royal Institution of Chartered Surveyors (RICS) each operate under a Code of Professional Conduct[8] and Rules of Conduct for Members.[9]

3.36   The RICS Rules are a brief set of principles, the most pertinent of which are concerned with ethical behaviour, competence and service. The RTPI Code is much more expansive and contains 29 articles by which its members are bound, and three Annexes. The Code expands on five core principles, each of which is relevant to the drafting of evidence in a planning appeal:

- competence, honesty and integrity;
- independent professional judgement;
- due care and diligence;
- equality and respect; and
- professional behaviour.

3.37   Without implying that any particular article of the Code is less significant than another, in its particular context, the following are evidently important aspects of the Code to be applied in the drafting of planning evidence:[10]

> '[3] Members must act within the scope of their professional competence in undertaking the professional planning services they are employed or commissioned to do.
>
> [4] Members must act with honesty and integrity throughout their career.
>
> ...
>
> [9] Members must not offer or accept inducements, financial or otherwise, to influence a decision or professional point of view with regards to planning matters.
>
> ...
>
> [11] Members must exercise fearlessly and impartially their independent professional judgement to the best of their skill and understanding.
>
> ...
>
> [13] Members must disclose their professional designation where appropriate to their employers, clients, colleagues or others and use their post-nominal letters, where held and where possible, in any professional correspondence as a mark of professional standing.'

---

[8]   MRTPI Code of Professional Conduct, last amended by the Board of Trustees in February 2016.
[9]   RICS Rules of Conduct for Members, version 7 with effect from 2 March 2020.
[10] The number in square brackets is the paragraph number in the original.

Professional duties and declarations by experts **3.43**

3.38 RTPI guidance says this:[11]

'Within this role you, as an expert, also have the opportunity to be persuasive and put forward arguments to support your viewpoint to ensure the best decision is made by the Inspector in the public interest. Your "duty" as an expert witness is always to the Inspector and overrides any obligation to the person or organisation that has instructed or paid you.'

3.39 Planning is a very broad area of practice which is heavily reliant on a substantial knowledge base which is itself interdisciplinary. Therefore, to act within professional competence is not simply a question of length of experience but is also a function of the type of experience.

3.40 Honesty, dealing with inducements and impartiality run together and are a constant theme. The code requires independent judgment, unaffected by client interest. It is for these essential reasons that professional witnesses are invited by the PINS guidance to endorse their written evidence with the following statement:

'The evidence which I have prepared and provide for this appeal reference APP/xxx (in this proof of evidence, written statement or report) is true [and has been prepared and is given in accordance with the guidance of my professional institution] and I confirm that the opinions expressed are my true and professional opinions.'

3.41 This will enable the Inspector and others involved in an appeal to know that the material in a proof of evidence, written statement or report is provided as 'expert evidence'. The Planning Inspectorate emphasise that the evidence should be accurate, concise and complete as to relevant fact(s)) within the expert's knowledge and should represent the witness's honest and objective opinion. If a professional body has adopted a code of practice on professional conduct dealing with the giving of evidence, then a member of that body will be expected to comply with the provisions of the code in the preparation and presentation (written or in person) of the expert evidence.

3.42 The PINS guidance indicates an acceptance that an expert may also appear as an advocate. The number of occasions on which that coincidence in fact happens must be very small. However, it is respectfully doubted whether the guidance is either correct or appropriate. An advocate's role does not involve his or her opinions and the advocate may not give evidence. An expert witness is the exact opposite – the expert's express purpose is to assist by giving opinions and evidence.

3.43 Expert evidence is often relied upon in civil and criminal cases. The courts have sought to direct the nature of that evidence:[12]

'The expert evidence should be the independent product of the expert uninfluenced as to form or content by the exigencies of litigation; The witness should provide expert unbiased opinion in relation to matters within his expertise and should never assume the

---

[11] RTPI Practice Advice (September 2018), p 3.
[12] *National Justice Compania Naviera SA v Prudential Assurance Co Ltd (The Ikarian Reefer) (No 1)* [1993] 2 Lloyd's Rep 68, [1993] 37 EG 158. headnote. This is a shipping case, not a planning case. However, the principles apply universally. These principles have been widely applied and expressly approved by the Supreme Court in *Kennedy v Cordia (Services) LLP* [2016] 1 WLR 597. They were also applied in *Gardiner & Theobald LLP v Jackson* [2018] UKUT 253 (LC), [2018] 5 Costs LR 987 in respect of the duties of Chartered Surveyors giving evidence to the Upper Tribunal (Lands Chamber).

3.44 *Written evidence and representations*

role of advocate. He should not omit to consider material facts which detract from his concluded opinion and he should make it clear when a question falls outside his own expertise. The opinion should state if it is provisional only, or subject to any qualification. If, after exchange of reports, the expert changes view, this should be communicated to the other side and the court without delay. Where the expert evidence refers to photographs, plans, calculations, analyses, measurements, survey reports or other similar documents these must be provided to the other party at the same time as the exchange of reports.'

3.44 These principles appear to be as helpful to the appeals process as they are to litigation. The case emphasises that the expert should never assume the role of advocate. A member of the public wandering into some planning inquiries might be forgiven for thinking that some experts are present in order to promote one side of a case. To a degree, that has become the culture of planning appeals over time, on all sides. To the extent that it occurs, it is unfortunate for at least the following reasons:

- it is plainly inconsistent with institutional codes of conduct, which undermines the function of those institutions;
- it tends to increase the range and cost of resolving issues;
- it reduces the effectiveness of the evidence for everybody; and
- it inhibits an important collateral benefit of planning appeals in improving knowledge, expertise, standards and in resolving issues which are of wider application than in the particular appeal.

3.45 The style of writing of decision letters tends not to engage with the credibility of expert witnesses. It is now quite rare to be able to gather from a decision letter that an Inspector was either particularly impressed by the work and learning of a witness, or particularly unimpressed. There are, no doubt, good reasons for that reticence, but it contrasts with the approach in litigation.

Fee agreements

3.46 There is presently a notable absence of rules, guidance and planning-specific guidance on the relevance of the fee structure under which an expert is engaged. In the context of valuation work in the Upper Tribunal (Lands Chamber), this conclusion was drawn in respect of valuation evidence which was given without a declaration of contingency fee on which the expert was engaged:[13]

'However, one thing is certainly clear. Whatever approach this tribunal decides to adopt on the issues raised by *Factortame*, it remains wholly unacceptable for an expert witness, or the practice for which he or she works, to enter into a conditional fee arrangement, without that fact being declared (and in sufficient detail) to the tribunal and any other party to the proceedings from the very outset of their involvement in the case. The tribunal will treat such a failure as a serious matter.'

3.47 A planning appeal is not a reference to the Upper Tribunal, though the same professionals might appear in both jurisdictions. However, it appears sensible to apply the conclusion in the *Gardiner* case to planning appeals. If a witness has an interest in the outcome of an appeal, then it should be declared. It is a matter for any

---

[13] *Gardiner & Theobald LLP v Jackson* [2018] UKUT 253 (LC), [2018] 5 Costs LR 987 at [81].

party to decide whether it is in their interests to call such a witness, having regard to the potential for the weight to be given to that evidence being affected by whatever interest is declared.

3.48 An interest in the outcome is not the same as remuneration for work done. An expert is, obviously, entitled to be paid without it being said that payment impairs impartiality.

DRAFTING – SPENDING LONGER PRODUCING LESS TEXT

Brevity

3.49 If the rules and guidance have been followed, then by the time a proof of evidence comes to be drafted and settled, it will be unnecessary to repeat much of the background to the appeal. It is burdensome for all if material is repeated without good reason. It is burdensome for the witness's own client, other witnesses and advocates who will need to read, digest and comment on material which is ultimately not needed. If that material appears within the final proof, then it will be burdensome to the other parties and the Inspector who will have to sift the material from the immaterial.

3.50 A sub-section of a book which seeks to promote brevity in written evidence and representations should not be long. Setting out the real points concisely will prove an aid to clearer thinking. Such was the conclusion of Winston Churchill in 1940. His four-point approach to avoiding the waste of time and energy is just as true 80 years later (see p 42).

Structure

3.51 Structure is essential. Structure allows the author to split and sift:
- known and agreed facts;
- disputed facts;
- methods, guidance and precedent; and
- opinions and discussion.

3.52 The same general principles apply to written representations, hearing statements and proofs of evidence. In respect of a proof of evidence, the main addition is the first section which is the author's qualifications and experience. A proof of evidence is personal to the author. Much of it may be written in the first person. In contrast, written representations and hearing statements are likely to be written in the third person, though there is no rule to that effect.

3.53 The Inspector needs to understand how the witness has approached all four of these elements and to know where the disagreements and common ground lie. If any of these elements are mixed, then they become difficult to disentangle. If there are disputed factual matters, then they have to be grappled with first because the opinions and discussion will be dependent on which facts are preferred or ultimately conceded.

3.54 *Written evidence and representations*

> (THIS DOCUMENT IS THE PROPERTY OF HIS BRITANNIC MAJESTY'S GOVERNMENT).
>
> S E C R E T.
> W.P.(G)(40) 211.   COPY NO. 51
> 9TH AUGUST, 1940.
>
> WAR CABINET.
>
> BREVITY.
>
> Memorandum by the Prime Minister.
>
> To do our work, we all have to read a mass of papers. Nearly all of them are far too long. This wastes time, while energy has to be spent in looking for the essential points.
>
> I ask my colleagues and their staffs to see to it that their Reports are shorter.
>
> (i) The aim should be Reports which set out the main points in a series of short, crisp paragraphs.
>
> (ii) If a Report relies on detailed analysis of some complicated factors, or on statistics, these should be set out in an Appendix.
>
> (iii) Often the occasion is best met by submitting not a full-dress Report, but an Aide-memoire consisting of headings only, which can be expanded orally if needed.
>
> (iv) Let us have an end of such phrases as these: "It is also of importance to bear in mind the following considerations......", or "Consideration should be given to the possibility of carrying into effect......". Most of these woolly phrases are mere padding, which can be left out altogether, or replaced by a single word. Let us not shrink from using the short expressive phrase, even if it is conversational.
>
> Reports drawn up on the lines I propose may at first seem rough as compared with the flat surface of officialese jargon. But the saving in time will be great, while the discipline of setting out the real points concisely will prove an aid to clearer thinking.
>
> W.S.C.
>
> 10, Downing Street.
> 9TH AUGUST, 1940.

3.54 The structure of a planning proof might be:

(1) Author's qualifications and experience.

(2) Site description.

(3) Site history.

(4) Description of the proposal.

(5) Reasons for refusal and grounds of appeal.

(6) The main issue(s).

(7) The development plan.

(8) Other material considerations.

(9) Analysis of the main issues.

    (a) Character and appearance.

    (b) Effects upon the setting of heritage assets.

    (c) Prematurity.

    (d) Need for and benefits of the proposal.

    (e) Planning balance.

        (i) Compliance with the development plan.

        (ii) Material considerations including national policy.

        (iii) The balance of considerations.

(10) Proposed conditions (if not being dealt with in the statement of common ground).

(11) Summary and conclusions.

This structure achieves the objective of confining the contentious material to an identifiable section. Here, the argument is to be contained in section 9. The preceding sections build the background and provide the material from which the author may draw out the analysis, discussion and opinions.

3.55 In a planning proof, the starting point is, and has to be, the development plan. The starting point is not national policy. The starting point is not emerging policy. National policy and emerging policy may be important and may ultimately be determinative in a particular case, but they are not the development plan which attracts statutory force. Development management decisions are to be taken in accordance with the development plan, unless material considerations indicate otherwise.

3.56 A planning proof may be very much dependent upon the work of other specialists, or it may contain much of its own specialist analysis, for example if the planning witness is dealing with design or sustainability. Those may be specialist topics within the planning witness's written evidence. The approach to such specialist topics is common to the various disciplines.

3.57 Similar principles apply to the structure to be given to other documents produced in support of a party's position on an appeal, including written representations and hearing statements.

A specialist's proof – facts, assessments and opinions

3.58 It is impossible to draft evidence without first of all accurately understanding the facts and accurately understanding policy and law. The starting point for

3.59 *Written evidence and representations*

a specialist's proof is to establish the facts and to state them. Those facts do not change, but how to analyse them and fit them into a policy framework is a process of reasoning. There may be more than one arguable line of reasoning. So, you are trying to show: (1) what the relevant facts are; (2) what the proposal needs to be measured against, ie relevant policies; and (3) what happens when you measure the facts against the policies. It may be desirable to consider a secondary case on a different factual basis to test the reasoning against the factual basis which is being contended for by another party. Such a counterfactual argument is secondary and should be considered after dealing fully with the primary case.

3.59 The nature of the proposal is a fundamental starting point so far as the facts are concerned. There should be no dispute about that, but an appeal scheme is not absolutely fixed. Changes to proposals between application and appeal stage are discouraged, but are nevertheless possible to the degree permitted by *Wheatcroft*.[14] There is no principle of law that prevents the imposition on a planning permission of conditions that would have the effect of reducing the permitted development below that for which permission had been applied for except where the application was severable. The test is not whether the development proposed in the application is severable but whether the effect of the conditional planning permission would be to allow development that was in substance not that for which permission had been applied for. The main, but not the only, criterion on which the judgement should be exercised is whether the development is so changed thereby that to grant it would be to deprive those who should have been consulted on the changed development of the opportunity of such consultation.

3.60 The beneficial and adverse effects of a proposal may be ascertainable facts, or they may be mixed questions of fact and opinion. For example, a proposal is either visible from a view point or it is not. That is a question of fact. If it is visible then its impact is a matter of assessment and opinion.

3.61 Very many matters of assessment are constrained by established guidance as to how they should be assessed. It will be a matter of fact that particular guidance exists, but there may be scope for different opinions about which of the available guidance is best applied, and how. Methodological debates between experts in the same discipline ought to be uncommon if the principles of expert evidence are faithfully applied. Nevertheless, experience shows that such debates are in fact common. When they do occur, it is helpful for:

- the experts to meet and prepare a joint statement on the methodological dispute rather than have a sequential exchange of proofs of evidence and rebuttal proofs;
- each expert to engage with the consequence of accepting the other expert's position on the method or guidance; and
- it to be clarified whether the experts contend that there is only one acceptable approach or whether each approach is of some assistance, but that there are good reasons to prefer one approach to another.

3.62 The first point is an exercise in focusing attention on the real differences and explaining what they are, and why. Such a joint statement, or statement of common

---

[14] *Bernard Wheatcroft Ltd v Secretary of State for the Environment* [1982] 43 P&CR 233, per Forbes J.

ground, also serves to marshal the rival contentions into one document rather than to require the Inspector to chase the arguments through several documents.

3.63 The second point addresses the materiality of the dispute. In other words, does it matter, and if so, to what extent? It also enables the parties and the Inspector to know what 'input' there will be to their wider consideration of the case, depending on which approach the Inspector ultimately prefers. It may mean that a planning witness has to proceed on the basis that if another side's witness is preferred, then that is determinative of the appeal.

3.64 The third point assists in understanding whether, on a particular issue, there is middle ground on which the Inspector could or should alight. This is not simply an exercise in splitting the difference but in clarifying whether there is assistance to be gained from the results of applying different methods or guidance.

3.65 All of these points are consistent with an expert's duties, none of which promote a rigid adherence to the approach which best suits the client.

Issues within issues

3.66 Can a main issue be broken down into its component parts? For example, if the reason for refusal identifies noise from the proposal as harmful to the amenity of current and future residents of adjoining property, that main issue might in fact comprise of the following disputed issues:

(1) the background noise level at night time is either [x; planning authority's case] or [y; appellant's case];

(2) the effectiveness of mitigation measures;

(3) the standard against which to assess the change in the noise environment; and

(4) the scope, effect and lawfulness of planning conditions.

3.67 Point (1) ought to be capable of being narrowed or eliminated by measurement and the collection of data in an agreed way. This shows the benefit of breaking down a disagreement on a main issue into component parts. Some components may well be resolvable and that which can be resolved without troubling the Inspector, should be. This is so even if further work is done after the service of a statement of case, for example if the respective experts meet and obtain new background noise levels on which they are able to agree. The timing of that agreement would not be ideal. It should have been possible to achieve it much earlier, but that in itself is not a good reason not to continue to attempt to narrow issues. The ideal course of events should not become the enemy of the helpful course of action now. An Inspector will not complain about experts who take sensible action to agree or narrow issues.

3.68 Point (2) is an example of a disputed issue which needs to be very clearly defined. To assist an Inspector, it is necessary to ensure that the parties address the same facts and so the appellant must be clear and precise about what is proposed, what the effects would be and why that is so, and how the particular effect contended for can be secured. Those taking the contrary view will have to ensure that they have fully understood what is proposed, the means by which its effects have been assessed and the merits of the measures to secure the alleged benefits.

3.69 *Written evidence and representations*

3.69 All of these matters ought to be clear from a combination of the application materials, the consultation responses and the statements of case. If they are not clear, then it is incumbent on the parties to say so.

3.70 Point (3) is, broadly, a dispute about method which is a type of dispute which is common to many technical disciplines. It is a question of how one should assess facts and what the threshold of acceptability is, or where on a scale of effects the particular proposal lies. If this is a genuine dispute which has to be resolved, then it is likely to be quite important to the outcome. However, this is a point which should be tested before the argument develops. If application of different methods or thresholds yields broadly similar outcomes, then the argument is not worth pursuing because the same or similar answer will result. Alternatively, if the application of different methods of assessment yields substantially different answers, then each party must actively engage with the outcome of both methods. It is unhelpful for each party to cling to their preferred method and to fail to consider the implications of the other method, if that is the one which is preferred by the Inspector.

3.71 Point (4) overlaps with planning evidence. A specialist witness will not deal with planning conditions or obligations which are not directed to the specialist's topic, but such a witness must fully engage with the conditions which might bear on that issue. This may be something as simple as a condition which limits hours of operation. Such a condition, if otherwise acceptable, may entirely eliminate the main issue and result in an award of costs. For these reasons alone, this component of the main issue may be not only important but determinative of the issue and whether the appeal is allowed, or not.

FORMAT AND PRACTICALITY

3.72 Both hearing statements and proofs of evidence, and their appendices, are read under pressure of time and with a desire to get to what is really going to make a difference to the case. Format and navigation aids can make a substantial difference to the impression and impact of a proof. Therefore, proofs are best bound separately from any supporting documents. Proofs should have both their pages and paragraphs numbered.

3.73 Appendices, and other inquiry materials, need to be in suitable folders, arranged in a manner which allows any particular passage to be found quickly. In practice, this requires the use of tabbed dividers and pagination of any document which does not have original pagination.

3.74 The Planning Inspectorate advises:
- use a font such as Arial or Verdana in a size of 11 point or larger;
- use **A4** paper wherever possible;
- number the pages of the documents;
- make sure photocopied and scanned documents are clear and legible;
- use black and white for documents unless colour is essential;
- put any photographs (both originals and photocopies should be in colour), maps, plans, etc, in a **separate appendix** and cross-reference them within the main body of the document;

- print documents on both sides of a page. Paper of good enough quality that something printed on one side of the page does not show through to the other side should be used;
- ensure that the scale and orientation of any maps and plans are shown clearly. If you are sending maps or plans by email or through GOV.UK you **MUST** specify the paper size;
- do not send original documents unless they are specifically asked for.

Digital documents and electronic bundles are discussed in Chapter 7.

Core documents

3.75 This is now a misnomer. For there to be *core* documents, there must be other documents which are not 'core'. If all documents are 'core documents' then there is nothing to surround the core. In practice, 'core documents' are frequently an amalgam of every document which the parties might ever refer to. The better term for the totality of these documents would be 'inquiry documents'. It would then be of considerable assistance to isolate from that list of documents a subset to which extensive or frequent reference is inevitably going to be made which are then genuinely core documents.

3.76 There is a tendency to provide more of a document than is actually required. There may be good reasons for supplying the whole of a document, but if there are no such good reasons then the inquiry, and the client, is assisted by the time taken to provide only the necessary extracts. It assists because it is then obvious which part of the document is germane to the inquiry. Extracts from published material must indicate the precise context with full titles, chapter headings and dates. A photocopy of the document's title page is sufficient to indicate its origin and publication date.

3.77 All main parties should start to number their own documents before the inquiry, and keep an up-to-date list to be completed and submitted before the close of the inquiry.

3.78 Sufficient copies of proofs should be prepared for all the main participating parties, the Inspector and a copy for use by the witness. Additional copies should be made available for inspection at the local planning authority's offices prior to the inquiry and for inspection and circulation at the inquiry. The number required will depend on the likely level of public interest. No document should be provided unless its relevance is explained so that the Inspector and the parties know why they have it and the point which it is intended to make.

SUMMARY PROOFS

3.79 A good way to learn quickly about a case is to read the summary proofs of evidence. This fact needs to be borne in mind because it means that the Inspector may well start preparation by reading the summary proofs. Perhaps the last part of the evidence which you write is the first thing that everybody reads. It may be the only thing that some people read. It would be unfortunate, therefore, if it is completed in a rush, just before a deadline.

3.80 *Written evidence and representations*

3.80 The summary proof should, therefore:

- start with a very short introduction to the witness. However, the main proof will include a full description of the witness's qualifications and experience and the witness will in most cases have been introduced to the inquiry by an advocate. The introduction should therefore be concise;

- pay attention to who else is going to give evidence and so provide only such background information as will be genuinely helpful. If there is a good statement of common ground, then such descriptive material will not be needed. If the evidence addresses a discrete and perhaps specialist topic, and other witnesses address the details of the scheme or the locality, then there is no need to do so in a summary proof. All that needs to be done is to state that you know that relevant background material has been covered elsewhere and then begin to get to the point;

- summaries should be provided when a proof exceeds 1,500 words. As a guide, summaries should not exceed 10% of the length of the proof; and

- get to the point – explain what the user of the summary proof will be interested in.

3.81 A summary proof is also unique in that it is the only document that is likely to be read aloud. It is likely that the witness' evidence in chief will be given, at least in part, by reading of the summary proof. This fact also needs to be borne in mind because people rarely write in the same style as they speak. Bullet points may be a helpful device to communicate information in a document but they might be less successful as an oral summary, or at least need some adaptation. A good summary needs an appropriate 'voice'. When read aloud, it should make the impact which is appropriate to its content.

3.82 The distinction is exemplified by the use of numerical references in a summary proof. An officer's report, a transport assessment or a main proof of evidence will understandably include precise referencing to application numbers or the long reference to a part of the National Planning Practice Guidance. But the reader of a summary proof will be uncomfortable, and the audience will be bored, to hear that reference read out; so leave it out. The detail is the main proof and that stands as the evidence in chief. The Inspector and the parties will have read the main proof. The purpose of the summary proof is to settle everybody in the inquiry into the topic areas on which they are about to be addressed and to state the general thrust and reasoning of the witness's evidence.

3.83 A summary proof may be a free-standing document or it may form a section of the main proof. There is nothing objectionable about having a section of the main proof with the title 'Summary and Conclusions'. It is not, however, enough to simply rely on 'Conclusions' because the conclusions will not say anything about what was done to arrive at those conclusions.

Chapter 4

Managing appeals and Rosewell

4.01 This chapter is about the route to an event, namely a hearing or an inquiry. It is particularly about the style of case management for inquiries which results from the Rosewell Review.[1]

4.02 The Rosewell Review concerned the way in which specific types of planning inquiries are planned and managed, principally s 78 appeals in respect of residential development. Enforcement was outside of the scope of the Review. The Review concluded that relatively simple changes could make the end-to-end process shorter and easier for the parties.

4.03 In terms of the timeline of an appeal, it is a time between making and setting out the case, and the busy times of finalising evidence and the immediate preparation for a hearing and inquiry. It is a time which serves to manage the case which is going to be heard.

4.04 The most significant changes are twofold. First, the way in which the Planning Inspectorate now goes about proactive management of an inquiry is directed to focusing attention on the main issues at a much earlier stage. Secondly, that case management provides for early decisions on the format of the inquiry. There are now choices to be made about the mix of inquiry and hearing formats for the presentation of the parties' cases on particular issues. The result of the Review has been to significantly reduce appeal timescales.

4.05 Where it is necessary to address social distancing in order to make arrangements for an inquiry, that topic may be addressed as part of the case management – see Chapter 7.

APPEAL TIMETABLES

4.06 Appeal timetables are generous to the parties, and as noted in Chapter 1, this generosity is to encourage resolution, not dispute.[2] First, the parties have always been working on their case for many months, if not years, before an appeal is notified and made. Each party has information available to know the other side's case in considerable, if sometimes incomplete, detail. This is unlike many other forms of dispute resolution. When a prosecutor commences a prosecution the nature of the defence is often unknown. In contrast, in planning appeals, the planning authority

---

[1] The Independent Review of Planning Appeal Inquiries (Main Report); Bridget Rosewell OBE (December 2018).
[2] See para 1.01 above.

will have been provided with all of the materials for a valid application, and may have influenced that application via pre-application discussions. The planning authority may have asked the applicant to produce further evidence or details. On the other side, the appellant will have the benefit of some, or all, of an officer's report; consultee responses; and third-party representations.

4.07 Secondly, the main parties should be able to foresee an appeal. The appellant is provided with an ample time period after a refusal in which to make an appeal. An appellant cannot be surprised by its own appeal. A planning authority will be able to spot those cases in which appeal is likely, such as when a refusal is contrary to officer recommendation or the proposal benefits from the presumption in favour of sustainable development in circumstances where the local plan is in difficulty.

4.08 Thirdly, the time periods to a site view (for written representations), to a hearing and to inquiry are measured in months and have in recent times extended to a year. Enforcement cases take, on average, more than a year. Even the target timescale for the expedited appeals under the Rosewell Review is six months.

4.09 Taken together, the general position is not that the parties are under pressure of time in an appeal, but that the planning process to the point of an appeal decision is too slow. It follows that when an appeal is made, the parties should be in a position to make progress.

SUMMARY OF DEADLINES

Written representations

4.10 Evidently, the written representations mode of determination is simplest.[3] The application documents are submitted with the appeal. If the appellant wishes to add to the information which was supplied with the application to the local planning authority (LPA), the appellant may do so. When appealing, the appellant should state their case with full particulars, copies of any documents referred to in the statement of case, and any other supporting evidence, including any expert reports.

4.11 If the LPA decides it needs to make further representations, it should send its full statement of case to the Planning Inspectorate (two copies if not sent electronically) within five weeks of the start date, or six weeks for enforcement, advertisement and discontinuation notice appeals.

4.12 If either the appellant or the LPA wishes to comment on any representations made at the five-week stage, they must send their comments to the Planning Inspectorate (two copies if not sent electronically) within seven weeks of the start date, or nine weeks for enforcement, advertisement and discontinuation notice appeals. These comments should be in the form of a concise response and should not introduce new material or technical evidence.

---

[3] Part 2 of the Town and Country Planning (Appeals) (Written Representations Procedure) (England) Regulations 2009, SI 2009/452.

Hearings

4.13 Within the hearing procedure, there is an important five-week stage (four weeks in Wales). This is five/four weeks after the Planning Inspectorate has sent the start date letter. At the five/four -week stage:

- the LPA is required to submit its full statement of case;

- the agreed statement of common ground is to be submitted;

- those who made representations on the application will have been notified of the appeal and will have an opportunity to comment on the appeal if they wish to, though the Planning Inspectorate will have received copies of the consultation responses from the application stage and will have regard to those.

4.14 In England, there is no opportunity for any party to provide a written response to the full statement of case. That is the end of the exchange of written evidence. The next stage is the hearing. In Wales, the situation is different. Within the six-week 'representation period', (measured from the start date letter), there is an opportunity to comment on another party's representations.[4] The *Procedural Guide – Wales*, explains the opportunity in this way:

> 'If either the appellant, the LPA/relevant authority or any interested person wishes to comment on any representations made at the 4 week stage, they must send their comments to us within 6 weeks of the start date. These comments should not introduce new material or technical evidence.'

4.15 The opportunity is for comment, not new material or technical evidence. Again, this is a more nuanced question than it appears from the guidance. For example, if the LPA has included an appeal decision within its full statement of case, the appellant may need to do more than simply comment on it. The comment might be: 'We note appeal decision [A], but the point relied upon has been overtaken by appeal decision [B] – attached'. In this circumstance, the Inspector needs to see appeal decision [B]. It is new material, but it cannot reasonably be turned away, not least because if appeal decision [B] is material to the decision, then an error of law may arise if the Inspector makes the decision without taking it into account.

ROSEWELL REVIEW

Scope

4.16 The scope of the review was confined to planning inquiries,[5] not hearings. Much of the Review addressed process within the Planning Inspectorate. For example, the administrative processes and information technology which underlie the submission and validation of appeals was the subject of the first recommendation. As a result, a new online portal was introduced. Increased pace was recommended at particular stages, such as the recommendation to issue a start letter within five

---

[4] See Town and Country Planning (Referred Applications and Appeals Procedure) (Wales) Regulations 2017, SI 2017/544, reg 24 which provides: 'The appellant, the local planning authority, and interested persons may send written comments on each other's representations to the Welsh Ministers so as to be received within the representation period.'

[5] Other than planning enforcement and listed building cases.

4.17 *Managing appeals and Rosewell*

working days of the receipt of each inquiry appeal. However, the bulk of the recommendations resulted in changing the progress of an appeal from one which was essentially backloaded to one which is now frontloaded and actively managed.

Focus and recommendations

4.17 The Rosewell Review broke up its consideration of the stages of an inquiry as follows:[6]

(1) Submission to start letter.

(2) Start letter to start of inquiry and also the notification letter to third parties.

(3) Inquiry to decision.

4.18 From the point of view of an appeal-participant, the key recommendations concerned the following:

- appellants to notify the LPA a minimum of 10 working days before an appeal under the inquiry procedure is submitted to the Planning Inspectorate;
- the Planning Inspectorate now expect: 'All documents must be submitted with the appeal. There is no ability to amend a scheme during the appeal process';
- the Planning Inspectorate will identify the inquiry date – not the parties;
- the inquiry date will be fixed from 13 to 16 weeks of the date of the start letter;
- not later than seven weeks after the start letter, there should be case management engagement between the appointed Inspector and the main parties, including any Rule 6 parties;[7]
- the statement of common ground will be prominent in case management and the aim is to identify both common ground and disputed issues early in the appeal process.

4.19 In combination with a range of administrative recommendations, the Review resulted in the adoption of the following targets, from receipt of appeal to decision:

- Inquiry appeals decided by the Inspector:
  - Receipt to decision – within 24 weeks – 90% of cases
  - Receipt to decision – within 26 weeks – remaining 10% of cases
- Inquiry appeals decided by the Secretary of State:
  - Receipt to submission of Inspector's report – within 30 weeks – 100% of cases

4.20 In summary, the current target timescales are (see Appendix 7):

---

[6] Sections 4, 5 and 6 of the Review.
[7] See further para 2.64 above on the role of third parties and Rule 6 status.

Pre notification	10 days before submission
Submission	
Start of Appeal	About 5–10 days after submission
Interested Parties Notified	1 week after start
Main Statement of Common Ground (Statement of Case of each party shared by PINS)	5 weeks after start
Case conference	7 weeks after start
Proofs of Evidence	4 weeks before inquiry
Inquiry	**13–16 weeks after the start**
Decision	24 weeks after start (max 26)

4.21 Compared to inquiries pre-Rosewell, this represents a halving of the timescale for a s 78 appeal by way of inquiry, from around 12 months to 6 months. The recommendations of the Rosewell Review were implemented promptly. They produced substantial practical changes to all stages of the appeal process for the inquiry procedure but they did so without any change in primary legislation, the procedure rules or regulations. The changes are changes of practice under the existing rules. They are changes to the way in which existing practices are performed rather than injecting new practice. It is a combination of improved administration and collaboration between parties.

4.22 In respect of Inspector case management, the Review concluded that there should be pre-inquiry engagement between the inspector, the main parties and Rule 6 parties in every inquiry appeal.[8] Not only is this likely to save resources and time, but it will also ensure that there is a greater focus on the issues that are in dispute at the inquiry.

4.23 This has resulted in telephone hearings with similar objectives to pre-inquiry meetings which are already a feature of large inquiries but were relatively scarce as events because they were thought only to be worthwhile for the longest and most complex work. The recommendation was:[9]

> '(a) In every inquiry appeal case, there should be case management engagement between the inspector, the main parties, Rule 6 parties and any other parties invited by the inspector, not later than 7 weeks after the start letter.
>
> (b) Following the case management engagement, the inspector should issue clear directions to the parties about the final stages of preparation and how evidence will be examined no later than 8 weeks after the start letter.'

Case management conferences

4.24 The key concept in holding a case management conference is simple, namely to bring the main parties together for a structured meeting with the appointed Inspector. The objectives of the meeting are to identify issues, settle the actions which

---

[8] Paragraphs 5.33 and 5.34, p 31.
[9] Recommendation 8, p 32.

4.25 *Managing appeals and Rosewell*

are necessary to progress evidence to a focused body of material which is consistent with the statement of common ground. The result should be an efficient and effective inquiry which satisfies the parties' need to be heard and provides the Inspector with the materials to reach a decision.

4.25 A typical agenda is:

1. Introduction by Inspector.
2. Purpose of the conference.
3. Likely main issues.
4. How the main issues and other matters will be dealt with.
5. Conditions.
6. Core documents.
7. Inquiry running order/programme.
8. Timetable for submission of documents.
9. Costs.
10. Any other procedural matters.

4.26 A good case management conference (CMC) requires careful preparation, including appropriate advance discussion between parties. It is an opportunity for a party to make progress in the prospects for its appearance at the inquiry. This is the first opportunity to address the Inspector. The crucial decision which is being made during the CMC is the number and the terms of the main issues. These will flow from the reasons for refusal, the statements of case and the draft statement of common ground, but the Inspector's main issues are invariably succinct and distil the issues to some commonly encountered phrases. To deal with this effectively, a party needs to hone very carefully how it would express the issue. This example illustrates the point.

(i) the effect of the development on the living conditions of the neighbouring occupiers;

(ii) whether or not the loss of the local heritage asset is acceptable; and

(iii) the effect of the development on protected species.

4.27 As a result of discussion during the CMC, the main issues were amended and agreed to be:

(i) the effect of the development on the living conditions of the neighbouring occupiers with regard to outlook, as well as noise and light generated by the development;

(ii) whether or not the loss of the local heritage asset is acceptable; and

(iii) the effect of the development on protected species with regard to light generated by the development.

4.28 The first and third main issues are more specific. The first main issue is concerned with three matters: outlook, noise and light. The third main issue was clarified as being specific to the effects of light on protected species. In this way it was possible to turn the general into the particular. The issues were, to some degree, nailed down.

4.29 The first issue was further refined or focused by the Inspector's post-conference note which recorded the following:

> 'With regard to the matter of living conditions, it was agreed that the parties would identify which properties might experience an impact from the development and what that impact might be. The possibility of this forming part of the statement of common ground was discussed, which the Council would lead on. The Inquiry would benefit from such an approach, in the interests of clarity and to assist the discussions that will take place on this issue.'

In this way, the LPA was invited to take the lead in recording which properties might be affected and so to clarify what this issue was actually about.

4.30 There is a pattern of Inspectors asking for a 'live inquiry schedule' being created and maintained. With respect to the originators of this tool, it appears to be a sharper instrument in its description than in use. The idea is to keep track of the evolving positions of the parties. That is, of course, vital for the reasons discussed in Chapter 5 as to the purpose of cross-examination. However, implementation of such a schedule is a layer of inquiry activity which can stretch the available resources of the parties, making it less useful than might initially be thought.

4.31 The CMC agenda will include 'rebuttal proofs' as an item for the Inspector to mention. They will generally be discouraged. The standard text in post conference notes is:

> 'There is no reference in the Rules or the Procedural Guide to supplementary or rebuttal proofs and none are encouraged.'

However, the use of a date for rebuttal proofs does provide a useful backstop for the provision of further evidence. Any evidence which is sought to be relied upon after that date is likely to require cogent explanation of the reasons why it was not and could not have been relied upon at the appropriate time.

4.32 An inquiry schedule or programme is not a new feature arising from the Rosewell Review. However, it has been given more prominence and has evolved from the previous practice of requesting advocates' time estimates. The initial task of preparing an inquiry programme has been passed to the parties. This is helpful in that it prompts consideration of the inquiry running order, namely which witnesses will be required at which times.

4.33 Post conference notes often include this text:

> 'You are also reminded that in order to support an effective and timely planning system in which all parties are required to behave reasonably, the Inspector has the power to initiate an award of costs in line with the Planning Guidance. Unreasonable behaviour may include not complying with the prescribed timetables.'

The point being made is that the parties are expected to co-operate and to achieve that which the post-conference note sets out, in accordance with a timetable which they had an opportunity to influence at the CMC. The sanction is costs, including those initiated by the Inspector. It is a helpful reminder, albeit that costs decisions initiated by Inspectors are very rare things.

4.34 *Managing appeals and Rosewell*

An effective and efficient Rosewell inquiry

4.34 The focus of the Review was upon improving the efficiency of the inquiry process such that it produced results which were effective in promoting the key aims of the appeals process, but achieving those outcomes in less time. The third element of the review, identified above, is concerned with the stage 'inquiry to decision'. How does the Review affect the inquiry, and how should the participants embrace those changes so that the inquiry is effective from their point of view, and from the point of view of the public interest? Like this:[10]

> 'In addition, the inspector may consider that a roundtable discussion would be the most appropriate way to consider some issues. We were told that some matters, such as consideration of the sites included in the 5 year land supply, seemed particularly well suited to roundtable discussion rather than cross-examination. This approach will leave the inquiry to focus on the key matters in contention, where cross-examination of witnesses is required.'

4.35 The recommendation was:[11]

> 'The inspector should decide, at the pre-inquiry stage, how best to examine the evidence at the inquiry and should notify the parties of the mechanism by which each topic or area of evidence will be examined, whether by topic organisation, oral evidence and cross-examination, roundtable discussions or written statements.'

4.36 The reason that the Review was able to tackle this part of the inquiry process and implement its recommendations without delay is that the inquiry rules arguably provide a wide discretion to Inspectors to conduct an inquiry as they see fit – more particularly:[12]

> '(1) Except as otherwise provided in these Rules, the inspector shall determine the procedure at an inquiry.
>
> ...
>
> (5) A person entitled to appear at an inquiry shall be entitled to call evidence and the appellant, the local planning authority and any statutory party shall be entitled to cross-examine persons giving evidence, but, subject to the foregoing and paragraphs (6) and (9), the calling of evidence and the cross-examination of persons giving evidence shall otherwise be at the discretion of the inspector.
>
> (6) The inspector may refuse to permit the–
>
> (a) giving or production of evidence;
>
> (b) cross-examination of persons giving evidence; or
>
> (c) of any other matter,
>
> which he considers to be irrelevant or repetitious; but where he refuses to permit the giving of oral evidence, the person wishing to give the evidence may submit to him any evidence or other matter in writing before the close of the inquiry.'

---

[10] The Review at paras 5.40 to 5.43, p 32.
[11] The Review – recommendation 9, p 32.
[12] Town and Country Planning Appeals (Determination by Inspectors) (Inquiries Procedure) (England) Rules 2000, SI 2000/1625, r 16.

4.37 Rule 16(1) is clear – the procedure is for the Inspector to decide. But it has to be read carefully in conjunction with r 16(5). This provides a right to call evidence, ie to conduct an examination in chief, and to cross-examine. That right is conferred on the appellant, on the LPA and any statutory party. Otherwise, ie in respect of other parties, the calling of evidence and cross examination is at the Inspector's discretion. The Inspector also has control over irrelevant or repetitious evidence. The Inspector can control the extent of the evidence and does not have listen to the same thing twice.

4.38 If a decision is taken to determine an appeal by inquiry, then the main parties have a right to call evidence, subject to the limitations within r 16. An inquiry which proceeds to deal with almost everything other than by the calling of witnesses is not an inquiry. It is a hearing by another name. However, the position is set to be amended in respect of planning appeals by reason of amendment to s 319A(2) of the Town and Country Planning Act 1990 so that the appeal procedure is determined as 'such one or more' of the ways of determining the appeal as appear appropriate (see s 20 of the Business and Planning Act 2020). Like amendments are to be made in respect of listed building and hazardous substances consents.

4.39 To have a right to do something is irrelevant to the question of whether it is sensible, useful or effective to do it. Rather, the key question for the main parties who are preparing for a CMC is how best, from their perspective, to resolve the issues, present their case and to persuade the Inspector.

4.40 Take a purely legal issue as an example, such as, the interpretation of a planning permission. What will be gained by asking questions of a planning witness which could be more clearly and efficiently communicated by short written submissions and an opportunity for each party to address the Inspector on the merits of their interpretation? Alternatively, if there are facts which it is fundamental to find and determine before a key issue can be decided, then cross-examination, may, in a particular case be preferred.

4.41 For a CMC, these questions require to be carefully thought through. Each party needs to know what it wants to do and to be able to explain clearly and concisely why that is so. This part of a CMC is a key point in the inquiry process.

Chapter 5

Inquiries

THE STRUCTURE AND PURPOSE OF THE INQUIRY

5.01 This chapter looks at inquiries of all types: appeals against refusal of permission, cases which are called-in or recovered for the Secretary of State's determination, enforcement, compulsory purchase order (CPO) and infrastructure inquiries. The largest proportion of inquiries are to determine appeals against refusal of planning permission by local authorities. Amongst those, the largest proportion is residential appeal work. While the overriding objectives of decision-making are the same for each type of inquiry, they differ in terms of practice in ways which range from the fundamental, such as which party presents its case first, to the more subtle such as the status of objectors.

5.02 First, the main types of inquiry and their broad structure and running order is identified. Secondly, each of the main elements of the inquiry is explained, in the approximate order in which they are likely to occur at the inquiry. Thirdly, the law in respect of procedural fairness is summarised. It is a common focus of concern for disappointed parties and is a key task for Inspectors. Lastly, some practical considerations are listed which may assist with the smooth presentation of a case and conduct of an inquiry.

Types of inquiry and running order

Section 78 appeals and call-in inquiries

5.03 Prior to the Town and Country Planning Appeals (Determination by Inspectors) (Inquiries Procedure) (England) Rules 2000 (the 2000 Rules),[1] the appellant in a s 78 inquiry called its evidence first, and those opposing the scheme, including the local planning authority (LPA), followed. The 2000 Rules reversed that order so that the LPA presents its case first.[2] This has the advantage that the inquiry is first informed about the reasons for refusal, which are the reasons which bring about the appeal. The same running order applies in respect of call-in inquiries[3] and recovered appeals.

---

[1] SI 2000/1625.
[2] Rule 16(4) of the 2000 Rules: 'Unless in any particular case the inspector otherwise determines, the local planning authority shall begin and the appellant shall have the right of final reply; and the other persons entitled or permitted to appear shall be heard in such order as the inspector may determine.'
[3] See r 15(4) of the Town and Country Planning (Inquiries Procedure) (England) Rules 2000, SI 2000/1624.

The structure and purpose of the inquiry **5.09**

5.04 In Wales, the Town and Country Planning (Referred Applications and Appeals Procedure) (Wales) Regulations 2017 (the 2017 Regulations)[4] are silent on running order. *The Procedural Guide – Wales* is similarly silent. Nevertheless, the practice in England and Wales is the same.

5.05 For most inquiries, it is convenient to hear each party's case as a whole. In some circumstances, the parties or the Inspector may canvas the alternative approach of organising the inquiry by issue or topic – the topic-based inquiry. If, say, the inquiry turned on the outcomes of three technical issues: highways impacts, noise and air quality, then the witnesses for each discipline might be called 'back-to-back' with the planning authority's highways witness followed by the appellant's highways witness. There are two main advantages. First, the inquiry can focus on one technical discipline at a time rather than moving back and forth between them. Secondly, there is scope to save costs for each party because the respective experts are often not required to be at the inquiry beyond the time required for the issue which they address.

5.06 The stages of the inquiry are detailed below, but, in summary, whichever arrangement is used, the inquiry will be opened by the Inspector who will explain the issues, the arrangements and the likely programme. The parties will then each provide an opening statement and then move into the evidence. The inquiry will conclude with a discussion of conditions and planning obligations, then turn to closing submissions and an accompanied site visit.

Enforcement

5.07 The Town and Country Planning (Enforcement) (Determination by Inspectors) (Inquiries Procedure) (England) Rules 2002 (the 2002 Rules)[5] provide for a running order for enforcement appeals which is the opposite of a s 78 inquiry: the appellant calls evidence first, and the LPA follows.[6]

CPO, highways, Transport and Works Act

5.08 There is a range of specialist inquiries to which specific inquiry procedure rules apply. For example, the Transport and Works (Inquiries Procedure) Rules 2004[7] apply in England and Wales to any inquiry held pursuant to s 11 of the Transport and Works Act 1992. The rules follow the same model and format as the 2000 Rules. However, owing to the complexity and length of most Transport and Works Act schemes and inquiries, the procedure adopted varies significantly from case to case. Linear schemes usually produce a range of objections which are specific to locations along a route and it is necessary to hold what amounts to a series of short inquiries into those issues.

5.09 There may also be over-arching issues which are fundamental to the scheme, such as whether the scheme is likely to be funded in a timely way, or some aspect of

---

[4] SI 2017/544.
[5] SI 2002/2685.
[6] See r 17(4) of the 2002 Rules.
[7] SI 2004/2018.

5.10 Inquiries

need may be questioned. These issues require different treatment, in part because the range and number of parties with an interest in those issues is likely to be different.

5.10 Other examples of inquiries which raise planning issues, albeit in varying contexts, include inquiries under the Compulsory Purchase (Inquiries Procedure) Rules 2007;[8] the Compulsory Purchase (Inquiries Procedure) (Wales) Rules 2010;[9] and the Electricity Generating Stations and Overhead Lines (Inquiries Procedure) (England and Wales) Rules 2007.[10] Again, the model and format is reflective of other inquiry procedure rules. It is necessary to consult the detail of the specific rules and the guidance produced by the relevant minister and the Planning Inspectorate (PINS). To illustrate the nature of the inquiry which can result, the procedure adopted at the Mid-Wales Windfarm Inquiry[11] is set out, with commentary *in italics*:

> '1. I held a conjoined public inquiry into the five section 36 applications and the section 37 application, commencing on 4 June 2013 and concluding on 30 May 2014. An Introductory Meeting was held on 28 November 2012 and a pre-Inquiry meeting (PIM) was held on 18 and 25 February 2013. The Inquiry was conducted in accordance with the Electricity Generating Stations and Overhead Lines (Inquiries Procedure) (England and Wales) Rules 2007.
>
> *[In a multi-party inquiry, co-operation between the parties and management of the issues and programme are only achievable by use of pre-inquiry case management hearings.]*
>
> 2. During the inquiry I was assisted by Inspector Emyr Jones BSc (Hons) CEng MICE MCMI in matters pertaining to Application F: the Llandinam 132kV Line.
>
> *[A good example of the use of a second Inspector or an assessor with specific expertise – here, an engineer.]*
>
> 3. In accordance with preferences expressed at the PIM the inquiry was conducted on a topic basis to a rolling programme, to a timetable approved by the Secretary of State under Rule 12.
>
> *[The inquiry was only sensibly capable of hearing matters by reference to topics and by references to the strategic search areas identified within Welsh onshore energy policy.]*
>
> 4. The opening session of the inquiry sat from 4 – 7 June 2013 and dealt with opening statements and the application and interpretation of relevant policy.
>
> *[Energy and planning policy were addressed immediately after hearing the parties open their respective cases.]*
>
> 5. Inquiry Session 1 sat from 3 September – 11 October 2013 and dealt with matters pertaining to SSA C. Site inspections were carried out on 13 and 14 October.
>
> 6. Inquiry Session 2 sat from 5 November – 5 December 2013 and dealt with matters pertaining to SSA B. Site inspections were carried out on 9 and 10 December.

---

[8] SI 2007/3617.
[9] SI 2010/3015.
[10] SI 2007/841.
[11] Report to the Secretary of State for Energy and Climate Change by A D Poulter BArch RIBA, 8 December 2014 (https://www.gov.uk/government/news/planning-decisions-for-six-powys-mid-wales-infrastructure-projects and https://itportal.beis.gov.uk/EIP/pages/projects/InspectorsReportEnglish.pdf).

7. Inquiry Session 3 sat from 21 January – 21 February 2014 and dealt with matters relating to the section 37 (Llandinam 132kV line) application. Site Inspections were carried out on 25 and 26 February.

   [*Not all parties needed to attend all parts of the inquiry. Strategic Search Areas C and B and the grid connection issues could be split out and heard over a period from September 2013 to February 2014.*]

8. Inquiry Session 4 sat from 18 March – 3 April 2014. It dealt with matters in common to all the applications and cumulative effects. A site inspection was carried out on 4 April 2014

   [*However, some issues crossed geographical areas and were required to be considered again on a cumulative basis.*]

9. The closing inquiry session sat from 20 May – 30 May 2014 and dealt with the planning balance, conditions, and closing statements.

   [*In the context of the mass of material heard over ten months, the parties were given six or seven weeks to prepare material on the planning balance and closing submissions.*]

10. With the agreement of the parties, the inquiry considered certain topics in a 'hearing' format through structured discussions led by the Inspector rather than through formal presentation and cross examination of evidence.'

    [*Rather like the Rosewell Review (see Chapter 4) concluded some six years later, the matters were heard by the method most appropriate to their nature and the issues between the parties. Each format was fairly obvious. However, contrary to the default position adopted by many Inspectors post Rosewell, landscape and setting issues were successfully dealt with by the formal calling of evidence – it could not have been effectively dealt with in any other way.*]

APPEARANCES

5.11 The persons entitled to appear at a s 78 inquiry or an enforcement inquiry in England are:

- the appellant;
- the LPA;
- statutory parties and councils in whose area the land is situated (eg the County Council);
- the Parish Council if it made representations on the application; and
- those with Rule 6 status.[12]

There is then a catch-all provision which gives the Inspector a discretion to permit any other person to appear, and that such permission shall not be unreasonably withheld. It is Inspectors' invariable practice to permit anybody to speak who indicates a wish to do so. The interaction between the principles of access and participation and fairness is a complicated one, discussed later in this chapter at para 5.90 ff.

---

[12] See further para 2.64 above on the role of third parties and Rule 6 status.

5.12 *Inquiries*

5.12 In Wales, the practical effect is the same, but the Regulations are more succinct: the appellant, LPA and any person invited by the Welsh Ministers may appear on their own behalf or be represented by any other person.[13]

5.13 Any person entitled or permitted to appear may do so on his own behalf or be represented by any other person. This means that the appearance may be by counsel. In other words, any person may instruct a barrister to present their case, or may instruct any other person, for example a solicitor, a planning consultant or simply a member of the community who is prepared to take on the task. There are no rules in this regard, but rather it is a matter for the person to decide having regard to their interest and what they wish to achieve by their appearance.

5.14 The Inspector may proceed with an inquiry in the absence of any person entitled to appear at it.[14] Whether an Inspector in fact does so will be a highly fact-specific question, turning on the reasons for the absence, their reasonableness and the effects of whatever decision is made upon other parties. Questions of adjournment and costs are also likely to arise.

FROM OPENING REMARKS TO CLOSING SUBMISSIONS

5.15 An inquiry is one event made up of identifiable parts and elements. They are all, however, directed to one outcome which is a consideration of the evidence as it stands at the end of the inquiry and making a decision on that evidence, against the relevant law and policy. To understand what is happening and how, it is necessary to be clear about the following:

- An opening statement is intended to explain, in a succinct way, the position which that party intends to demonstrate by the end of the inquiry.

- The evidence will not be the same at the beginning and end of the inquiry. If it were, the inquiry would be pointless, witnesses would not be needed and the Inspector would only require submissions from each side to explain the merits of the case, as they would put them.

- Closing submissions must address the evidential position after the evidence has been presented and tested and may not ignore concessions made, errors identified, changes in case or changes in emphasis.

- The opening statement and the closing submissions are, therefore, book ends between which a well-run case comprises chapters of evidence which tell a coherent story which does not leave plot-holes or take inexplicable turns in the narrative.

5.16 The opening of an inquiry will be a period of around an hour in which the Inspector explains why everybody is there and what the issues are and the parties explain what they are going to contend for and, in outline, why that is going to be shown to be correct.

---

[13] See reg 38 of the 2017 Regulations.
[14] See for example r 16(11) of the 2000 rules, or r 17(11) of the 2002 rules, or reg 39 of the 2017 Regulations.

From opening remarks to closing submissions **5.22**

5.17 In part, the opening of an inquiry is also an opportunity to explain why another party or parties is not correct. But it is not a time for argument. The opportunity to show that a particular contention is without a proper foundation or is otherwise misconceived comes during the course of the evidence and in drawing those points together in closing submissions.

5.18 There is, therefore, a route from the start to the finish. In a well-considered case, that route will have been set out with sufficient particularity during the application process and in stating a case. The opening of an inquiry is a point by which the issues have been sifted and sorted in order to focus the energy of the inquiry on the evidence which is about to be called. During the course of the inquiry, the contentions of the parties will variously strengthen and weaken and it is those changes which are to be captured and argued in the closing submissions.

5.19 The opening of an inquiry is procedurally important. The Inspector will ask about notification and will wish to be assured that there has been notification of those who had objected to or supported the application.[15] Each set of inquiry rules will require that site notices are placed.[16] Failure to notify will almost inevitably lead to adjournment because of the obvious risk of prejudice to interested persons. The waste of costs is likely to arise in consequence.

5.20 At the start of an inquiry in England the Inspector shall identify what are, in her or his opinion, the main issues to be considered at the inquiry and any matters on which she or he requires further explanation from the persons entitled or permitted to appear.[17] In Wales, the Inspector must identify the matters on which she or he requires representations.[18] In practical terms, the approach is likely to be the same in England and Wales, but the difference is real, not just semantic. In Wales, the Regulation refers to 'the matters', not to the main matters or the main issues. The Inspector in Wales 'must', therefore, identify all of the matters on which representations are required. This is clearly a broader and less focused approach and does not give the parties an indication of which issues are likely to be determinative. However, there is nothing in the regulation to prevent the identification of main issues and as a matter of practice Inspectors do so.

5.21 There is a further contrast between England and Wales. In England, any person entitled or permitted to appear shall not be precluded from referring to issues which they consider relevant to the consideration of the appeal but which were not issues identified by the Inspector as main issues.[19] So, in the English inquiry, the parties have to at least direct their minds to whatever issues may come up, having regard to the representations which have already been made during the application and appeal stages. As the South Oxfordshire example shows (see paras 3.15–3.23 above), the inquiry may turn on a matter which is not the subject of a reason for refusal.

5.22 However, in Wales there is no equivalent provision to expressly address the status of non-main issues. Again, in practice, it is highly unlikely that an Inspector

---

[15] See r 10 of the 2000 Rules.
[16] See r 10(6) of the 2000 Rules.
[17] See r 16(2) of the 2000 Rules.
[18] Regulation 45 of the 2017 Regulations.
[19] See r 16(2).

5.23   Inquiries

would shut out a representation, though an Inspector would give a clear indication about the level of detail or the time to be expended on it. This is not forbearance but is the essence of being an independent tribunal. The Inspector is there to listen, to evaluate and to be open to the evidence, the argument and to be persuaded. The Inspector has neither pre-determined any issue, is not hostile to any case nor required to ignore any apparent lack of merit or the scope for time and expense to be wasted. The balance between those competing interests is one for the Inspector to strike.

5.23   In summary, at the opening of an inquiry, the Inspector typically:

(1)   identifies herself or himself;

(2)   takes the names of all those who appear or who wish to be heard;[20]

(3)   checks that those who intend to rely on a proof of evidence have the relevant proofs and appendices;

(4)   checks the drawings and application documents on which the decision was made, or would have been made in non-determination or call-in inquiries;

(5)   addresses time estimates and programme;

(6)   outlines the procedure to be adopted for giving of evidence;

(7)   indicates likely timings for short adjournments during the day;

(8)   explains the role and purpose of a conditions session;

(9)   asks whether there is to be any planning obligation submitted to the inquiry under s 106 of the Town and Country Planning Act 1990 (TCPA 1990); and

(10)   asks for closing submissions in writing.

5.24   Closing submissions are invariably sought in writing no matter what the length of the Inquiry. In fact, the rules in England only anticipated written closing submissions for inquiries of two weeks or more,[21] but the regulation in Wales[22] accurately reflects the practice in that closing submissions are required to be in writing. The regulation is arguably too tightly drafted not least because it is impractical to provide written closing submissions in a short inquiry, and there is nothing to suggest that inquiries should not be short. Moreover, it is the appellant's right to respond to the contrary submissions. Those responses will necessarily be oral. The inquiry is an oral proceeding, as consideration of the giving of evidence shows.

ORAL EVIDENCE

5.25   Consider the modes of communication which may be encountered in a typical day: a 10-word tweet; a map showing a site location; the editorial in a newspaper; a phone call with family member; 50 minutes of conversation over a meal. The quality, depth, nuance and impact of those communications are very widely different. They are not just marginally different; they are fundamentally different to the point of being essentially incomparable.

---

[20]   An 'appearance' and being 'heard' are not the same thing – see further at r 11 of the 2000 Rules which addresses those entitled or permitted to appear.
[21]   Rule 16(14) of the 2000 Rules
[22]   Regulation 45(15).

5.26 The opportunity to communicate, face to face, is the gold standard. It makes available all of the layers and codes of language which have evolved in society for some thousands of years and which may include:

- idiom;
- the colloquial;
- humour;
- varied pace; and
- varied tone.

All of this is supplemented by, for example:

- facial expression;
- posture;
- demeanour;
- charm; and
- choice of clothing

If this was not so, theatre would not exist, nor would Parliament. We could simply read King Lear and Hansard; this suggestion only has to be stated to show why hearing and seeing contribute as they do.

5.27 It is not necessary to do anything in particular to address any of these features of oral communication and evidence. Indeed, it is likely to be counter-productive for a witness to try to be someone or something which they are not. Rather, the main point is to understand the opportunity which has been provided, to prepare the material for that opportunity and to use it effectively to persuade the inquiry of the honest, professional opinion on the point or position at issue. This is what the giving of evidence in chief is about – using the opportunity to speak and explain, face to face, using all the means and modes of communication which are available. This is the time at which the witness, assisted by an advocate, has all of the means and modes in one place: the written material, the plans, the tables, the photographs, the chance to clarify orally, to simplify, to point, to smile, to show that the witness is comfortable with her or his opinion and can meet the contrary case.

5.28 To adopt some sort of style in answering questions which is other than straightforward and clear was shown to be counter-productive in a case in the High Court (which is not a planning case, but which makes the point).[23] These extracts from the judgment show that an over-prepared script was spotted easily and was unconvincing, but answers to questions made (by the same witness) promptly, candidly and openly were wholly convincing.

> '81. Mr Colwill adopted a style of giving evidence that became increasingly common throughout the trial for the majority of the witnesses for Energy Solutions. I was unaware of the architect of this when I drafted the judgment distributed to the parties on 6 July 2016, although in further disclosure in July 2016 following the Supplemental Agreements and win bonus issues, it appears that witness training was provided by a company called Bond Solon. Whether that training was responsible for the style of giving evidence, I do

---

[23] *Energy Solutions EU Ltd v Nuclear Decommissioning Authority* [2016] EWHC 1988, per Fraser J.

5.29 *Inquiries*

not know. Mr Colwill was the first to use it. This was, at times, to avoid the question and embark upon something of a corporate presentation. The linguistic device adopted for this approach was, usually, to state that it was necessary to put a question "in context" and then embark upon an exposition that was essentially sketching out the Claimant's case, and avoiding giving a clear answer to sensible questions from Mr Giffin QC for the NDA. I found this increasingly unhelpful.

82. Mr Colwill was the first proponent of this technique, and other witnesses for Energy Solutions adopted it to a greater or lesser degree, such that a pattern seemed to emerge. This had obvious disadvantages. Preparation by a witness is undoubtedly necessary in a case such as this with so much material, covering so many different technical areas, but if preparation involves refining an approach to keep witnesses' oral evidence as close to a pre-ordained script as possible, it risks being counter-productive. This became more pronounced (or noticeable) during the evidence of the different witnesses, and it approached its nadir during Ms Wilson's evidence.

83. Ironically, I found Mr Colwill's style of giving evidence when he was cross-examined on 26 July 2016 (about matters which could potentially go substantially to an attack on his credit) to be far more persuasive than it had been during the trial in November 2015. Perhaps the lack of time for extensive preparation, or witness training, was a good thing. Certainly where before there had been long pauses, requests to put matters "in context", careful consideration of questions and equally careful non-answers, on 26 July 2016 he answered promptly, candidly and openly, and I found what he had to say wholly convincing.'

Effective evidence in chief

5.29 Giving oral evidence is at least three-way communication. The advocate and the witness are responding to each other. There is an important audience: the Inspector. Both the advocate and the witness will be responding to what the Inspector is, or is not, doing or saying. This is fundamentally different to communication in writing. It is also fundamentally different to oral responses to an Inspector's questions at a hearing.

5.30 The large majority of evidence given at inquiries is from witnesses who are giving evidence in the course of their professional work. However, that is very far from universally so. The evidence of an appellant may be key to persuading an Inspector of the need for the development. The evidence of an objector may be uniquely compelling by reason of long local knowledge: 'Local people are encouraged to take part in the inquiry process. Local knowledge and opinion can often be a valuable addition to the evidence given by the appellant and the LPA.'[24] The objector whose land is proposed to be taken compulsorily is perfectly placed to explain why it is not proportionate to do so, for example if that land is the objector's home or livelihood. The credibility of a factual witness may be the matter on which the success of a legal ground of appeal stands or falls in an enforcement inquiry. However, the following considerations are important to the effective oral presentation of any evidence, whether expert, professional or lay.

5.31 Giving evidence in chief is the first opportunity for a witness to make an impact on the inquiry. It creates the first impression on the Inspector, on the advocate for any opposing party, on any witness who is to give contrary evidence, and on the

---

[24] PINS, *Guide to taking part in a planning and listed building consent appeals by an inquiry – England* (September 2019) at [9.1].

assembled public. All will respond to the content and cogency of the evidence given. A point which comes across clearly and persuasively may be left alone because it seems to be unanswerable. Any weakness will be detected straight away. To achieve more of the former and less of the latter, it is essential to:

- prepare;
- respond;
- be clear; and
- be concise.

The focus is on the witness and the evidence which the witness is giving. The focus is not on the advocate, not on another party's case and not on the Inspector's questions, concerns or interests. All of that comes later.

5.32 The advocate's role is to facilitate the clearest delivery of the witness' evidence. This is done by the following:

- Introducing the witness. This is likely to be the only time when the advocate leads the witness, stating the relevant qualifications and experience and asking whether that is correct.

- The remainder of the evidence in chief will comprise a combination of reading parts of a summary proof and responses to open questions: 'Please give your opinion on the consistency of policy ABC with the Framework'; 'What role does the hedgerow play for bats?'.

- Taking the Inspector to key tables, plans, photographs or similar materials to develop and explain the point. This enables the witness to show how the conclusion is justified and well supported. It is a means of making sure that the Inspector and the other parties really understand what is being said, and why. This is the only guaranteed opportunity to do this because the witness cannot control the areas which are cross-examined upon, nor the Inspector's questions. If the witness is not cross-examined on a point then she cannot be re-examined on it.

5.33 To achieve this level of clarity, both the witness and the advocate need to prepare. Preparedness is sometimes thought to require re-reading of the witness' proof of evidence and any contrary evidence, which it does. But it is a mistake to omit to also re-read and actively think about:

- *The related evidence.* So, if highways impacts give rise to noise or air quality objections, then the specialist noise and air quality witnesses need a clear understanding of where the key highways data are to be found in the inquiry documents and to be able to give coherent explanations of how the parts of the evidence fit together, rather than treating each as a silo of its own.

- *The history of the application or the particular issue.* The witness needs to have the story in mind, not just the final chapter. There may have been twists and turns in the available evidence and in the parties' positions. These are important in understanding how the position presented at the inquiry was actually arrived at.

- *The relationship with relevant policies.* The witness may not be the relevant witness to explain the function of the policy or conduct any sort of balance, but

5.34 *Inquiries*

the witness not only needs to know what the policy target is, but also where it comes from and its status: development plan, Framework, guidance from a statutory body etc.

5.34 Typically, witnesses at an inquiry prepare more thoroughly than for a hearing, though some would contest that proposition. The discipline is in all senses quite different. The reality is that a witness preparing evidence for an inquiry knows that an expert witness will be assisting an advocate on the other side, or sides. It is obvious to the witness that the preparation of the evidence requires a forensic and robust approach which will withstand the scrutiny of a peer, a specialist advocate and an experienced professional sitting as an Inspector. In seeing where all of the preparatory effort is ultimately to be examined, the witness produces evidence which is better than would otherwise be the case.

5.35 In practical terms, the following will assist the witness:

- Labelling or distinguishing the folders in the inquiry documents which are of particular relevance. If folder 4 of the core documents contains the relevant development plan policies, mark it so that it can be spotted instantly.
- 'Flagging' documents and parts of documents not only helps in navigating materials, it is a thought process in itself which helps to work through arguments and responses. There are two sides of any document which are likely to help the witness: the top and the right-hand edge: use them differently and to help. The top can be used to flag the document, and the side can be used to flag key parts of the document. Any such system aids clear thinking, clear explanation and therefore helps the inquiry.

5.36 Evidence in chief should not be overly lengthy. In almost all cases there will be a proof of evidence which the Inspector and the main parties have read carefully. Time estimates for evidence in chief normally fall in the bracket between 20 minutes and one and half hours, depending very much on the nature and extent of both the evidence and the range of matters which need to be explained or which are in issue. The Inspector may refuse to permit the giving or production of evidence; (b) cross-examination of persons giving evidence; or (c) presentation of any other matter, which he considers to be irrelevant or repetitious.[25]

5.37 The main parties will always call witnesses who have prepared and exchanged proofs of their evidence, but it is worthwhile to note the exception. It is not a requirement of the rules that a witness sends a proof of evidence. For example, r 14 of the 2000 Rules provides:[26]

> 'Any person entitled to appear at an inquiry who proposes to give, or to call another person to give, evidence at the inquiry by reading a proof of evidence shall simultaneously send …'.

5.38 This does not require a proof to be sent. Rather, if the witness is to give evidence by reading a proof, then a copy must be sent. Of course, an opposing party

---

[25] See r 16(6) of the 2000 Rules; r 17(6) of the 2002 Rules, and; reg 45(7) and (9) of the 2017 Regulations. But note that where the Inspector refuses to permit the giving of oral evidence, the person wishing to give the evidence may submit to him any evidence or other matter in writing before the close of the inquiry.
[26] The position is the same in Wales: reg 44(1) of the 2017 Regulations.

and the Inspector are likely to object in vigorous terms if a witness is sprung on the inquiry without notice of what they are going to say. However, the drafting of the rule, when correctly understood, injects helpful flexibility into the inquiry process. For example, an issue may arise without notice during the course of an inquiry, from either a main party, the Inspector or an objector. It may be that somebody can answer the point by reference to either a document which is before the inquiry, by introducing a document which provides the answer, or by simply explaining the answer orally. Whether this can be done without prejudice to a party to the inquiry is a highly case-sensitive question. However, it is common for information to be required in order to inform the Inspector, but for that information to be uncontentious. It would be onerous and wasteful to require a proof of evidence when it was not needed.

5.39 It is possible to give evidence in chief by reference to video or audio recording, played at the inquiry. Generally, the Planning Inspectorate will return any audio/video evidence sent in advance of the inquiry but a written summary may be sent which will be seen by the Inspector, the appellant, statutory parties, any Rule 6(6) party and the LPA. It is strongly advisable to send a copy of the material which is proposed to be played to the other parties. They will not want to be surprised by material simply brought to the inquiry. It is also helpful to state the total length of material which is proposed to be played. The shorter the material, the more likely it is to be accepted and the less likely it is to prompt concerns about poor use of inquiry time. PINS Guidance makes clear that it is the responsibility of the party wishing to play the material to contact the LPA to find out whether it has suitable equipment at the venue to access the evidence, or if it will allow you to use your own. The equipment must be suitable to play the evidence so that everyone can see/hear it.[27] If the evidence is accepted by the Inspector it will become part of the inquiry evidence and will be retained by the Inspector.

5.40 Evidence is rarely given on oath, save in enforcement inquiries where the inquiry involves a dispute between the appellant and the LPA about the facts. Then, it is usual for the evidence to be given under oath (which the Inspector will administer) or after 'affirming'.

Objectives of cross examination and its conduct

A right to cross-examine?

5.41 There is, generally, a right to cross-examine. It was established in the 1992 rules,[28] and is present in the same form in r 16(5) of the 2000 Rules:

> 'A person entitled to appear at an inquiry shall be entitled to call evidence and the appellant, the local planning authority and any statutory party shall be entitled to cross-examine persons giving evidence, but, subject to the foregoing and paragraphs (6) and (9), the calling of evidence and the cross-examination of persons giving evidence shall otherwise be at the discretion of the inspector.'

5.42 The right is not unlimited. The Inspector may, as would be expected, refuse to permit cross-examination which is irrelevant or repetitious. The same position

---

[27] PINS guidance at [8.2].
[28] Rule 14(3) of the Town and Country Planning (Inquiries Procedure) Rules 1992, SI 1992/2038, now revoked.

5.43 *Inquiries*

applies in respect of other forms of inquiry and in Wales.[29] Whether it is fair to allow or disallow cross-examination will depend on all of the circumstances. The courts will be very slow to intervene.[30]

5.43 There is not, however, a right to cross-examine which is contained in any statute. The right is contained in statutory instruments: the rules and the regulations. In any event, the 1990 Act gives the decision on whether to hold an inquiry to the Secretary of State. There is no right to a public inquiry, so the entitlement contained in the rules is contingent on a decision to hold an inquiry.

5.44 The following account is that of an advocate, but it is aimed at the perspective of a witness. It is the advocate's task to immerse herself or himself in the witness' world, to understand it, and to examine it.

Purpose

5.45 Cross-examination has purpose. Its practice is rooted in 600 years of the Bar and parameters set by the Code of Conduct (see para 5.64 ff below).

5.46 The purpose of cross-examination in a planning inquiry will vary from case to case and from witness to witness. For each, there is likely to be more than one purpose.

5.47 The clue to the first purpose lies in the very term 'cross-examination'. The purpose is to examine the witness's evidence. In large part it is a comparative exercise, cross-referencing what is said to other material. This has been called 'probing'. PINS refer to it in the criteria on mode of appeal as 'testing'. But there is no real need for a secondary term because the primary term captures the purpose: examination.

5.48 An expert and professional witness appears at an inquiry to explain her or his conclusions or opinion and it is that explanation, assessment, modelling or reasoning which gives rise to the first purpose of cross-examination, which is to examine the conclusions by reference to the material which is said to support it. This may be as simple as identifying the assertion within the evidence and asking where one finds the material which supports it.

5.49 To undertake cross-examination in the fields which are in issue in a planning inquiry requires experts who are highly experienced and advocates who are specialist. It is a time-consuming and expensive exercise. Why does a party want to cross-examine? It must be a potent reason to justify the effort and the expense. The answer is straightforward: to persuade, and to know that the Inspector has heard the case comprehensively put. The answer is not simply 'to test' or because there is a factual dispute. Those reasons may also be in play, but the overarching purpose is to persuade by the answers which are given by the witnesses on both sides.

5.50 It is sometimes said in response to the criteria for determining the mode of appeal that there is a need to cross examine on a particular topic. The dominant

---

[29] See reg 45(6) of the 2017 Regulations.
[30] *Bushell v Secretary of State for the Environment* [1981] AC 75 (HL), discussed in respect of procedural fairness at para 5.100 below.

thinking is that there is a need for one party to show that another party is incorrect in its position on some part of the case. That may be true, but fails to give the necessary additional emphasis to the need for each side to have the contrary case put to their witness. The elucidation of the case is through the cases being put to the witness and from the strength of the respective positions emerging from the response. The two ways in which a case is presented and illuminated by cross-examination are first that the witness has to grapple with any suggested flaws in her or his own evidence, and secondly, that the witness has the opportunity to respond to the case being put by the opposing party.

5.51 A witness whose evidence responds convincingly to the case put in cross-examination has probably won the argument on that issue. So, the right to cross-examine at an inquiry is also a right to be cross-examined. Any party which has faith in its case will wish to give consideration to the benefits of being able to explain, directly, to the other side why it is correct on determinative issues.

5.52 The cross-examination required and suitable to a planning inquiry is determined by the subject matter. The issues arising from a factual dispute as to the immunity from enforcement action are different in character to a dispute as to the method to determine the appropriate background noise level. However, in both cases, the Inspector is an experienced tribunal who will be able to move quickly through the points and the issues.

Practice

5.53 Now to consider the practice of cross-examination. Though the evidence in chief is led largely from the summary, cross-examination is on the whole of the proof of evidence.[31] Indeed, cross-examination may be on any document before the inquiry which is relevant to an issue within the witness's evidence.

5.54 A witness, and an Inspector, may expect questions in cross-examination to be focused and direct. In large measure, they will be closed questions, namely questions which indicate or state what the answer is expected to be: 'Today is sunny, isn't it?'; 'Lunch is at 1pm, isn't it?', not 'How is the weather today?'; 'When is lunch time?'. It follows that most questions are capable of being answered either in the affirmative or in the negative. 'Yes' and 'no', or, 'I would agree ...' will therefore be the style of answers which the inquiry expects to hear. The inquiry is entitled to such an answer if the question is clear and precise. If an equally clear response is not forthcoming, then courteous persistence will follow along with a gradual reduction in the credibility of the answers if they remain evasive. The answer should be given, then explained or any necessary qualification should be given. There may be partial agreement with the proposition put. If so, that should be stated and the position explained: 'Yes, lunchtime will be 1pm I expect, but I don't eat lunch'.

5.55 It is because direct, or closed, questions are both permitted and are predominant in cross-examination that the evidence becomes focused on what matters to the party cross-examining and that party's case can be put. The use of closed questions is fundamental and is the essence of the right which is contained

---

[31] This is the effect of r 16(6) of the 2000 Rules; reg 45(8)(b) of the 2017 Regulations.

5.56 *Inquiries*

within the rules. It provides the opportunity for a party to obtain a clear answer to a precise question which is so unlikely to be obtained by any other means.

5.56 Obtaining a clear answer to a precise question has a profound impact on the inquiry, which is this. An advocate is obliged to put his client's case. If that case changes as a result of answers given by witnesses, then so too does the case that may properly be put to other witnesses. This is a purpose and consequence of cross-examination which has to be understood in order to grasp the powerful nature of the inquiry process. It works like this.

5.57 Witness A is called by the appellant to address impacts on the local highway network. Witness A concedes an error in the highway modelling and that the residual impacts on the highway network would be severe.

5.58 Witness B is called by the planning authority to give planning evidence, including the planning balance. The cross-examination of Witness B by the appellant can no longer be on the basis of the appellant's case as it was opened. The cross-examination must now be on the basis that severe residual impacts on the local highway network are part of the planning balance.

5.59 Evidently, the appellant is in considerable difficulty in this stark scenario. The same principle applies to any concession made – if the evidence moves on, so does the case which may then be put to subsequent witnesses. Further, the same principle applies to the submissions which may properly be made at the close of the inquiry, as emphasised above.

5.60 A witness will not be assisted by her or his own advocate during cross-examination. The exceptions include the provision of a document reference if that is needed because cross-examination is not a test of memory. Also, it may be appropriate to intervene if a question is beyond the scope of that witness' evidence or is more properly considered to be within the scope of the evidence of another witness to be called.

5.61 To set out areas or types of cross-examination is apt to mislead the reader to the view that those areas are comprehensive and complete. Good cross-examination is a discipline of its own and no attempt is made to describe it here.[32] Obviously, omissions may be highlighted. They may be wholesale omissions or omissions of emphasis. If an opinion is based on one factual assumption then the witness may be asked to deal with an alternative set of facts. As has been highlighted and emphasised, a witness may properly expect to have the contrary case put to them on the principal controversial points.

5.62 A witness may ask, 'how should I give my evidence?'. Such a simple question raises many of the issues which are addressed in the rules which frame an advocate's conduct. These are the parameters which frame the conduct of the advocate. They are summarised generally here, in respect of the interactions with witnesses, and also more broadly so far as relevant to planning inquiries.

---

[32] For a discussion of the benefits and purpose of cross-examination see the article by Lionel Read QC (1997) JPEL 24.

Oral evidence **5.68**

5.63 In preparing to give evidence, a witness and an inquiry team can properly expect guidance and leadership from the appointed advocate. If the advocate is a barrister, he or she will provide that guidance within the scope of the professional duties which are a hallmark of the Bar. There is no good reason why other advocates should operate differently.

5.64 Since the fourteenth century, barristers have imposed on themselves a set of rules which regulate their duties to the court, their client and how they may approach written and oral evidence. The judges oversaw those rules, and so did the Inns of Court. The Inns consolidated some of their regulatory role in the General Council of the Bar. The Bar Standards Board (BSB) maintains a Handbook, last revised on 3 February 2020 (version 4.4). The current code of conduct is issued by the BSB as Part 2 C of the Handbook (see Appendix 9). It is supported by guidance documents from the Ethics Committee. These are the parameters within which the oral evidence is examined.

Parameters

5.65 The Code of Conduct refers to duties to the court and clients. 'Court' is given a wide definition. It means any court or tribunal or any other person or body whether sitting in public or in private before whom a barrister appears or may appear as an advocate. On this definition, the Code of Conduct applies to a planning inquiry as it would in the Crown Court, so far as relevant.

5.66 In planning inquiries, there are some key points of conduct for advocates. They are arranged here by reference to the client, witnesses, argument and fees. They, and similar if less stringent rules in other professions, are fundamental to the proper functioning of a public inquiry. For a person who is to participate in a public inquiry, in whatever capacity, some familiarity with these rules is necessary in order to understand much of the preparation and conduct of an inquiry.

5.67 In respect of the client:

- promote fearlessly and by all proper and lawful means the client's best interests and do so without regard to the advocate's own interests or to any consequences for the advocate, or to any other person, and the advocate's professional client may not limit the advocate's discretion as to how the interests of the client may best be served;

- protect the confidentiality of each client's affairs, except for such disclosures as are required or permitted by law or for which the client gives informed consent; but

- the forgoing duties are subject to the advocate's duty to the inquiry and to act with honesty, integrity and maintaining independence;

5.68 In respect of witnesses:

- not to do or say anything which could be interpreted as manufacturing or in any way influencing the content of the evidence that the expert is to give in the witness box;

- not to call witnesses to give evidence or to ask the inquiry to consider documents which the advocate knows or is instructed are untrue or misleading, unless the advocate makes the true position known;

5.69 *Inquiries*

- allied to the last point, not to knowingly or recklessly mislead or attempt to mislead anyone;
- not rehearse, practise with or coach a witness in respect of their evidence;
- must not make statements or ask questions merely to insult, humiliate or annoy a witness or any other person;
- not to make a serious allegation against a witness for whom there has been an opportunity to cross-examine unless that witness was given a chance to answer the allegation in cross-examination; and
- unless you have the permission of the representative for the opposing side or of the court, you must not communicate with any witness (including your client) about the case while the witness is giving evidence.

5.69 In respect of opinions and arguments:

- not put forward a personal opinion of the facts or the law unless you are invited or required to do so by the Inspector;
- not to make any contention which the advocate does not consider to be properly arguable.

5.70 In respect of fees:

- not make, or offer to make, payments to any witness which are contingent on their evidence or on the outcome of the case;
- only propose, or accept, fee arrangements which are legal.

5.71 From this summary, it can be seen that the advocate retains her or his independence throughout and takes responsibility for the proper conduct of the client's case. The advocate is bound to use all proper and lawful means to advance the client's best interests. This is done with honesty and with integrity. This means that it is done via the evidence of the witnesses, not via the advocate manufacturing or influencing the content of the evidence – that is for the witnesses. That evidence is not to be rehearsed or practised.

5.72 These are the parameters within which the oral evidence is presented. They are a presumption on which the procedure rules are built.

Inspector's questions and third parties

5.73 An Inspector ought to have only a small number of questions on the main issues. The proofs of evidence, statement of common ground and the oral evidence should have addressed the points which arose in the Inspector's mind during the preparation for the inquiry. If there are questions on main issues, they are likely to be either factual clarification or a really important question which goes to the heart of the case; a question which nobody else had dared to ask. It follows that very great attention and focus should be given to the answer to such questions.

5.74 In the author's view, it is not appropriate for third parties to ask questions of witnesses. Third parties are, as matter of universal practice, given an opportunity to make oral representations. In a concession to participation and public involvement, a third party may give any evidence they wish without notice to the inquiry or to any party. It is a significant degree of latitude which is extended with a view to removing formality which might otherwise inhibit participation. However, the opportunity to be heard, at the Inspector's discretion, is not to be confused or conflated with the right to appear or the opportunity to appear as a result of applying to do so as a Rule 6 party. Those who will appear do so on a level playing field in which they disclose their case, exchange their evidence and are bound by the same rules and practice in giving evidence and making submissions. The result is a fair proceeding. To give the opportunity to ask questions to a person who has not followed any of the disciplines which were observed by the parties who appear is neither consistent with the rules nor fair. Of course, consistency with the rules and fairness tend to be the same thing.

Re-examination

5.75 It is particularly important that the witness does not discuss the case with anybody during the period from the start of the cross-examination until the re-examination has concluded. This is often referred to as the term 'purdah', which is not really apt, but has become commonplace.[33] This is to avoid the impression that a witness has been prompted to give an answer in re-examination or to put right something which was said in answer to a question in cross-examination. It is likely to be a serious breach of relevant codes of conduct for a member of a professional institution to seek to influence evidence in this way. However, the fact that a witness is in 'purdah' after completing evidence in chief is well known and not problematic in practice.

5.76 This practice does not extend to preventing all communication whatsoever. It is concerned with avoiding discussion of the case. Witnesses still need to eat, drink and travel. Nevertheless, it is good practice for a witness to take meals away from other inquiry participants until re-examination is complete.

5.77 Re-examination may occur before or after an Inspector asks questions. It is preferable that it takes place after an Inspector's question because this avoids a potential need to re-examine twice: once after the parties' cross-examinations and once after the Inspector's questions, if anything arises from those answers.

5.78 Re-examination is in many respects the most taxing part of both giving evidence and calling evidence. This is because of the proper limitations on the exercise which are:

---

[33] In the context of political purdah, in *R (on the application of ClientEarth) v Secretary of State for the Environment, Food and Rural Affairs* [2017] EWHC 1618 (Admin), Garnham J described the term in this way:

'It is necessary to identify what "Purdah" is and, as importantly, what it is not. "Purdah" is a word of Indian origin. It describes the curtain once used to screen Hindu or Muslim women from the sight of men or strangers. According to the Concise Oxford Dictionary, the word is used figuratively to describe the Indian system of secluding women of rank from public view.

The word has been adopted in English to describe the period before an election in which ministers, public servants, councillors and officials are expected to refrain from taking controversial decisions. That policy serves an important function in protecting the electoral process from interference, intended or accidental, by those holding elected public office. Purdah is, in effect, a self-denying ordinance imposed by local or central governments on its officers and members.'

5.79 *Inquiries*

- the topics or matters to be examined are limited to those matters which have been cross-examined upon. Therefore, it is not possible to simply pick up a point which was forgotten in evidence in chief. Nor is it possible to go on a journey through those points which that party simply wants to emphasise; and

- the questions being asked are open questions, not the closed questions which will have been prevalent during cross-examination. It is not possible for the advocate to ask a question which contains the answer. If such a question is asked, it is improper, will be objected to, and the Inspector will ignore both the question and the answer – so the exercise is pointless.

5.79 However, re-examination is an important opportunity for the witness and for the party calling the evidence. It presents an opportunity to:

- add to a good answer and make it better;
- build on a failure or flaw identified by the witness;
- return the focus of the case and of the Inspector to matters which are important to your case;
- clarify; and
- correct potential misunderstanding of fact or of emphasis.

5.80 The first two points illustrate the two-way nature of cross-examination. The advocate plans a cross-examination to make and secure the points which establish the client's case on the particular issue. But, often, the advocate does not succeed and the witness in fact strengthens and reinforces her or his opinion by the answers which are given. In other words, the cross-examination in fact exposes the flaw on the other side. This is the opportunity to build on that development in the evidence, to underscore it for the Inspector and to de-stabilise the evidence of any witness who is yet to give contrary evidence.

5.81 A re-examination in which the advocate and the witness have such a good understanding of the material and the thinking which is behind it becomes an engaging and compelling conversation. The advocate is a low-key interviewer, picking up topics and guiding that conversation. The witness is able to occupy the space provided and have the last word in that part of the evidence.

5.82 There are of course those examples which are better characterised as rescue missions, about which little can be helpfully said.

CONDITIONS, OBLIGATIONS AND SITE VISITS

5.83 Typically, planning conditions are considered at the end of the evidence and before closing submissions. Typically, accompanied site visits take place after the closing submissions and after the inquiry has closed. However, there can be considerable variation in this order of events, simply to take account of the circumstances of the case and the preferences of the parties and the Inspector. For example it is often helpful to:

Conditions, obligations and site visits **5.87**

- have an earlier accompanied site visit.[34] If there is to be evidence about what can been seen or what something is, then it assists the Inspector to see it first and hear the evidence second. It is always possible to do a second site visit if that is desirable. It may also fit the programme: for example if the evidence runs short on one day, then the time might be used to undertake a site visit;

- have more than one conditions session, the first of which is during the first half of the inquiry. If there is a long list of proposed conditions, it assists the parties to run through them once with the Inspector and return with a revised draft in the light of the contributions of the parties, interested persons and the Inspector.

5.84 A discussion of planning conditions and any planning obligation offered by way of a deed under s 106 of TCPA 1990 will take place during the inquiry and before it closes. The Inspector will be careful to explain that such discussion is undertaken so that the necessary information may be gathered so that in the event the Inspector decides to allow the appeal, she or he is equipped to draft an appropriate set of conditions. The discussion is without prejudice to any party's position on the main issues.

5.85 Nevertheless, the 'conditions session' is a very important stage in the inquiry process. First, the evidence may have revealed that a concern is capable of being addressed satisfactorily by a planning condition. There is an interaction between the oral evidence and the conditions session. Secondly, the tests to be applied in law and in policy are a potential source of legal challenge to any permission which may be granted. If a condition is in some material respect outside of the powers to impose planning conditions then there is a possibility that the entire process of the inquiry will have been wasted and need to be repeated after quashing of the decision.

5.86 It is convenient for any planning obligation to be provided to the Inspector and to the parties along with the proofs of evidence, which will usually be four weeks before the inquiry opens. However, the guidance in this regard is less demanding: not later than 10 days before the inquiry opens.[35]

5.87 The Inspector may make an unaccompanied inspection of the land before or during an inquiry without giving notice of his intention to the persons entitled to appear at the inquiry.[36] However, if either the LPA or the appellant request it, then the Inspector shall carry out an accompanied site visit.[37] If, at the appointed time, a party has not attended the location for the start of the site visit, the Inspector is not obliged to defer it.[38]

---

[34] This is accommodated by the rules which leave it in the Inspector's discretion when to have an accompanied site visit, but the date and time of that site visit is to be announced in the inquiry: r 17(3) of the 2000 Rules. In respect of site visits, the rules for enforcement inquiries are the same – see r 18 of the 2002 Rules.
[35] See the Procedural Guide at, for example Appendix F.1; See also 'Taking part in a planning inquiry' PINS Sept 2019 at Annex A (enforcement); Annex B (non-recovered appeals).
[36] Rule 17(1) of the 2000 Rules.
[37] Rule 17(2)(b) of the 2000 Rules.
[38] Rule 17(4) of the 2000 Rules.

5.88 *Inquiries*

5.88 There are no regulations which specifically address site visits in Wales. The regulations are silent on the topic. The practice will not be materially different to that which has been long standing in England and in Wales.

5.89 In practical terms: think about agreeing an itinerary, on a plan; decide who is going so that the Inspector may be informed; arrange access; have the necessary clothing and any necessary personal protective equipment available.

PROCEDURAL FAIRNESS

5.90 The starting point is the Franks Committee – more formally the Committee on Administrative Tribunals and Inquiries (1957) (Cmd 218), which produced the Franks Report. It is difficult to grasp fully or to understand the nature of planning inquiries without appreciating the thinking which went into their creation. Craig[39] captures the essence in this way:

> 'Witnesses who gave evidence before the Committee were divided as to the role of inquiries. One group saw inquiries as part of the process of administration, as an extension of departmental decision-making in specific areas, which should be relatively free from controls other than those imposed by Parliament. A different view was expressed by those who saw the inquiry as akin to a judicial process, in which the inspector who undertook the hearing was in the position of a judge. The corollary of this latter approach was that the procedures by which the inquiry was run should be modelled on the judicial process, at least to the extent that this entailed the decision being taken directly on the evidence presented at the inquiry. The Franks Committee rejected both positions:
>
>> "Our general conclusion is that those procedures cannot be classified as purely administrative or purely judicial. They are not purely administrative because of the provision for a special procedure preliminary to the decision – a feature not to be found in the ordinary course of administration – and because this procedure, as we have shown, involves the testing of an issue, often partly in public. They are not on the other hand purely judicial, because the final decision cannot be reached by the application of rules and must allow the exercise of wide discretion in the balancing of public and private interests. Neither view at its extreme is tenable, nor should either be emphasised at the expense of the other."
>
> Instead of attempting to model the inquiry procedures on either of the preceding views the Franks Committee drew up recommendations which attempted to balance the conflicting interests. What emerged were proposals concerning the pre-inquiry stage, the procedure at inquiry, and post-inquiry practice.'

5.91 Its interaction with the procedure rules which followed is described in the leading case on procedural fairness in planning inquiries in this way:[40]

> 'It, inter alia, considered and made recommendations as to the procedure to be followed in relation to inquiries, stressing the need for an authority seeking to acquire land to inform those affected of its reasons for doing so in order that they might be better able to prepare and present their case (paragraphs 280, 281) and that the right of individuals to state their case cannot be effective unless the case of the authority is adequately presented at the inquiry paragraph 306).

---

[39] Paul Craig, *Administrative Law* (Sweet and Maxwell, 2012).
[40] *Fairmount Investments Ltd v Secretary of State for the Environment* [1976] 1 WLR 1255.

Procedural fairness **5.96**

Following their report, the Compulsory Purchase by Local Authorities (Inquiries Procedure) Rules 1962 (S.I. 1962 No. 1424) were made. They do not apply, we were told, to acquisitions under Part III of the Housing Act 1957. They only have legal effect in relation to local inquiries held under the Acquisition of Land (Authorisation Procedure) Act 1946 and no similar rules have been made in relation to acquisitions under Part III. Nevertheless we were told that in practice local authorities seeking to acquire under Part III have regard to them.

They embody certain recommendations of the Franks Committee designed to secure fairness and natural justice. Under them an acquiring authority has to serve on "statutory objectors" who include the owners of the land affected, a written statement of their reasons for making the order (rule 4(4)) and the inspector appointed to hold the inquiry can allow the reasons stated to be altered and added to "but shall (if necessary by adjourning the inquiry) give every statutory objector an adequate opportunity of considering any fresh reason …" (rule 7(5)).

Similar provisions are contained in the Town and Country Planning (Inquiries Procedures) Rules 1974 (S.I. 1974 No. 419).

Their object clearly was to ensure that the requirements of natural justice were met, and that an objector knew what case he had to meet.'

5.92 Natural justice, or procedural fairness in adversarial proceedings means that any participant is entitled to know the case which he has to meet and to have a reasonable opportunity to bring evidence and make submissions in relation to the opposing case. These principles were the foundation of the finding by the House of Lords in *Fairmount Investments*. A point relied upon by an Inspector which had not been part of the council's case in a CPO inquiry prejudiced Fairmount because it had not had an opportunity to refute the Inspector's point.

5.93 What may give rise to procedural unfairness is usefully illustrated by the examples to be found in the first instance cases.

5.94 In *Castleford Homes Ltd*[41] the judge had to consider whether the appellant ought reasonably to have been alert to the need to address a point about a local area of play. It did not matter that the Inspector was unaware of Castleford Homes' misapprehension as to the true position of the council. Castleford Homes ought to have been given an opportunity to address the point.

5.95 There was a different result in respect of the next case in which a disappointed appellant sought the assistance of the High Court. In *Tatham Homes Ltd* the main issues did not include the effects of overlooking and privacy. Local residents, however, did take the point and the Inspector agreed, dismissing the appeal. It was foreseeable that residents' concerns might result in the dismissal of the appeal and it was also evident that the Inspector's site visit might support the residents' case.

5.96 A further case has been referred to in the context of the importance of statements of common ground: *Poole*.[42] This was a case about a tree, a statement of common ground, a witness who changed her position and an Inspector who refused an adjournment. A statement of common ground had been agreed in respect of the

---

[41] *Castleford Homes Ltd v Secretary of State for Environment, Transport and the Regions* [2001] EWHC Admin 77, [2001] PLCR 29.
[42] *R (on the application of Poole) v Secretary of State for Communities and Local Government* [2008] EWHC 676 (Admin), [2008] JPL 1774.

5.97 *Inquiries*

use of a planning condition to protect trees in the vicinity of proposed development. In evidence, the planning authority's witness resiled from that position. The appellant sought an adjournment, which was refused. In cross-examination of the planning authority's witness, agreement was again reached that the issue could be dealt with by an appropriate planning condition. The Inspector nevertheless dismissed the appeal on the ground of future adverse effect on trees. The appellant applied to the High Court on the basis that it had been procedurally unfair to refuse the opportunity to call evidence on an issue which had been the subject of common ground, and then to dismiss the appeal on that issue.

5.97 The court gave valuable guidance on the interaction between the common law rules of procedural fairness and the procedural rules governing the conduct of planning inquiries. He said, at [40]:

> 'However, it is most important when deciding whether the parties at an inquiry have had a fair opportunity to comment on an issue raised by an inspector of his or her own motion, and whether they could reasonably have anticipated that an issue had to be addressed because it might be raised by an inspector, to bear in mind the highly focused nature of the modern public inquiry where the whole emphasis of the Rules and procedural guidance contained in circulars is to encourage the parties to focus their evidence and submissions on those matters that are in dispute.'

5.98 There are two judgments in *Hopkins Developments Ltd*. In the first, of Jackson LJ, five principles of procedural fairness are identified:

> '(1) Any party to a planning inquiry is entitled (i) to know the case which he has to meet and (ii) to have a reasonable opportunity to adduce evidence and make submissions in relation to that opposing case. (2) If there is procedural unfairness which materially prejudices a party to a planning inquiry that may be a good ground for quashing the inspector's decision. (3) The 2000 Rules are designed to assist in achieving objective (1)(i), avoiding pitfall (1)(ii) and promoting efficiency. Nevertheless the Rules are not a complete code for achieving procedural fairness. (4) A rule 7 statement or a rule 16 statement identifies what the inspector regards as the main issues at the time of his statement. Such a statement is likely to assist the parties, but it does not bind the inspector to disregard evidence on other issues. Nor does it oblige him to give the parties regular updates about his thinking as the Inquiry proceeds. (5) The inspector will consider any significant issues raised by third parties, even if those issues are not in dispute between the main parties. The main parties should therefore deal with any such issues, unless and until the inspector expressly states that they need not do so. (6) If a main party resiles from a matter agreed in the statement of common ground prepared pursuant to rule 15, the inspector must give the other party a reasonable opportunity to deal with the new issue which has emerged.'

5.99 The second judgment of Beatson LJ is more discursive, less often cited, but just as important in understanding what the opportunity to be heard really is. He held:

- it is a commonplace that in the context of administrative decision-making the ascertainment of what procedures are required is acutely sensitive to context and the particular factual situation. Fairness is thus a flexible concept, as well as, of course, being subject to any particular requirements in primary and secondary legislation;
- the 'right to be heard' limb of the principle of natural justice had been expanded to new situations but the procedures required in those situations might be less onerous and less formal because of the nature of the decision that is to be made; and

- what is required is an opportunity to be heard, an opportunity to participate in the procedure by which the decision is made.

5.100 This may or may not require cross-examination. The Inspector's discretion is very wide, for the reasons given in *Bushell*:[43]

> 'To over-judicialise the inquiry by insisting on observance of the procedures of a court of justice which professional lawyers alone are competent to operate effectively in the interests of their clients would not be fair. It would, in my view, be quite fallacious to suppose that at an inquiry of this kind the only fair way of ascertaining matters of fact and expert opinion is by the oral testimony of witnesses who are subjected to cross-examination on behalf of parties who disagree with what they have said. Such a procedure is peculiar to litigation conducted in the courts that follow the common law system of procedure; it plays no part in the procedure of courts of justice under legal systems based upon the civil law ... So refusal by an inspector to allow a party to cross-examine orally at a local inquiry a person who has made statements of facts or has expressed expert opinions is not unfair *per se*."

5.101 The general position is clear – the decision is for the Inspector who has significant discretion. That decision will not be unfair *per se* if cross-examination is refused. But this does not tell us what should guide a decision to allow or refuse cross-examination, and it does not tell us when it would be unfair.

PRACTICAL MATTERS

Interested persons

5.102 Interested people may appear and give evidence at the Inspector's discretion. The Planning Inspectorate would very rarely refuse a request to appear at the inquiry, nor would an Inspector refuse an opportunity for an interested person to be heard.

5.103 An evening inquiry session is sometimes held if there are a significant number of interested people who cannot attend during the daytime inquiry sessions. This is at the discretion of the Inspector and dependent on there being a suitable inquiry venue. They ought to be exceptional. There is a limit to the number of relevant points to be made, and their repetition does not improve them.

5.104 It is convenient to have at least copies of the summaries of the proofs available for members of the public who attend the inquiry. A laptop with copies of other documents is one solution which provides some access with less risk of wasted copying costs.

Inquiry rooms

5.105 There is guidance from the Planning Inspectorate.[44] Note:

---

[43] *Bushell v Secretary of State for the Environment* [1981] AC 75 (HL), per Lord Diplock at 97.
[44] https://assets.publishing.service.gov.uk/government/uploads/system/uploads/attachment_data/file/669224/venue_and_facilities.pdf and see Appendix 8 for the layout of an inquiry room.

5.106 *Inquiries*

- Matching the size of the inquiry room to the space required by the Inspector, the parties and the public makes a difference to the dynamics of an inquiry. If it is too cramped that will become frustrating. Too large is better than too small providing that audibility is properly addressed.
- Audibility is key. If a sound system is necessary for all participants to take part, then it must be provided.
- External noise may be a factor.
- An adequate quantity and quality of chairs and tables is required.
- Council chambers, depending upon their layout, are often poor venues for the parties in a longer inquiry.

5.106 There is the vital matter of the Inspector's chair, for which specific guidance is given, namely the chair should, whenever possible and where specifically requested by the Inspectorate, have:

- seat back height and tilt adjustment;
- seat height adjustment;
- swivel mechanism; and
- castors or glides.

Welsh language

5.107 On 30 March 2016 the Welsh Language Commissioner introduced new Welsh Language Standards. These are a set of requirements that aim to improve the bilingual services that the people of Wales can expect to receive from their Government. The Standards clearly set out what the responsibilities are in terms of providing bilingual services, ensuring the Welsh language is not treated any less favourably than the English language. The Standards are an important opportunity to improve customer service and provide better policy outcomes for the people of Wales. The Standards are legally binding and must be adhered to by all.

5.108 Members of the public are welcome to speak in Welsh at events organised by the Planning Inspectorate in Wales. Publicity (including formal notices) will make clear that contributions from the public will be welcome in both Welsh and English. The local authority will provide Welsh translation facilities for all parties to the appeal.

5.109 Those who wish to speak Welsh should let the Inspectorate know beforehand so that the local authority can arrange for a translation service to be provided for the event. This request will be made in the formal notices and letters. Requests may be made on the day although these may delay the start of the event.

ADJOURNMENT

5.110 At the end of each day, the Inspector will announce the time and location to which the inquiry is adjourned, the relevant rule being: 'The inspector may from time to time adjourn an inquiry and, if the date, time and place of the adjourned inquiry

Adjournment **5.110**

are announced before the adjournment, no further notice shall be required.' This is procedurally significant in that the rule avoids the need for any sort of notification of the adjournment provided that it is stated in open inquiry before the inquiry adjourns. On the other hand, if there is no announcement, the rule requires notification. So, if an inquiry 'goes part-heard' to several weeks hence, perhaps because more time is needed, then no further notification is required provided that the appropriate announcement is made at the inquiry before it adjourns.

Chapter 6

Hearings

OVERVIEW

6.01 A hearing is not an inquiry. It is subject to its own procedural rules which are materially different to those in respect of inquiries, in both the preparation of the evidence and the conduct of the hearing itself. It is an inquisitorial process which places very considerable burdens on the Inspector to understand and explore the competing cases. A hearing procedure may be used in respect of a particular issue within an inquiry (see further at para 4.38 above).

Rules

6.02 There are two sets of hearing procedure rules in England: one set for enforcement cases,[1] and one set for s 78 appeals and s 20 Listed Building Act (Planning (Listed Buildings and Conservation Areas) Act 1990) cases.[2]

6.03 The position is slightly different in respect of hearings in comparison to inquiries in that there is only one set of rules for each type of case (enforcement/not enforcement). However, in contrast to the position in respect of inquiries, there are no separate rules for hearing cases which are determined by the Secretary of State rather than directly by the Inspector.

6.04 In Wales, there is one set of Regulations which address enforcement, s 78 and s 29 Listed Building Act cases, regardless of the mode of determination[3].

Notification of hearing

6.05 In England, a hearing date is to be fixed not later than 12 weeks after the starting date, unless this is impracticable in which case it should be fixed on the earliest date thereafter;[4] 10 weeks after the start date in Wales.[5] In practice, it is often the case that the hearing date is fixed later than required by the statutory instruments.

---

[1] Town and Country Planning (Enforcement) (Hearings Procedure) (England) Rules 2002, SI 2002/2684 ('the 2002 Hearing Rules').
[2] Town and Country Planning (Hearings Procedure) (England) Rules 2000, SI 2000/1626 ('the 2000 Hearing Rules').
[3] Town and Country Planning (Referred Applications and Appeals Procedure) (Wales) Regulations 2017, SI 2017/544 ('the 2017 Regulations').
[4] Rule 7(1) of the 2000 Hearing Rules; r 6(1) of the 2002 Hearing Rules.
[5] The 'representations period' is a defined term in the Regulations, being six weeks from the start date (reg 3(1)); Part 5 of the Regulations deals with hearings and reg 29(1) requires that the date be fixed no later than four weeks after the end of the representations period, thus making a total of 10 weeks from the start date.

6.06 The hearing date will be notified at least four weeks before the hearing, unless the parties and the Planning Inspectorate agree otherwise.[6] The Planning Inspectorate will require the local planning authority (LPA) to give notice of:

- the hearing date, time and venue;
- a description of the appeal-site location and the development proposed; and
- details of where one may inspect the completed questionnaire and details of the appellant's case.[7]

In Wales, having regard to the nature of the appeal, different parts of the hearing may be held at different locations.[8]

Appearances

6.07 The appellant and the LPA are entitled to take part in a hearing, along with any person invited to take part by the Welsh Ministers and those parties may represent themselves or be represented.[9]

INQUISITORIAL PROCEEDINGS

6.08 In England and Wales, the procedure at the hearing is described in similar but not identical ways:

England[10]	Wales[11]
Except as otherwise provided in these Rules, the Inspector shall determine the procedure at a hearing.	The appointed person presides at any hearing and must determine the procedure at the hearing, subject to these Regulations.
A hearing shall take the form of a discussion led by the Inspector and cross-examination shall not be permitted unless the Inspector considers that cross-examination is required to ensure a thorough examination of the main issues.	A hearing is to take the form of a discussion led by the appointed person and cross-examination is not to be permitted.
Where the Inspector considers that cross-examination is required under paragraph (2) he shall consider, after consulting the appellant and the LPA, whether the hearing should be closed and an inquiry held instead.	Where the appointed person considers that cross-examination is required the appointed person must consider (after consulting the appellant) whether the hearing should be closed and an inquiry held instead.

---

[6] Rule 7(2) of the 2000 Hearing Rules; reg 29(4) of the 2017 Regulations.
[7] Rule 7(5) and 7(6) of the 2000 Hearing Rules; r 6(5) and 6(6) of the 2002 Hearing Rules; reg 29(4) and (5) of the 2017 Regulations.
[8] Regulation 29(3) of the 2017 Regulations.
[9] Rule 9 of the 2000 Hearing Rules; reg 31 of the 2017 Regulations.
[10] Rule 11(1) and (2) of the 2000 Hearing Rules; Rule 11(1) and (2) of the 2002 Hearing Rules.
[11] Regulation 33(1)–(3) of the 2017 Regulations.

6.09 Hearings

6.09 The following key features of a hearing emerge from these rules:

- *The nature of the procedure is in the Inspector's gift.* It is therefore highly flexible and will be adapted to the circumstances of the issues in the case, the way in which the parties have approached those issues, the number of parties, and the extent to which they are represented, and if so, by whom.

- *The Inspector will lead a discussion.* While it is evident, and indeed obvious, that the hearing is under the control of the Inspector, 'a discussion' is also a broad term and results in great flexibility in the ways in which issues are addressed;

- *Cross-examination is not permitted.* This implies, and is established as a matter of practice, that examination in chief will be not be permitted either. However, all parties are present to ask and to answer questions, so this aspect requires further elaboration;

- *The Inspector may be of the view, for a wide variety of reasons, that cross-examination is required.* The words 'to ensure a thorough examination of the main issues' are present in the English Rules but not in the Welsh Regulations. The difference is probably immaterial. The Inspector is always seized of the procedure and may change the mode of appeal at any time if the circumstances require it and the Inspector has given the parties an opportunity to be heard on any change in procedure which the Inspector is minded to make. Curiously, the Welsh Regulations require consultation with only the appellant before change of mode of appeal to inquiry whereas the English Rules require consultation with both the appellant and the LPA. In fairness, all parties will have to be given the same opportunity to be heard on that question regardless of the provisions in the rules.

6.10 All of this amounts to an inquisitorial procedure. It is to be distinguished from an 'adversarial' procedure. The terms 'inquisitorial' and 'adversarial' have particular meanings in this context. An inquisitorial hearing places the burden on the tribunal to investigate, to probe, to challenge and to put the contrary positions. In an adversarial hearing, the parties take on much of that role by questioning and arguing the parties' cases.

The Inspector's duty at a hearing

6.11 Section 78 of the 1990 Act confers a right to appeal against the refusal of an application for planning permission. Section 79(2) provides that 'Before determining an appeal under Section 78 the Secretary of State shall, if either the appellant or the local planning authority so wish, give each of them an opportunity of appearing before and being heard by a person appointed by the Secretary of State for the purpose'. This is the way that Pill LJ introduced the ratio of the Court of Appeal's decision in *Dyason*.[12]

6.12 The Court referred to the 'statutory right to be heard' in Circular 15/96 (now cancelled). In para 1 of the Circular, it was stated that 'the appeal process is designed to be as efficient and user-friendly as possible, involving the best possible use of resources, whilst upholding the principles of fairness, thoroughness and consistency'. Paragraph 18 of the Circular provided:

---

[12] *Dyason v Secretary of State for the Environment and Chiltern* (1998) 75 P&CR 506.

Inquisitorial proceedings **6.14**

'The hearings procedure is simpler and quicker than that for inquiries. It enables the parties to present their case fully and fairly in a more relaxed and less formal atmosphere than at an inquiry. It usually takes the form of a round-the-table discussion led by the Inspector. Without formal cross-examination or advocacy, hearings can be much less daunting for unrepresented parties. Where one or other of the parties has exercised their right to be heard, the Department's policy is to promote the use of hearings in preference to inquiries for appropriate cases. Hearings are not suitable for all planning appeals, particularly where a substantial number of third parties wishes to speak or where formal cross-examination is required.'

6.13 Paragraphs 2 and 3 to Annex 2 of the Circular provided:

'2. This code contains the procedure which the appellant and the local planning authority should follow when a hearing is to be held. The procedure is intended to save the parties time and money and to allow the Inspector to lead a discussion about the issues. The aim is to give everybody, including interested third parties, a fair hearing and to provide the Inspector with all the information necessary for his decision, but in a more relaxed and less formal atmosphere than at a local inquiry. Although the code does not have statutory force, all parties to a hearing are expected to comply with it.

3. A hearing is suitable where the development is small-scale; there is little or no third party interest; complex legal, technical or policy issues are unlikely to arise; and there is no likelihood that formal cross-examination will be needed to test the opposing cases.'

6.14 In the following five paragraphs, which merit citation in full, the Court set out the ingredients of a fair hearing, and explained that the objective of thoroughness is not capable of being dispensed with in pursuit of a relaxed hearing:

'It is clear that at a hearing there is to be no formal cross-examination and that a hearing is the suitable procedure where "there is no likelihood that formal cross-examination will be needed to test the opposing cases". The intention is to make the procedure "less daunting for unrepresented parties". It is intended to "eliminate or reduce the formalities of the traditional local inquiry".

Planning permission having been refused, conflicting propositions and evidence will often be placed before an Inspector on appeal. Whatever procedure is followed, the strength of a case can be determined only upon an understanding of that case and by testing it with reference to propositions in the opposing case. At a public local inquiry the Inspector, in performing that task, usually has the benefit of cross-examination on behalf of the other party. If cross-examination disappears, the need to examine propositions in that way does not disappear with it. Further, the statutory right to be heard is nullified unless, in some way, the strength of what one party says is not only listened to by the tribunal but is assessed for its own worth and in relation to opposing contentions.

There is a danger, upon the procedure now followed by the Secretary of State of observing the right to be heard by holding a "hearing", that the need for such consideration is forgotten. The danger is that the "more relaxed" atmosphere could lead not to a "full and fair" hearing but to a less than thorough examination of the issues. A relaxed hearing is not necessarily a fair hearing. The hearing must not become so relaxed that the rigorous examination essential to the determination of difficult questions may be diluted. The absence of an accusatorial procedure places an inquisitorial burden upon an Inspector.

I have come to the conclusion that the danger that the required fair hearing did not occur in this case is such that the decision must be quashed. In the final paragraph of his affidavit, the Inspector states that he "respectfully suggests that the applicant is confused as to the relevant procedure for a hearing of the sort I conducted with a public inquiry in which,

6.15 *Hearings*

> as he deposes, he had previously taken part". I am prepared to accept that the remark was directed only to the point the Inspector had considered in his previous paragraph, that is the expected length of the hearing, but if there is any suggestion that the requirements at a "hearing" are fundamentally different from those at a "public local inquiry" that suggestion is to be resisted. A fair and thorough investigation can in my judgment be expected by a party who has the right to be heard whichever procedure is followed.
>
> ...
>
> In reaching the conclusion I have, I am not encouraging long decision letters. Where a decision is challenged, however, the Court will need to enquire, by reference to the decision letter, whether there has been a sufficient consideration of the merits of the case put forward by a party and of any challenge to it. In leading the discussion at the hearing, the duties of the Inspector may be extensive especially when dealing with an unrepresented person who, relaxed as he is expected to be, may be diffident about repeating points which the Inspector says he has read in the documents or seeking to challenge or have challenged an assertion made by someone else around the table. The applicant said that, having been told by the Inspector that he had read the business plan, he did not take the Inspector through it."

6.15 From these five paragraphs may be extracted the following summary:

- whatever procedure is followed, a fair and thorough investigation can be expected by a party who has the right to be heard;
- the strength of a case can be determined only upon an understanding of that case and by testing it with reference to propositions in the opposing case;
- the strength of what a party has to say has to be listened to;
- a party's contentions have to be assessed for their own worth, in relation to opposing contentions;
- at a hearing propositions are to be examined as rigorously as if there was cross-examination;
- a relaxed hearing is not necessarily a fair hearing;
- failure to provide a fair and thorough investigation nullifies the statutory right to be heard; and
- the absence of inquiry procedure places an inquisitorial burden upon an Inspector.

6.16 The hearing procedure therefore places a considerably greater burden on the Inspector than the inquiry procedure. Preparation for a hearing effectively requires that the Inspector prepares each side of the case (and there may be more than two sides) as if the Inspector were presenting the case for that side of the case. That is what is meant by the inquisitorial burden being on the Inspector. It is this context which should inform the preparation which each contributor to a hearing undertakes and also inform the way in which that contribution is made at the hearing.

Late evidence

6.17 The scheme of the procedure rules is to exchange all of the evidence and representations by the five-week stage. By then, a statement of common ground should be agreed and the main parties have prepared and exchanged their respective full statements of case. For new evidence which is material to the case to emerge after this stage, or worse still, at the hearing, is potentially problematic.[13] The Planning Inspectorate takes a strong line, and uses the term 'exceptional circumstances' to describe the test which it applies to deciding whether such material should be accepted, and gives a costs warning. The Procedural Guide explains:[14]

> 'Appellants, local planning authorities and interested people should not try to "get around" the rules by taking late evidence to the hearing.
>
> If, exceptionally, a party feels that further evidence should be taken into account this may be taken to the hearing. Inspectors do have discretion whether to accept late evidence.
>
> Before deciding whether, exceptionally, to accept it, the Inspector will require:
>
> - an explanation as to why it was not received by us in accordance with the rules; and
> - an explanation of how and why the material is relevant; and
> - the opposing party's views on whether it should be accepted.
>
> The Inspector will refuse to accept late evidence unless fully satisfied that:
>
> - it is not covered in the evidence already received; and
> - it is directly relevant and necessary for his or her decision;
> - it would not have been possible for the party to have provided the evidence when they sent us their full statement of case; and
> - it would be procedurally fair to all parties (including interested people) if the late evidence were taken into account.
>
> If the Inspector accepts late evidence this may result in the need for an adjournment. The other party may make an application for costs or the Inspector may initiate an award of costs. This would be on the basis that the necessary adjournment had directly caused another party to incur expenses that would not otherwise have been necessary.'

6.18 The strong line can become unduly rigid and counter-productive. On occasion, even the submission of a very short document which is merely explanatory or which provides clarification is met with a strict rule against anything further being expressed on paper. This misses the point of hearings and inquiries. There is no point in holding a hearing or an inquiry if the evidence and the arguments do not develop. Hearings and inquiries are full of new evidence – it is oral evidence. If that process can be assisted by a document which aids explanation, or even corrects a mistake, then that is to be welcomed, not turned away. Rather, the objective of the Planning Inspectorate's approach, quite rightly, is to avoid the late introduction of material to bolster the case on any of the issues to be decided in the appeal. The difference between those documents which are helpful, clarify and are not prejudicial and those which are 'offside' is a difference which is usually obvious, but for which criteria are not easily set out.

---

[13] Indeed, the 2017 Regulations provide that 'In deciding an appeal the Welsh Ministers or the appointed person as the case may be, may disregard any representations, documents, evidence or information received after the relevant time limits.' See reg 12.

[14] See Appendix E9 to the Procedural Guide *Planning Appeals – England* July 2020 (https://assets. publishing.service.gov.uk/government/uploads/system/uploads/attachment_data/file/897145/ Procedural_Guide_Planning_appeals_version_10.pdf).

6.19 *Hearings*

FORMAT, ROLES AND BEING EFFECTIVE

6.19   In summary, at the opening of a hearing, the Inspector typically:

(1)   identifies herself or himself;

(2)   takes the names of all those who appear or who wish to be heard;[15]

(3)   checks that the parties have copies of each other's statements of case;

(4)   checks the drawings and application documents on which the decision was made, or would have been made in non-determination or call-in inquiries;

(5)   addresses time estimates and programme;

(6)   outlines the agenda;

(7)   explains the role and purpose of a conditions session;

(8)   asks whether there is to be any planning obligation submitted under s 106 of the Town and Country Planning Act 1990 (TCPA 1990); and

(9)   makes arrangements for a site view, and may explain that evidence may continue to be heard during the site visit.

6.20   The hearing will proceed through an agenda. For each main issue, an Inspector may seek to summarise each party's case and ask whether each case has been properly understood. This exercise requires that:

- a party's representative has undertaken this exercise for themselves, in advance, so that the way in which one would want the case to be fully and accurately summarised is crystal clear. If this is done 'on the hoof', listening to the summary from the Inspector and trying to think through whether it has been accurately captured, then there is a real risk that matters will be missed or the thrust of the case altered from that which the party might choose; and

- the Inspector is listened to very carefully.

6.21   Listening is a skill. To deploy it effectively in a hearing, it is necessary to pay close and focused attention to what is being said. Taking a written note is not only desirable in itself, it also assists with focused listening.

6.22   In circumstances where the parties are not present together in the same venue, listening and participation is still more of a skill. Being effective in telephone or video hearings is dealt with in Chapter 7.

6.23   If the Inspector's summary could be materially improved, then say so. A right to be heard is exactly that, and the opportunity to be heard on whether the summary is accurate will be offered only once.

6.24   There is an opportunity to make closing arguments. The appellant has the last word. This is an opportunity which is sometimes seen to be wasted. It is not an opportunity for repetition and certainly not an opportunity to introduce new material.

---

[15] An 'appearance' and being 'heard' are not the same thing – see further, for example, at rr 6 and 11 of the 2000 Rules. Some parties are entitled to appear; others are permitted to do so. A person may be heard though they do not appear as a party.

Rather, it is an opportunity to bring together the key points in an integrated way, after having dealt with each of the main issues separately in accordance with the Inspector's agenda. Issues often relate to or overlap with each other in ways which may not have been fully brought out during the course of the evidence. The opportunity to address the Inspector at end of hearing is the time when this can be done.

6.25 Sometimes, in the absence of social-distancing requirements, it is suggested that final arguments be heard on site. This is likely to be unsatisfactory because there will be a sense of needing to conclude quickly, the conditions are unlikely to be conducive to focused listening and note taking will be similarly impaired.

CONDITIONS AND SITE VISIT

6.26 Typically, planning conditions are considered at the end of the evidence.

6.27 A discussion of planning conditions and any planning obligation offered by way of a deed under TCPA 1990, s 106 will take place before adjourning for an accompanied site visit. It is convenient for any planning obligation to be provided to the Inspector and to the parties along with the proofs of evidence, which will usually be four weeks before the inquiry opens. However, the guidance in this regard is less demanding: not later than 10 days before the inquiry opens.[16]

6.28 The Inspector will be careful to explain that such discussion is undertaken in order that the necessary information may be gathered so that in the event the Inspector decides to allow the appeal, she or he is equipped to draft an appropriate set of conditions. The discussion is without prejudice to any party's position on the main issues.

6.29 Nevertheless, the 'conditions session' is a very important stage of the hearing for the same reasons as in respect of an inquiry (see paras 5.83–5.89 above).

6.30 The Inspector may adjourn the hearing to the appeal site, and continue there, but such an approach must not place any party at a disadvantage.[17] The Inspector must inspect the appeal site if the appellant or the LPA request it.[18] As for attendance at a site view, if the appellant or the LPA indicate that they wish to be present at the site view, then the Inspector shall announce the date and time at which the site view is to be undertaken and it shall be in the company of both the appellant and the LPA and any other person entitled or permitted to appear at the hearing.[19]

6.31 There are no regulations which specifically address site visits in Wales. The regulations are silent on the topic. The practice will not be materially different to that which has been long standing in England and in Wales.

6.32 In practical terms: think about agreeing an itinerary, on a plan; decide who is going so that the Inspector may be informed; arrange access; have the necessary clothing and any necessary personal protective equipment available.

---

[16] See the Procedural Guide at, for example, section 2.6, p 7.
[17] Rule 12(1) of the 2000 Rules.
[18] Rule 12(2) of the 2000 Rules.
[19] Rule 12(4) of the 2000 Rules.

Chapter 7

Remote events and electronic documents

THE ISSUES

7.01 Recording and broadcasting of proceedings has taken place in respect of longer, larger inquiries and at the examination in public of development plan documents. This has enabled participation by observation. However, it had never resulted in a person who is entitled or permitted to be heard doing so without being in the same room as the Inspector, the parties and those members of the public or press who wish to attend and observe.

7.02 In March 2020 the Planning Inspectorate postponed inquiries and hearings because it became incompatible with guidance on social distancing to avoid the transmission of Covid-19. The result is the Written Ministerial Statement (WMS)[1] of Robert Jenrick (Secretary of State for the Ministry of Housing, Communities and Local Government), made on 13 May 2020. The WMS addresses four topics:

- virtual events;
- digital documentation;
- site visits; and
- publicity and community engagement.

7.03 The policy is straightforward: moving to digital events and processes is critical to driving the planning process forward and will support economic recovery, so opportunities for virtual hearings and processes are to be maximised. The key material paragraphs are:

'**Virtual working and planning – Responding to Covid-19 Restrictions**

Introduction

The planning system has a vital role to play in enabling the delivery of housing and economic growth that will support the UK's economic recovery. It is important that the system continues to operate effectively, ensuring that all those involved, including local authorities, the Planning Inspectorate, developers, statutory consultees, local communities and others can engage in the process while adhering to the Government's guidance on social distancing.

This Statement sets out the Government's expectations for how the planning system should be operating during the COVID-19 emergency. It applies to applications and appeals under the Town and Country Planning Act; Development Consent Orders under

---

[1] https://www.parliament.uk/business/publications/written-questions-answers-statements/written-statement/Commons/2020-05-13/HCWS235/.

the Planning Act 2008; the Compulsory Purchase Order regime and to development plans, including neighbourhood plans and spatial development strategies.

The role of digital

Local planning authorities and the Planning Inspectorate drive the planning process forward and should ensure that it continues to operate effectively to support economic recovery. Moving to digital events and processes will be critical. This means adapting to working virtually, including virtual hearings and events (such as using video-conferencing and/or telephone) and making documents available for inspection online. The Government expects everyone involved in the planning process to engage proactively.

The Government considers that the current legislative framework allows for virtual hearings. It is confident that processes can be put in place in the vast majority of cases to allow for the participation of all parties. The Government recognises that the method by which hearings and events are conducted is a matter for the Inspectorate, operating in accordance with their legal obligations, and it expects these arrangements to be made as the default method of operation in the vast majority of cases. The Government recognises that in exceptional circumstances it may not be fair to proceed virtually and that alternative arrangements may be needed. These alternative arrangements should be taken forward speedily, where possible, taking into account the Government's guidance on social distancing.

The Government expects opportunities for virtual hearings and processes to be maximised. It will draw from current and emerging practice to inform policy and process in the longer term.

Virtual events

The Government fully supports the Planning Inspectorate's programme for moving to digital inquiries, hearings, meetings and other events. Digital events present opportunities to increase participation in planning processes which are important for local communities and will minimise the impacts of delays to planning decisions which might otherwise occur due to the requirements for social distancing.

...

Digital documentation

...

As restrictions are eased, planning authorities and others should integrate the range of methods that are available to them into their approaches to ensure all sections of the community are reached as thoroughly as is practically possible.

Site Visits

Site visits, whether conducted by local authorities, planning inspectors or statutory consultees, are an important part of the process of considering development proposals and plans. Where site visits are required or necessary, they should be undertaken in line with the Government's guidance on social distancing and safety requirements.

...

Publicity and community engagement

...

Local planning authorities (and applicants of EIA development under the TCPA) now have the flexibility to take other reasonable steps to publicise applications if they cannot discharge the specific requirements for site notices, neighbour notifications or newspaper publicity. These steps will notify people who are likely to have an interest in the application and indicate where further information about it can be viewed online. These steps can include the use of social media and other electronic communications and must be proportionate to the scale and nature of the proposed development.

7.04 *Remote events and electronic documents*

...

Guidance and Advice

The Planning Inspectorate has published and regularly updates guidance on its work during the COVID-19 social distancing measures, which can be viewed here (https://www.gov.uk/guidance/coronavirus-covid-19-planning-inspectorate-guidance).'

7.04 The issues in the WMS derive from the Covid-19 emergency and have a clear policy objective to drive the planning system forward. However, the ambition is not new. The Rosewell Review argued strongly for reform in this regard, leading to its Recommendation 14, in this way:

'In common with all other stages of the inquiry appeal process, there is very limited and often ineffective use of technology in most inquiries. We understand that at present accessible wifi is not always available and the use of visual technology for the projection of plans, maps and other visual material is also often limited and ineffective.

Using technology offers cost savings and increased transparency, and every effort should be made to maximise its use.

...

In our view, and as a minimum requirement, a good internet connection should be available for everyone at every inquiry venue. It would also be in the interests of all parties to have one central web-based library of all documents, with a consistent referencing system, to deliver benefits for all parties involved in the process by reducing or eliminating the need for paper documents and allowing faster identification of the evidence being considered. This would also improve the transparency of the process and the evidence for the public and other interested parties, who do not always have ready access to this information at present.

However, many respondents pointed to the opportunity to go much further in terms of the use of technology, for example:

- using transcription technology to generate records of oral evidence – this could offer particular benefits for inspectors who are writing a report to the Secretary of State on a recovered appeal or called-in application
- making webcasts of the inquiry available (ideally live webcasts)
- allowing witnesses to appear via video link
- providing pre-loaded devices for those attending the inquiry to view the evidence being discussed

A number of these advances are already being used, or are under active consideration, by other organisations who conduct similar events.

...

Recommendation 14

The Planning Inspectorate should ensure that its programme for improving operational delivery through greater use of technology fully exploits the opportunities available to enhance the efficiency and transparency of the inquiry event, such as the use of transcription technology for inspectors and publishing webcasts of proceedings.'

7.05 In summary, therefore, the issues and objectives are now:

(1) Documents:
- increasing transparency (not reducing it);
- saving resources by allowing documents to be used more efficiently;

Digital documents **7.09**

- co-operation between parties in producing electronic materials.

(2) Virtual observation:
- making it possible to see and hear what the Inspector, representatives, witnesses and public are doing and saying;
- achieving this without convening at a venue, or using an arrangement which ensures that those attending the venue do so safely;
- taking account of varying access to technology and reliable connections.

(3) Virtual appearances and being heard virtually:
- making it possible to see, hear *and to address* the Inspector, representatives, witnesses and public;
- achieving this without convening at a venue or using an arrangement which ensures that those attending the venue do so safely;
- taking account of varying access to technology and reliable connections.

(4) Site visits:
- undertaking an unaccompanied site visit if the Inspector or the main parties consider it necessary to do so;
- undertaking a site visit as a part of a hearing, if the Inspector or the main parties consider it necessary to do so;
- undertaking an accompanied site visit during an inquiry or after it has closed.

DIGITAL DOCUMENTS

7.06 The first observation to make is that nobody has suggested, still less required, that all documents should be produced only in digital form. Paper is a technology which has very many advantages, the continued role for which is not in doubt. Rather, the issue is how and to what extent may the appeal process be enhanced and made more effective by use of digital documents, for all participants.

7.07 Planning appeals, like many other forms of dispute resolution and decision-making, have changed gradually and followed changes in technology. This has been so throughout the history of planning appeals. For example, when it became possible to copy documents quickly, many more documents were supplied to many more parties. That, in turn, brought its own changes and challenges. In the same way, the ability to transmit large documents electronically to the Planning Inspectorate is now a well-established part of the fabric of planning appeals and the use of 'the portal' to make appeals is unremarkable.

7.08 However, there has been only recent and modest change to use of electronic documents at hearings and inquiries. Inspectors may quite frequently attend an inquiry with core documents in only electronic form, but parties and witnesses more frequently rely on hard copies.

7.09 The scale of the disputed issues, the technical evidence and the number of active participants varies very greatly, and with that variation there is a similar

7.10 *Remote events and electronic documents*

need to deal proportionately with digital documents. Similarly, the resources of the parties vary from case to case. The production of digital documents to a very high specification may become a barrier to access to the appeals system.

7.10 Conversely, a digital library may become the 'go to' source of documents and a key tool for all. By the close of the Mid-Wales Windfarm Inquiry in May 2014,[2] the Inspector spoke for all participants in stating that the inquiry website had become the document library for all. In that instance, it was not feasible to move a single party's inquiry documents in one vehicle. Electronic working was therefore essential. That is an extreme example in terms of size of schemes, number of schemes, number of parties and length of inquiry. However, it is a clear illustration that an appropriately resourced major inquiry could work effectively in 2014.

7.11 At the other end of the scale, a 'one-day' hearing will not have a bespoke website, nor will almost all inquiries. The approach is, therefore, to be proportionate. To fail to do so is contrary to the objective of making the appeal process both more transparent and efficient. For the straightforward case, it may well be sufficient to rely upon a modest collection of key documents comprising individual pdfs of the application documents, the hearing statements, extracts from the development plan and a collated folder of consultation responses.

7.12 The Planning and Environmental Bar Association has drawn on the courts' approaches to digital documents. It has proposed arrangements which would suit a typical one-week inquiry, along these lines.

7.13 A digital bundle should be:

- complete;
- paginated continuously;
- navigable through bookmarking;
- searchable through optical character recognition (OCR);
- capable of electronic mark-up/notation; and
- accessible by Inspectors, inquiry participants and members of the public.

7.14 So, the digital bundle should:

- be in PDF format;
- not be password protected or otherwise 'locked for editing';
- a single unified file;
- be numerically paginated, including index pages and any intervening blank pages as part of the single PDF document (and not skipped);
- pagination must be electronic (not hand-written);

---

[2] Report to the Secretary of State for Energy and Climate Change by AD Poulter BArch RIBA, 8 December 2014 (https://www.gov.uk/government/news/planning-decisions-for-six-powys-mid-wales-infrastructure-projects and https://itportal.beis.gov.uk/EIP/pages/projects/InspectorsReportEnglish.pdf).

- each internal document must be bookmarked, with a label in the form: reference number; document's title (abbreviated where necessary); and date of publication (in the form dd.mm.yyyy). Each part should be separated by a hyphen. For example: '1.1 – Application Form – 01.04.2020';
- each PDF file must be searchable (and all scanned documents must have been processed by OCR software or similar to allow this);
- the index page must be hyperlinked to the pages or documents referred to;
- the default page view size of all pages must be 100%;
- the resolution on the electronic bundle must be reduced to between 200 and 300 dpi to prevent delays whilst scrolling from one page to another (and the PDF should have been 'flattened'); and
- text on all pages must be selectable to enable comments and highlights to be imposed upon the text.

7.15 As to contents, the Statement of Common Ground Pro Forma, para 14 recommends:

> 'The Core Documents should comprise only those documents to which you will be referring. Where any documents on which it is intended to rely are lengthy, only relevant extracts need to be supplied, prefaced with the front cover of the relevant document and should include any accompanying relevant contextual text.'

If this important advice is followed, then file sizes can be reduced and page numbers reduced where possible.

7.16 The digital bundle should also aim to distinguish those documents which are essential to consideration of the main issues (as identified by the Inspector) from those which are merely relevant background documents (eg application technical reports). One approach to arrangement of documents is:

Inspectorate Correspondence
- Inspector's CMC Letter identifying Main Issues etc
- Subsequent Inspector Directions

Appeal Documents
- Appeal Form
- LPA Questionnaire
- Appellant's Statement of Case
- LPA's Statement of Case
- Rule 6 Party's Statement of Case (where applicable)

Proofs of Evidence
- Appellant's Planning Proof of Evidence and Appendices
- Appellant's Other Proofs of Evidence and Appendices

7.16 *Remote events and electronic documents*

- LPA Planning Proof of Evidence and Appendices
- LPA's Other Proofs of Evidence and Appendices
- Rule 6 Party's Proofs of Evidence and Appendices (where applicable)

Statements of Common Ground

- Main/Planning Statements of Common Ground
- Other Statements of Common Ground

CD1 Application Documents

- Application Forms and Covering Letters
- Planning Statement
- Design and Access Statement (where applicable)
- Submitted Plans
- Technical Reports Relevant to Main Issues
- Other Application Documents submitted prior to validation

CD2: Additional/Amended Reports and/or Plans submitted after validation

- Additional Plans submitted, including relevant correspondence
- Additional Technical Reports Relevant to Main Issues
- Other Correspondence submitted after validation

CD3: Committee Report and Decision Notice

- Committee Report and Minute of Committee Meeting
- Decision Notice
- Consultation Responses Relevant to Main Issues
- Other Consultation Responses

CD4: Development Plan

- Development Plan Documents and Spatial Development Strategies
- Inspectors' Reports following Examination of above
- Neighbourhood Development Plans
- Examiner's Reports and LPA Decision Notices following Examination of above
- Consultation/Submission Documents and Evidence Base Documents (e.g. SHMAs)

CD5: Emerging Plan

- Most Recent Draft Version of DPD/SPS
- Correspondence/Evidence Base Documents relevant to Main Issues
- Most Recent Draft Version of NDP
- Correspondence/Evidence Base Documents relevant to Main Issues

CD6: Relevant Appeal Decisions
- Full Appeals Index and Table of Relevant Paragraphs Justifying Inclusion
- Appeal Decisions

CD7: Relevant High Court and Appellate Court Judgments
- Full Judgments Index and Table of Relevant Paragraphs Justifying Inclusion
  ○ Judgments

CD8: Appellant Additional Documents
- Documents submitted by the Appellant, not included above but relevant to Main Issues (e.g. Government Statements, Specialist Reports)
- Relevant Application/Appeal Correspondence

CD9: Local Planning Authority Documents
- Documents submitted by LPA, not included above but relevant to Main Issues (e.g. Government Statements, Specialist Reports)
- Relevant Application/Appeal Correspondence

CD10: Other Documents
[As required]

VIRTUAL EVENTS

7.17 As has been highlighted, there are two principal tasks: (1) to enable observation; and (2) to enable oral contribution. The focus here is on effective oral contribution to a virtual event because that is the area in which the main difficulties lie. In the author's view, those difficulties are not capable of being fully overcome in the context of important decision-making which truly requires the full range and scope of communication and interaction which only direct and face-to-face communication can provide. Virtual events 'make do' when there is no choice.

7.18 In principle, virtual events are no different. They provide an opportunity to be heard, to persuade, to clarify, to challenge and reach accommodation and resolutions. The structure of any event remains the same. The roles remain the same. It is the way in which those roles are performed which is modified.

7.19 During the initial period of Covid-19 restrictions from March to June 2020, the courts considered and used a variety of software platforms to conduct their business. The Crown Courts and the magistrates' courts have expanded the use of a bespoke video platform (Cloud Video Platform). Microsoft Teams began to be preferred as a means of video conferencing. From this general background of change in courts and tribunals, practitioners have prepared a variety of helpful guides from which the following points have been collated:

7.20 *Remote events and electronic documents*

- Use a device which is on a steady surface.
- Google Chrome has been recommended as the better browser to use.
- Join early, not just in time.
- Neutral backgrounds or backgrounds which are not distracting are preferable.
- Work from a location which is quiet and has a reliable, strong connection.
- It assists to have a second device on which to work with documents.
- Ensure that the microphone is suitable for use, ie test it on a call to be sure that other parties may hear you well.
- Use 'mute' when not contributing.
- Use 'mute' if you are typing near the microphone, failing which other users will be 'rattled'.
- Sharing screens carries real danger of inadvertent disclosure of information.
- Business attire is appropriate.
- Do not eat.
- Do not smoke.
- Only drink water.
- Do not use a phone.
- If you are an active participant, only move away from the screen after agreeing this with the Inspector.

7.20 Beyond the practicalities, the key objective is to do and seek to achieve everything which you would do and seek to achieve if the event were not a virtual event. The parties' cases remain as important as ever and there is no suggestion that the quality of the process is to be diminished by reason of the change in mode. It follows, therefore, that additional care and preparation are necessary in order to make the contributions as effective, but as succinct as possible.

7.21 An event may very usefully be a hybrid – a combination of attending at a venue and attending by video or audio. Good case management conferences should identify how the particular features of the case are best addressed. Experience of hybrid court hearings shows that:

- to have certain participants present before the Inspector can improve the quality of the event, but it is unnecessary for others to attend in person;
- choices may be made about the relative benefits of having particular witness present in person; and
- good quality, common, electronic documents are essential.

7.22 Likewise, it is open to each party to decide how best to arrange its appearance at an event. Depending upon the scale of the event and the issues, it may assist to gather some or all of a party's representatives and witnesses and clients in an appropriate venue, rather than for each of them to work remotely. Thus, the event may as a matter of fact be a virtual event but some of the benefits of interactions between members of an inquiry or examination team are retained by those people working together in an appropriate building. This has been shown to be effective in, for example, appearances at the entirely virtual examination of the South Oxfordshire Local Plan, which was the first of its kind.

SITE VISITS

7.23 On the assumption that a site may be reached by car, and the visit is conducted outdoors, then safe protocols are capable of being adopted for accompanied site visits.

7.24 A potential difficulty arises if a site visit cannot be safely undertaken, but a main party requests that the Inspector undertakes a site visit. The rules require that a site visit is undertaken if a main party requests it and moreover, it is likely to provide material information without which it is difficult to reach a robust decision.

Chapter 8

Costs

LEGAL BASIS

8.01 Section 250(5) of the Local Government Act 1972 gives power to the Secretary of State to make an order as to the costs of the parties at public inquiries, generally. It is a power which applies to public inquiries which are concerned with planning matters, and also to inquiries which are not concerned with planning. In respect of planning appeals, the section is applied within the Planning Acts and is specifically amended to suit the objectives of the planning system.[1]

8.02 So, in respect of appeals which derive from the Town and Country Planning Act 1990 (TCPA 1990), s 250 of the 1972 Act is applied by TCPA 1990, Sch 6 with the adaptation that the costs of holding the inquiry shall be defrayed by the Secretary of State. As modified by Sch 6 of TCPA 1990, the relevant power is:

> 'The [Secretary of State] causing an inquiry to be held under this section may make orders as to the costs of the parties at the inquiry and as to the parties by whom the costs are to be paid, and every such order may be made a rule of the High Court on the application of any party named in the order.'

8.03 The primary legislation is silent about the exercise of the discretion to make costs orders. The section does not require that costs applications should be decided on the basis that costs normally follow the event, nor does the section preclude such an approach.

8.04 A similar observation was made in *R v Secretary of State for the Environment, Ex p Westminster City Council*:[2]

> 'The power to award costs in these inquiries is in very wide terms. The relevant subsection, subsection (5) of section 250 of the Local Government Act 1972, provides that:
>
>> "the Minister causing an inquiry to be held under this section may make orders as to the costs of the parties at the inquiry and as to the parties by whom the costs are to be paid, and every such order may be made a rule of the High Court"
>
> So, there is little restriction on the power that the Secretary of State has under the subsection but, he has issued circulars which, from time to time, have set out the basis upon which he makes such awards. The relevant one, although it was not actually in force at the time of these proceedings, is Circular 2 of 1987, which sets out in similar

---

[1] TCPA 1990, Sch 6, para 4 specifically applies s 250(2)–(5) of the 1972 Act.
[2] [1989] 1 PLR 23 at 27, per Farquharson J.

Aims, objectives and purpose **8.07**

terms the earlier provisions. That states [para 5]: 'In planning proceedings the parties are normally expected to meet their own expenses and costs are awarded only on grounds of unreasonable behaviour'. There is some further reference to earlier circulars, but nothing more turns on that. That is the basis upon which the Secretary of State makes his award, and it is really that term which we have had to review in this case. Has it been established that there are grounds upon which the Secretary of State could have so concluded, namely, that the Westminster City Council, in relation to this matter, have been guilty of unreasonable behaviour and therefore properly subject to an order for costs?'

8.05 There is a right to challenge a costs decision. There is a small number of such cases each year in which the Planning Court considers the lawfulness of a costs decision. They succeed if it can be shown that the decision is mistaken in fact, materially misunderstood the costs guidance or failed to give adequate reasons. However, challenges to the rationality of costs decisions face a very high hurdle and such grounds of challenge are seen to enjoy very low prospects. This is unsurprising because, at its root, the statutory power and the discretion provided to the decision-maker are so broad.

8.06 The long-standing policy has been to operate the costs regime such that the parties bear their own costs. A costs award is only made if there has been unreasonable behaviour which has caused expense. The costs regime is therefore one of policy and guidance, not statute. The dominant characteristic of both policy and guidance (so far as they are different) is their flexibility. The result is a restricted and narrow basis for costs awards. This has a number of benefits in furthering the objectives of the planning system, namely:

- parties and interested persons may participate in appeals with no costs risk, provided that they act reasonably;
- satellite disputes about costs are suppressed and discouraged by reason of the restricted and narrow regime, thus focusing attention on the planning merits – it helps to avoid cases becoming about costs, not merits;
- there is a control and a sanction available to suppress unreasonable behaviour;
- an award of costs is itself a criticism because it is based on a finding of unreasonableness, which parties are likely to seek to avoid; and
- the regime provides a mechanism of putting a party back in the financial position which they would have been in, but for the unreasonable behaviour of another party.

AIMS, OBJECTIVES AND PURPOSE

8.07 The costs regime has been in place and been practiced for nearly 50 years. It is a part of the planning system which has seen little change in its overall aims, objectives and purpose. However, the pruning of guidance which took place in both England and Wales post 2012 has removed much of the material which explains what the costs regime is intended to achieve. For example, in Wales, the aims of the costs regime are expressed as:[3]

---

[3] Development Management Manual Section 12 Annex: Award of costs.

8.08 *Costs*

- to encourage all those involved to behave in a reasonable manner, instil a greater sense of discipline and follow good practice in terms of timeliness and in the presentation of full and detailed evidence to support their case;
- to encourage local planning authorities (LPA) to exercise properly their development management responsibilities, to rely only on reasons for refusal that stand up to scrutiny on the planning merits of the case and not to add to development costs through avoidable delay; and
- not to deter people from exercising their statutory right of appeal.

8.08 In England, the aims are explained thus:[4]

'Parties in planning appeals and other planning proceedings normally meet their own expenses. All parties are expected to behave reasonably to support an efficient and timely process, for example in providing all the required evidence and ensuring that timetables are met. Where a party has behaved unreasonably, and this has directly caused another party to incur unnecessary or wasted expense in the appeal process, they may be subject to an award of costs.

The aim of the costs regime is to:

- encourage all those involved in the appeal process to behave in a reasonable way and follow good practice, both in terms of timeliness and in the presentation of full and detailed evidence to support their case
- encourage LPAs to properly exercise their development management responsibilities, to rely only on reasons for refusal which stand up to scrutiny on the planning merits of the case, not to add to development costs through avoidable delay,
- discourage unnecessary appeals by encouraging all parties to consider a revised planning application which meets reasonable local objections.'

8.09 The aims in England and Wales are the same, save in respect of the third bullet point where there is a significant difference. In Wales, the long-standing position is stated that mere appeal should not be discouraged by the threat of an adverse costs award. In England, the opposite position is articulated. It is positively stated that the costs regime is in place to discourage appeals which are unnecessary. It is an aim of the costs regime to send applicants back to the planning authority with a revised planning application. There are two aspects to this aim: (1) negotiation and dialogue should be exhausted before appeal; and (2) the costs regime is aimed at resolution of reasonable local objection. The problem with (2) is the absence of reference to the planning balance because all development is almost always capable of reasonable objection but the decision is a function of a proper understanding of all of the material facts and policies and applying one to the other. The third bullet point sits uneasily with the second.

8.10 The purpose of the costs regime was better articulated in the cancelled Circulars, for example[5] (emphasis added):

---

[4] See National Planning Practice Guidance (NPPG), para 028.
[5] Annex 1, para 5 to DoE Circular 8/93 and Welsh Officer Circular 23/93 (Not in force) *Award of Costs Incurred in Planning and Other (Including Compulsory Purchase Order) Proceeding.* The former Welsh Office Circular 23/93 remained in force until 2017. It was in the same terms as the former Department of Environment Circular 8/93, revoked by Circular 03/2009, which was itself withdrawn on 7 March 2014 and replaced by the NPPG.

'This discipline is not intended to deter people from exercising their statutory right of appeal, but rather to ensure that other parties, notably the planning authority (and, indirectly, the local taxpayer) are *not put to unnecessary expense as a result of unreasonable use of the right of appeal*. Where complex or technical issues of legal precedent or procedure arise, the Secretary of State, in deciding whether behaviour is unreasonable, will take into account the extent to which an appellant obtained professional advice. Where the planning authority drew the appellant's attention to relevant facts (see paragraph 6 of Annex 3), the Secretary of State will also take that into account. The guidance is intended both to support planning authorities in the proper exercise of their statutory responsibilities and to reflect the principle that *the planning system should not prevent, inhibit or delay development which could reasonably be permitted*, in the light of the development plan, so far as it is material to the application, and of any other material considerations.'

This reflects the principle that the planning system should not prevent, inhibit or delay development which could reasonably be permitted. It is a concept which is carried forward and indeed strengthened in current national policy: see paras 11c and 11d of the National Planning Policy Framework.[6]

SCOPE AND NATURE OF THE COSTS JURISDICTION

Two different regimes – planning appeals and CPO etc

8.11 The power in s 250(5) of the Local Government Act 1972 is deployed in different ways depending on the context of the determination which the minister has to make. The general rule in planning appeals is that the parties will meet their own costs of the appeal. In contested objections to orders affecting interests in land, such as compulsory acquisition, the general rule is that a successful objector is awarded costs, to be paid by the promoter.

8.12 In respect of planning appeals, the costs jurisdiction is different to that in civil litigation. In civil proceedings the starting point is that the unsuccessful party pays the reasonable costs of the successful party. In contrast, an award of costs in a planning appeal is firstly concerned with whether a party has incurred costs as a result of unreasonable behaviour. The unreasonable behaviour may be in respect of either, or both of, the substance of the appeal or conduct of the party during the course of the appeal, which is referred to as a procedural award. It is therefore possible that the fact that a party has been unsuccessful is indirectly relevant to the award of costs in that it may be shown that a party's case is unreasonable. However, the mere fact that a party lost on a particular point or issue is not the test.

8.13 The former Circular guidance captured the nature of the costs jurisdiction in this way:[7]

'The principle that the parties normally meet their own expenses means that, in proceedings to which this guidance (except Annex 6) applies, awards of costs do not necessarily "follow the event". A decision on a costs application, when made, does not follow directly from the result of the appeal itself. An appellant is not awarded costs

---

[6] https://gov.uk/guidance/national-planning-policy-framework.
[7] Annex 1, para 2 to DoE Circular 8/93 and Welsh Officer Circular 23/93 (Not in force) *Award of Costs Incurred in Planning and Other (Including Compulsory Purchase Order) Proceeding*.

8.14 *Costs*

simply because the appeal succeeds. Nor are the planning authority awarded their costs simply because the appeal fails. An award against a successful party may very occasionally be justified. (For example, a partial award may be made against a successful appellant for behaviour resulting in procedural delay.)'

8.14 So far as planning appeals are concerned, the costs regime applies to:

- planning appeals under TCPA 1990, s 78;
- planning applications referred to the Secretary of State under TCPA 1990, s 77;
- enforcement notice appeals under TCPA 1990, s 174;
- listed building consent appeals under Planning (Listed Buildings and Conservation Areas) Act 1990 (the Listed Buildings Act), s 20;
- listed building consent applications referred to the Secretary of State under Listed Buildings Act, s 12;
- listed building enforcement notice appeals under Listed Buildings Act, s 39;
- conservation area consent applications referred to the Secretary of State under Listed Buildings Act, s 74(2)(a);
- conservation area consent appeals under Listed Buildings Act, s 74(3);
- conservation area enforcement appeals under Listed Buildings Act, s 74(3);
- advertisement appeals, including 'discontinuance notice' appeals, under TCPA 1990, s 220;
- orders under TCPA 1990, s 220 and the Town and Country Planning (Control of Advertisements) Regulations 2007[8] designating, revoking or modifying Areas of Special Advertisement Control;
- appeals under TCPA 1990, s 195;
- completion notices requiring confirmation by the Secretary of State under TCPA 1990, s 95;
- purchase notice references to the Secretary of State under TCPA 1990, ss 139 and 140;
- listed building purchase notice references to the Secretary of State under Listed Buildings Act, ss 33 and 34;
- tree preservation order purchase notice references to the Secretary of State under TCPA 1990, s 198(4)(b);
- tree replacement enforcement notice appeals under TCPA 1990, s 208;
- appeals under Planning and Compensation Act 1991, s 22 and Sch 2, against refusal of an application for registration of an old mining permission; or against determination of an area of land or conditions different from those set out in the application; or against determination of conditions to be attached to a registered old mining permission;
- hazardous substances applications referred to the Secretary of State under Planning (Hazardous Substances) Act 1990 (the Hazardous Substances Act), s 20 and Regulations;

---

[8] SI 2007/783.

Scope and nature of the costs jurisdiction **8.17**

- hazardous substances consent appeals under Hazardous Substances Act, s 21 and Regulations;
- appeals under Hazardous Substances Act, s 25 and Regulations against hazardous substances contravention notices;
- opposed highways or public rights of way orders under TCPA 1990, Part X;
- orders under TCPA 1990, ss 97 and 98 and Sch 5 revoking or modifying a planning permission;
- orders under Listed Buildings Act, ss 23 and 24, revoking or modifying listed building consent;
- orders under TCPA 1990, s 220 and Town and Country Planning (Control of Advertisements) Regulations 2007 revoking or modifying a grant of advertisement consent;
- discontinuance orders under TCPA 1990, ss 102 and 103 and Sch 9;
- prohibition orders and orders (after suspension of winning and working of minerals) for protection of the environment, under TCPA 1990, Sch 9;
- orders under Hazardous Substances Act, ss 14 and 15 and Regulations, revoking or modifying hazardous substances consent.

Compulsory purchase and other objections based on property rights

8.15 The second regime is in respect of those proceedings in which an objector is protecting a right or an interest, particularly an interest in land. There is a distinction between cases where appellants take the initiative, such as in applying for planning permission or undertaking development allegedly without planning permission, and cases where objectors are defending their rights, or protecting their interests, which are the subject of a compulsory purchase order (CPO). If a statutory objector to such an order is successful, an award of costs will be made in her or his favour unless there are exceptional reasons for not doing so.

8.16 This is a further illustration of the flexibility of the power in s 250(5) of the Local Government Act 1972. In compulsory purchase proceedings, if the objector is successful, the promoter will pay the objector's costs, save in exceptional circumstances. It is not a jurisdiction based on unreasonable behaviour. In other words, because the fundamental policy considerations are quite different as between planning appeals generally and the right of a person to defend interests in land, the costs regimes which are adopted and implemented by the government are wholly different in character: same power, different policy.

8.17 The National Planning Practice Guidance (NPPG) provides that costs will be awarded in favour of a successful remaining objector unless there are exceptional reasons for not making an award: [9]

> 'Compulsory purchase and analogous orders seek to take away a party's rights or interest in land. Further information on compulsory purchase orders can be found in the Guidance on compulsory purchase process and the Crichel Down Rules for the disposal of surplus

---

[9] See NPPG, para 057.

8.18 *Costs*

land acquired by, or under the threat of, compulsion. Where objectors are defending their rights, or protecting their interests, which are the subject of a compulsory purchase or analogous order, they may have costs awarded in their favour if the order does not proceed or is not confirmed.

For the purposes of this Part, "remaining objector" means a person who is defending their rights, or protecting their interests, which are the subject of a compulsory purchase or analogous order, and who has made a "remaining objection" within the meaning of section 13A(1) of the Acquisition of Land Act 1981.

Costs will be awarded in favour of a successful remaining objector unless there are exceptional reasons for not making an award. The award will be made by the Secretary of State against the authority which made the order.

Normally, the following conditions must be met for an award to be made on the basis of a successful objection:

(a) the claimant must have made a remaining objection and have either:

- attended (or been represented at) an inquiry (or, if applicable, a hearing at which the objection was heard); or
- submitted a written representation which was considered as part of the written procedure; and

(b) the objection must have been sustained by the confirming authority's refusal to confirm the order or by its decision to exclude the whole or part of the claimant's property from the order.

In addition, a remaining objection will be successful and an award of costs may be made in the claimant's favour if an inquiry is cancelled because the acquiring authority have decided not to proceed with the order, or a claimant has not appeared at an inquiry having made an arrangement for their land to be excluded from the order.'

The last paragraph is a useful and just correction to the position which prevailed before amendment to the guidance which meant that if an inquiry was cancelled, the work done by an objector in preparing for the inquiry was not recoverable, even though the objector's arguments were successful.[10]

8.18 The regime applies to analogous orders under the Planning Acts which affect rights in land, including:[11]

- orders under TCPA 1990, ss 97 and 98, revoking or modifying a planning permission;
- orders under Listed Buildings Act, ss 23 and 24, revoking or modifying listed building consent;
- orders under TCPA 1990, s 220 and Town and Country Planning (Control of Advertisements) Regulations 2007, revoking or modifying a grant of advertisement consent;
- orders under TCPA 1990, ss 102 and 103 and Sch 9:

---

[10] *R (on the application of Bedford Land Investments Ltd) v Secretary of State for Transport and Bedford Borough Council* [2015] EWHC 3159 (Admin).
[11] See NPPG, para 064.

(a) requiring discontinuance of a use of land (including the winning and working of minerals), or imposing conditions on the continuance of a use of land; or

(b) requiring the removal or alteration of buildings or works; or

(c) requiring the removal or alteration of plant or machinery used for winning or working of minerals; or

(d) prohibiting the resumption of winning or working of minerals; or

(e) requiring steps to be taken for the protection of the environment, after suspension of winning and working of minerals;

- orders under Hazardous Substances Act, ss 14 and 15, revoking or modifying a hazardous substances consent, or refusal of an application under s 17(1) of the Act for continuation of a consent, on change of control of land;
- a petition under Local Government Act 1972, s 125, as substituted by Housing and Planning Act 1986, s 43, relating to compulsory acquisition of land on behalf of parish or community Councils.

8.19 There is, in addition, a range of orders under legislation other than the Planning Acts to which the same regime applies, including:

- orders under Highways Act 1980, s 26 creating a footpath or bridleway over land;
- orders under Highways Act 1980, ss 118–119A (as amended by the Transport and Works Act 1992);
- orders under National Parks and Access to the Countryside Act 1949, s 65 regarding access to land;
- orders under Wildlife and Countryside Act 1981, s 29 relating to special protection of certain areas of special scientific interest.

Unreasonable behaviour

8.20 The NPPG provides:[12]

> 'The word "unreasonable" is used in its ordinary meaning, as established by the courts in *Manchester City Council v SSE & Mercury Communications Limited* [1988] JPL 774.
>
> Unreasonable behaviour in the context of an application for an award of costs may be either:
>
> - procedural – relating to the process; or
> - substantive – relating to the issues arising from the merits of the appeal.
>
> The Inspector has discretion when deciding an award, enabling extenuating circumstances to be taken into account.'

8.21 In *Manchester City Council*, the court explained the meaning of 'unreasonable'. Oddly, the NPPG says nothing about the content of that case. What is clear from *Manchester City Council*, is that it is necessary to have regard to the picture as a whole, as the court explained (emphasis added):

---

[12] See NPPG, para 031.

8.22 *Costs*

'Ground 2(d) was merely a repetition of the allegation that in making his decision as to the question of costs the Secretary of State should have looked only at the evidence called by the city council to support its decision, and not at the picture as a whole. *As indicated, it seemed that **in order to decide whether a party had acted unreasonably**, and whether the evidence on which it had relied should be regarded as substantial **it would nearly always be necessary to have regard to the picture as a whole**.'*

PROCEDURE

8.22 There is a power to award costs regardless of the mode of appeal. Formerly, there was no costs jurisdiction in written representations appeals, but the position since 2009 has been that costs may be awarded in inquiry, hearing and written representations cases.

8.23 For written representations, an application for costs can be made by letter or by the Planning Inspectorate (PINS) application form.[13]

8.24 For hearings and inquiries, the application is to be made before the Inspector closes it. Notice of a costs application and its basis should be given in advance of the hearing or inquiry unless the unreasonable behaviour arises during the hearing or inquiry. This allows the Inspector to prepare to hear the application and allows the other party to prepare a response.

CURRENT GUIDANCE

8.25 In England the relevant guidance as to costs is contained in the NPPG. In Wales, the Development Management Manual addresses costs in planning appeals in its Chapter 12.3 and cross-refers to an Annex in respect of 'Awards of Costs'. In comparison to the NPPG and the former guidance, the current Welsh guidance is skeletal and its utility is doubtful.

8.26 Attention is drawn to the following key paragraphs of the NPPG.[14]

'**Local planning authorities**

When might an award of costs be made against a local planning authority?

Awards against a local planning authority may be either procedural, relating to the appeal process or substantive, relating to the planning merits of the appeal. The examples below relate mainly to planning appeals and are not exhaustive. The Planning Inspectorate will take all evidence into account, alongside any extenuating circumstances.

What type of behaviour may give rise to a procedural award against a local planning authority?

Local planning authorities are required to behave reasonably in relation to procedural matters at the appeal, for example by complying with the requirements and deadlines of the process. Examples of unreasonable behaviour which may result in an award of costs include:

---

[13] https://assets.publishing.service.gov.uk/government/uploads/system/uploads/attachment_data/file/519803/costs_application_form_3.pdf
[14] https://www.gov.uk/guidance/appeals#the-award-of-costs--general

Current guidance **8.26**

- lack of co-operation with the other party or parties
- delay in providing information or other failure to adhere to deadlines
- only supplying relevant information at appeal when it was previously requested, but not provided, at application stage
- not agreeing a statement of common ground in a timely manner or not agreeing factual matters common to witnesses of both principal parties
- introducing fresh and substantial evidence at a late stage necessitating an adjournment, or extra expense for preparatory work that would not otherwise have arisen
- prolonging the proceedings by introducing a new reason for refusal
- withdrawal of any reason for refusal or reason for issuing an enforcement notice
- failing to provide relevant information within statutory time limits, resulting in an enforcement notice being quashed without the issues on appeal being determined
- failing to attend or to be represented at a site visit, hearing or inquiry without good reason withdrawing an enforcement notice without good reason
- providing information that is shown to be manifestly inaccurate or untrue
- deliberately concealing relevant evidence at planning application stage or at subsequent appeal failing to notify the public of an inquiry or hearing, where this leads to the need for an adjournment

(This list is not exhaustive.)

When might a local planning authority's handling of the planning application or enforcement notice prior to the appeal lead to an award of costs?

If it is clear that the local planning authority will fail to determine an application within the time limits, it should give the applicant a proper explanation. In any appeal against non-determination, the local planning authority should explain their reasons for not reaching a decision within the relevant time limit, and why permission would not have been granted had the application been determined within the relevant period.

If an appeal in such cases is allowed, the local planning authority may be at risk of an award of costs, if the Inspector or Secretary of State concludes that there were no substantive reasons to justify delaying the determination and better communication with the applicant would have enabled the appeal to be avoided altogether. Such a decision would take into account any unreasonable behaviour on the part of the appellant in causing or adding to the delay.

For enforcement action, local planning authorities must carry out adequate prior investigation. They are at risk of an award of costs if it is concluded that an appeal could have been avoided by more diligent investigation that would have either avoided the need to serve the notice in the first place, or ensured that it was accurate.

What type of behaviour may give rise to a substantive award against a local planning authority?

Local planning authorities are at risk of an award of costs if they behave unreasonably with respect to the substance of the matter under appeal, for example, by unreasonably refusing or failing to determine planning applications, or by unreasonably defending appeals. Examples of this include:

- preventing or delaying development which should clearly be permitted, having regard to its accordance with the development plan, national policy and any other material considerations.

8.27 Costs

- failure to produce evidence to substantiate each reason for refusal on appeal
- vague, generalised or inaccurate assertions about a proposal's impact, which are unsupported by any objective analysis.
- refusing planning permission on a planning ground capable of being dealt with by conditions risks an award of costs, where it is concluded that suitable conditions would enable the proposed development to go ahead
- acting contrary to, or not following, well-established case law
- persisting in objections to a scheme or elements of a scheme which the Secretary of State or an Inspector has previously indicated to be acceptable
- not determining similar cases in a consistent manner
- failing to grant a further planning permission for a scheme that is the subject of an extant or recently expired permission where there has been no material change in circumstances
- refusing to approve reserved matters when the objections relate to issues that should already have been considered at the outline stage
- imposing a condition that is not necessary, relevant to planning and to the development to be permitted, enforceable, precise and reasonable in all other respects, and thus does not comply with the guidance in the National Planning Policy Framework on planning conditions and obligations
- requiring that the appellant enter into a planning obligation which does not accord with the law or relevant national policy in the National Planning Policy Framework, on planning conditions and obligations
- refusing to enter into pre-application discussions, or to provide reasonably requested information, when a more helpful approach would probably have resulted in either the appeal being avoided altogether, or the issues to be considered being narrowed, thus reducing the expense associated with the appeal
- not reviewing their case promptly following the lodging of an appeal against refusal of planning permission (or non-determination), or an application to remove or vary one or more conditions, as part of sensible on-going case management.
- if the local planning authority grants planning permission on an identical application where the evidence base is unchanged and the scheme has not been amended in any way, they run the risk of a full award of costs for an abortive appeal which is subsequently withdrawn

(This list is not exhaustive.)'[15]

8.27 This guidance is illustrated in an appeal decision.[16] The Inspector decided as follows:

'The Council in defending the second reason for refusal stated that it had "... no evidence to contradict that presented in the Daylight and Sunlight Assessment ...". The Council's case asserts that because there would be some reduction in the receipt of light via a glazed door serving one room at 46 Radnor Walk (No 46) that the development would have an unacceptable effect on the living conditions of the occupiers of No 46. However, the affected room at No 46 is also served by a window, with the receipt of light via that window having been assessed as not being adversely affected by the development. I consider

---

[15] See NPPG, paras 046–049.
[16] 39 to 47 Shawfield Street, London APP/K5600/W/17/3183855; Grahame Gould BA MPhil MRTPI.

that the case made by the Council has failed to demonstrate that the effect on the living conditions of the occupiers of No 46 would be so severe as to warrant the withholding of planning permission. While I am mindful that the members of the Council's planning committee undertook a site visit, I consider that the Council's appeal evidence has failed to substantiate that the loss of light associated with the development would seriously harm the living conditions of the occupiers of the neighbouring properties.

...

I therefore consider that the Council's case with respect to the alleged adverse effect on the receipt of light was deficient, having regard to the second (production of evidence) and third (vague and inaccurate assertions) grounds of unreasonable behaviour referred to in paragraph 049 of the PPG.

This is an example of a LPA failing to substantiate a reason for refusal.

8.28 The Guidance continues:

'When might an award of costs not be made against a local planning authority?

Where local planning authorities have exercised their duty to determine planning applications in a reasonable manner, they should not be liable for an award of costs.

Where a local planning authority has refused a planning application for a proposal that is not in accordance with the development plan policy, and no material considerations including national policy indicate that planning permission should have been granted, there should generally be no grounds for an award of costs against the local planning authority for unreasonable refusal of an application.

Appellants

When might an award of costs be made against an appellant?

Awards against appellants may be either procedural in regard to behaviour in relation to completing the appeal process or substantive which relates to the planning merits of the appeal. The examples below are not exhaustive. The Planning Inspectorate will take all evidence into account, alongside any extenuating circumstances.

What type of behaviour may give rise to a procedural award against an appellant?

Appellants are required to behave reasonably in relation to procedural matters on the appeal, for example by complying with the requirements and deadlines of the appeals process. Examples of unreasonable behaviour which may result in an award of costs include:

- resistance to, or lack of co-operation with the other party or parties in providing information,
- discussing the application or appeal, or in responding to a planning contravention notice
- delay in providing information or other failure to adhere to deadlines
- only supplying relevant information at appeal when it was requested, but not provided, at application stage
- introducing fresh and substantial evidence at a late stage necessitating an adjournment, or extra expense for preparatory work that would not otherwise have arisen
- prolonging the proceedings by introducing a new ground of appeal or issue
- not completing a timely statement of common ground or not agreeing factual matters common to witnesses of both principal parties

8.28 *Costs*

- failing to attend or to be represented at a site visit, hearing or inquiry without good reason providing information that is shown to be manifestly inaccurate or untrue
- deliberately concealing relevant evidence at planning application stage or at a subsequent appeal. withdrawal of an appeal without good reason

(This list is not exhaustive.)

What type of behaviour may give rise to a substantive award against an appellant?

The right of appeal should be exercised in a reasonable manner. An appellant is at risk of an award of costs being made against them if the appeal or ground of appeal had no reasonable prospect of succeeding. This may occur when:

- the development is clearly not in accordance with the development plan, and no other material considerations such as national planning policy are advanced that indicate the decision should have been made otherwise, or where other material considerations are advanced, there is inadequate supporting evidence the appeal follows a recent appeal decision in respect of the same, or a very similar, development on the same, or substantially the same site where the Secretary of State or an Inspector decided that the proposal was unacceptable and circumstances have not materially changed in the intervening period
- in enforcement and lawful development certificate appeals, the onus of proof on matters of fact is on the appellant. Sometimes it is made plain by a recent appeal decision relating to the same, or a very similar development on the same, or substantially the same site, that development should not be allowed. The appellant is at risk of an award of costs, if they persist with an appeal against an enforcement notice on the ground that planning permission ought to be granted for the development in question
- lack of co-operation on any planning obligation

(This list is not exhaustive.)

Can an award of costs be made if the appellant withdraws an appeal?

Yes, if the appeal is withdrawn without good reason. Appellants are encouraged to withdraw their appeal at the earliest opportunity if there is good reason to do so.

If an appeal is withdrawn without any material change in the planning authority's case, or any other material change in circumstances relevant to the planning issues arising on the appeal, an award of costs may be made against the appellant if the claiming party can clearly show that they have incurred wasted expense as a result.

Statutory consultees

When might an award of costs be made against a statutory consultee?

Statutory consultees play an important role in the planning system: local authorities often give significant weight to the technical advice of the key statutory consultees. Where a local planning authority has relied on the advice of the statutory consultee in refusing an application, there is a clear expectation that the consultee in question will substantiate its advice at any appeal.

Where the statutory consultee is a party to the appeal, they may be liable to an award of costs to or against them.

Where a local planning authority has placed significant weight on the view of the statutory consultee in its reasons for refusal, the local planning authority may wish to request the statutory consultee attends the inquiry or hearing, or makes written representations, to defend its position as an interested party.

Where it is considered that the evidence of the statutory consultee is relevant to the determination of the appeal, the Inspector may use powers under section 250(2) and (3) of the Local Government Act 1972 to summon the statutory consultee to an appeal held as an inquiry, which may make them a party at the inquiry.

Where the Mayor of London or any other statutory consultee exercises a power to direct a planning authority to refuse planning permission, this party will be treated as a principal party at the appeal, and may be liable for an award of costs if they behave unreasonably or have an award of costs made to them.

Any allegations of unreasonable behaviour directed at a statutory consultee should be drawn to their attention at an early stage.

Statutory consultees must, at the earliest opportunity, notify the planning authority if their evidence or advice changes from that provided during the determination of the application to which the appeal relates.'[17]

EXAMPLES OF COSTS DECISIONS

8.29 To recap, the appeal decision itself will not be affected in any way by the fact that an application for costs has been made. The determination of a costs application is a separate jurisdiction. A decision whether to award costs is usually taken by the Planning Inspector, or Secretary of State, after the end of the appeal process.

8.30 It is therefore necessary for an applicant for an award of costs to demonstrate two matters. First, that a party in the appeal has behaved unreasonably. Secondly, it has to be shown that the unreasonable behaviour has caused wasted expense. These are examples of costs decisions made by Inspectors, which illustrate the approaches, in practice.

8.31 In an application for costs made by a planning authority in an enforcement notice case, the LPA applied for costs. Its sole ground for applying for costs was that the appeal was unreasonable.[18] That ground was not further particularised. In the absence of any particularisation, the appellant was unable to respond substantively. The appellant submitted that merely submitting an appeal was not unreasonable. The Inspector declined to make an award of costs and gave his reasons as:

> 'In fifteen years as a Planning Inspector this is the most pathetic application for costs I have ever had the misfortune to adjudicate on. The Guidance is clear that there is a right of appeal and this is expressly reiterated in respect of enforcement notices. It continues by saying that the parties in appeals are normally expected to meet their own expenses. The Guidance says costs may be awarded where a party has behaved unreasonably and it says unreasonable behaviour may be either procedural, relating to the process, or substantive, relating to the issues. Examples are given. It then makes absolutely clear that: "An application will need to clearly demonstrate how any alleged unreasonable behaviour has resulted in unnecessary or wasted expense."
>
> It is clear that the Council has failed to heed the advice that it has referred to. It has not offered any reason why the mere act of submitting this appeal might be said to constitute unreasonable behaviour. In the context of a statutory right of appeal it would be quite extraordinary for me to make an award of costs against an Appellant merely because they had exercised their right of appeal against such a notice ...'

---

[17] See NPPG, paras 050–055.
[18] Land at parcel 1212, Leigh Lane, Bath APP/F0114/C/16/3153305; Pete Drew BSc(Hons) DipTP (Dist) MRTPI.

8.32 *Costs*

The Inspector then went on to make some further observations about the Council's case. He noted the power to make an award of costs where no application has been made by another party. He gave serious consideration to whether he should do so in this case. He cited misconceptions in the Council's case and its understanding of policy. He also considered that the application for costs was unreasonable:

> 'Put bluntly this application for costs is so frivolous as to be a complete waste of public resources.'

Nevertheless, the Inspector exercised his discretion not to initiate an award for costs against the planning authority.

8.32 Unreasonable behaviour has to be shown to be causative of wasted expense. In a residential appeal, the planning authority relied upon heritage harm.[19] The appellant applied for costs on the basis of errors of approach in the planning authority's heritage evidence:

> 'In this case, the Council refused permission on the grounds of the harm they considered arose from the scheme to the setting of nearby heritage assets. The reason for refusal could have been better constructed so as to properly detail the assets considered to be affected. What is more, the Proof of Evidence (POE) of the Council's heritage witness refers to heritage assets within the Manthorpe Conservation Area (as does the reason for refusal), but it then fails to define the significance of one of the principal listed buildings in the form of St John the Evangelist Church. This error of omission is unreasonable given the premise of the Council's stance on harm to the setting of heritage assets within the conservation area.
>
> However, I do not consider that this resulted in unnecessary or wasted expense on the part of the applicants. Paragraph 128 of the National Planning Policy Framework requires applicants to describe the significance of any heritage asset affected, including any contribution made by their setting. To follow the process set out in the Framework, the applicants would have had to have carried out an assessment of the significance of heritage assets, irrespective of the Council's omission.'

8.33 In this case, the Inspector found unreasonable behaviour by the planning authority. Its heritage assessment unreasonably made errors in its assessment. But the appellant was no worse off. The appellant had to undertake the same assessment regardless of whether the planning authority did it correctly, incorrectly or at all. In this case, the costs application failed because the appellant could not show causation.

8.34 Significantly more profound failings in supporting a case with evidence resulted in a partial award of costs in a recovered appeal.[20] The GLA issued a direction to the LPA (Lewisham) to refuse consent on the basis that the affordable housing provision was insufficient. Considerable evidence was given in support of the appellant's viability case. The GLA appeared at the inquiry, represented by the same Leading Counsel who represented the LPA. The background was:[21]

> 'On day 2 of the Inquiry, following cross-examination of the Council's construction costs witness, the advocate representing the Council and the Greater London Authority (GLA)

---

[19] Land to the North of Longcliffe Road, Grantham APP/E2530/W/17/3173367; Cullum JA Parker BA(Hons) MA MRTPI IHBC.
[20] Land at former car parks, Tesco Store, Conington Road, Lewisham APP/C5690/W/18/3205926; Paul Jackson BArch(Hons) RIBA.
[21] Inspector's Report on costs, para 1.

Examples of costs decisions **8.36**

advised that due to a conflict of interest, the GLA would no longer be represented. The GLA however wished to continue with their objections as an unrepresented principal party. Later in the afternoon, following cross-examination by the appellant of [a further witness] for the GLA, the Council formally withdrew its objections to the proposal on viability grounds. The Council took no further part in the Inquiry.'

The appellant submitted that:

'In substantive terms, the GLA produced no evidence which met or came close to the requirements of the PPG on the issue of construction costs to support its reason for refusal.

Its "evidence" failed to meet the threshold properly to be called "evidence". It failed to engage with the agreed evidence of others that the construction costs were fair and reasonable and during the proceedings failed to read understand or engage with evidence which clearly established that its evidence was incorrect and unreasonable.'

8.35 The Inspector recommended that a partial award of costs should be made against the GLA, and the Secretary of State agreed. The basis for that conclusion was:[22]

'There is no dispute that the GLA wished to be represented by Counsel at the Inquiry. The GLA was the instigator of the refusal by Lewisham and provided 2 professional witnesses who had prepared a large volume of written evidence. I consequently give very little weight to the idea that the GLA could not themselves be responsible for potentially incurring costs. Nothing suggests that the GLA simply intended to appear as an interested party and "make a statement".

It became clear very quickly that the Council's evidence was not going to convincingly support the contention that there was a viability case for a much higher level of affordable housing. At that point, at 1145 on day 2, the withdrawal of the Council's case, and Counsel for the GLA, meant that the onus for proving the viability case would be entirely in the GLA's hands. The GLA persisted with its case, unrepresented. In cross-examination, the GLA witnesses, in putting forward their case, could provide no more than assertion and generalised assumptions and admitted they had not carried out any detailed examination of the appellant's submissions. Indeed the professional witnesses for the GLA acknowledged that much of the appellants' detailed evidence had not been read.

....

The PPG states that "Where the Mayor of London or any other statutory consultee exercises a power to direct a planning authority to refuse planning permission, this party will be treated as a principal party at the appeal, and may be liable for an award of costs if they behave unreasonably or have an award of costs made to them". It further states that costs may be awarded if there is a failure to produce evidence to substantiate each reason for refusal on appeal; and vague, generalised or inaccurate assertions are made about a proposal's impact, which are unsupported by any objective analysis.

One of the main aims of the costs regime is to encourage all those involved in the appeal process to behave in a reasonable way and follow good practice, both in terms of timeliness and in the presentation of full and detailed evidence to support their case. I conclude that the GLA's behaviour in further pursuing its grounds of objection without any credible evidence, following the withdrawal of the Council, was unreasonable behaviour that led to unnecessary and wasted expense.'

8.36 The Inspector emphasises one of the main aims of the costs regime. This is the disciplining effect and aim in action. In this case, it very quickly became clear that

---

[22] Inspector's Report on costs, paras 28, 29, 33, 34.

8.37 *Costs*

there was no evidence pointing the other way on the main viability issues and that the appellant's evidence was reasonable. But the GLA ploughed on. It is a fairly stark example of a public body simply failing to produce evidence to support its position. Mere assertion will be quickly uncovered and is highly likely to be an expensive error.

CALL-IN

8.37 In the case of 'called-in' planning applications, referred to the Secretary of State under TCPA 1990, s 77, and other referred applications (as specified in sub-paragraphs (2), (5), (7) and (22) of Annex 7), the decision by the Secretary of State to call-in an application for his own determination places the parties in subsequent inquiry proceedings in a different position from that in a planning appeal. In call-in proceedings the participation of the parties is primarily to assist the Secretary of State in the process of reaching his decision on the planning issues identified in his statement under Rule 6 of the relevant Inquiries Procedure Rules. Unlike the situation in a planning appeal, the LPA is not defending its formal decision to refuse planning permission, or its failure to determine the application within the prescribed period. The applicant has a right to apply for planning permission. In these circumstances, it is not envisaged that a party may be at risk of an award of costs for unreasonable behaviour relating to the substance of the case or action taken prior to the call-in decision.[23]

INTERESTED PARTIES

8.38 As regards the costs of interested parties, the Guidance states:

> '*When might an award of costs be made against an interested party?*
>
> Interested parties who choose to be recognised as Rule 6 parties under the inquiry procedure rules, may be liable to an award of costs if they behave unreasonably. They may also have an award of costs made to them.
>
> It is not anticipated that awards of costs will be made in favour of, or against, other interested parties, other than in exceptional circumstances. An award will not be made in favour of, or against interested parties, where a finding of unreasonable behaviour by one of the principal parties relates to the merits of the appeal. However an award may be made in favour of, or against, an interested party on procedural grounds, for example where an appeal has been withdrawn without good reason or where an unnecessary adjournment of a hearing or inquiry is caused by unreasonable conduct. In cases dealt with by written representations, it is not envisaged that awards of costs involving interested parties will arise.'[24]

AMOUNT OF THE AWARD

8.39 Costs awards do not specify the quantum of costs awarded. Rather, a costs award will state whether the award is a full award or a partial award. In the case of a

---

[23] See para 9 of Annex 1 of the Procedural Guide.
[24] See NPPG, para 056.

partial award, the context of the application will indicate the nature of the costs which are the subject of the award.

8.40 It is for the party which benefits from the award to identify and quantify the work and related costs claimed and to invite the other party to agree. In the absence of agreement, the costs fall to be assessed by the court. An application for detailed assessment of the costs should be made to the Senior Courts Costs Office.

Chapter 9

Applications and appeals against Secretary of State decisions

9.01 A person with a sufficient interest in an appeal decision has access to the court to apply for relief if it is shown that an error of law has caused prejudice and it cannot be said that the decision would be the same without the error. To unpack that one sentence is the work of one or more books. They have already been written,[1] so the task here is not to repeat that work but to provide some general orientation for those participants in a planning appeal who contemplate taking the matter further or who wish to consider their involvement in consequent proceedings. Case-specific legal advice is essential.

RIGHTS

9.02 There is always a right of access to the High Court to challenge an appeal decision as being wrong in law. This will either be as a result of a statutory provision which provides for the right and its limitations (a statutory review), or it will be as a result of a common law right of judicial review. Some of the main and typical examples are as follows.

9.03 The work of the Planning Court derives very largely from the exercise of two rights: (1) to challenge the appeal decisions pursuant to ss 288 and 289 of the Town and Country Planning Act 1990 (TCPA 1990); and (2) to challenge the grant of consent by local planning authorities by way of judicial review. The scope of the potential claimants is quite different for these two rights. This is because any party may challenge an appeal decision, be that the appellant, the local authority or any person who has a proper interest in the decision. In contrast, it is only those with a proper interest who will apply to the court in respect of the grant of consent by a local authority.[2] A disappointed applicant will not apply for judicial review because the applicant may appeal to the Secretary of State.

9.04 Other rights to apply to the court from decisions taken by Inspectors or a Secretary of State are encountered with lower frequency. For example, if the Secretary of State for Transport makes an order under the Transport and Works Act 1992, s 22 of that Act provides that a person aggrieved who desires to question its validity on the ground that it is not within the powers of the Act or that any requirement imposed under the Act (or the Tribunals and Inquiries Act 1992) has not been complied with,

---

[1] See, for example, Michael Fordham QC *Judicial Review Handbook* (Hart Publishing).
[2] Save in the extremely rare circumstance of a local authority which realises that it has granted consent in error and applies to quash its own decision.

may make an application for the purpose to the High Court. A further example is s 63 of the Planning (Listed Buildings and Conservation Areas) Act 1990 on materially the same grounds as those which are found in s 22 of the Transport and Works Act 1992.

9.05 In common with all of the Planning Acts and with the rules in respect of judicial review, the court has a permission stage, or filter. Generally, permission is required to be granted before the court proceeds to determine the substantive merits.[3] The validity provisions of the Planning Acts were amended in 2015 to add permission stages.[4] However, this is not universally the case even after the 2015 amendments. There is no permission stage for a s 22 challenge under the Transport and Works Act 1992, for example.

9.06 Statutory reviews are generally subject to 'drop-dead' time limits: in short, a day late is simply too late. Judicial review in planning cases is subject to a six-week time limit which, on application, the court may extend. These short illustrations seek to emphasise to any party which does not have legal advice on receipt of an appeal decision, that it may become necessary to give urgent consideration as to:

- Whether there is a pre-action protocol which should be followed prior to the issue of any proceedings. Generally, pre-action correspondence is not entered into in statutory reviews, but it is a feature of the Civil Procedure Rules (CPR) in respect of judicial review (see the Pre-Action Protocol for Judicial Review).[5] This Protocol sets out a code of good practice and contains the steps which parties should generally follow before making a claim for judicial review.

- Time limits – when will the appeal decision be legally secure and no longer capable of legal challenge (on which day does time start to run; which days count towards the time limit; when does the court day end etc)?

- What is the applicable right to apply for statutory review, and is any other claim form needed for judicial review in addition?

- Permission – is the permission of the court required in order for a claim to proceed, and if so what are the prospects of permission being granted?

- Concession – if a clear legal error has been identified, will the claim be conceded by one or more parties?

- Remedies – what the relevant relief might be in respect to any particular alleged legal error: would the decision be quashed and the appeal be re-heard; would the decision go back to the Secretary of State but without the need for a further inquiry; can a defective condition be remedied; would a planning obligation by deed rectify an error?

VENUE AND TIMESCALES

9.07 Challenges to planning appeal decisions are to be made to the High Court. The High Court is organised into divisions. Within the Queen's Bench Division there

---

[3] Though there is a half-way house in which the court sometimes orders a hearing at which the permission stage will be dealt with in a way which rolls-up the two stages.

[4] Amendments made by Criminal Justice and Courts Act 2015, s 91 and Sch 16 to: TCPA 1990, ss 284, 287, 288; Planning (Listed Buildings and Conservation Areas) Act 1990, ss 62, 63; Planning (Hazardous Substances) Act 1990, s 22; Planning and Compulsory Purchase Act 2004, s 8.

[5] https://www.justice.gov.uk/courts/procedure-rules/civil/protocol/prot_jrv.

9.08 *Applications and appeals against Secretary of State decisions*

are specialist courts and lists. The Administrative Court is the specialist court which hears public law cases in which the decisions of public bodies may be reviewed. Until 2014 the Administrative Court handled planning and environmental cases as part of its generalised workload. A difficulty in that approach was that planning cases took many months to be heard with resultant delays to development which might ultimately be shown to be entirely lawfully consented. The solution was to establish a specialist list called the Planning Court, with a Planning Liaison Judge who is a specialist in planning and environmental law.

9.08 Planning Court cases may be issued and heard in designated regional courts throughout England and Wales, and in London.

9.09 The establishment of the Planning Court was accompanied by amendment to the Civil Procedure Rules, adding Part 54 II 'Planning Court'. An additional Practice Direction 54E was introduced. It provides for target timescales for the Planning Court as follows:

> '3.4 The target timescales for the hearing of significant (as defined by paragraph 3.2) Planning Court claims, which the parties should prepare to meet, are as follows, subject to the overriding objective of the interests of justice—
>
> (a) applications for permission to apply for judicial review or planning statutory review are to be determined within three weeks of the expiry of the time limit for filing of the acknowledgment of service;
>
> (b) oral renewals of applications for permission to apply for judicial review or planning statutory review are to be heard within one month of receipt of request for renewal;
>
> (c) applications for permission under section 289 of the Town and Country Planning Act 1990 are to be determined within one month of issue;
>
> (d) planning statutory reviews are to be heard within six months of issue; and
>
> (e) judicial reviews are to be heard within ten weeks of the expiry of the period for the submission of detailed grounds by the defendant or any other party as provided in rule 54.14.'

9.10 A significant Planning Court claim is one which relates to developments which have significant economic impact either locally or beyond their immediate locality, or which raise important points of law, or in which there is significant public interest, or by reason of the volume or nature of technical material are best dealt with by judges with significant experience of handling such matters. If a case is designated as a significant Planning Court claim, then the timescales in the Practice Direction apply. However, it is also the practice of the Court to proceed expeditiously with any planning or environmental claim, whether it is significant or not. Hence it appears that it is a reasonable target to determine permission to appeal within three weeks where the decision is made on the papers, or one month where a hearing is required, as in enforcement cases under TCPA 1990, s 289. The Planning Court meets the targets, and does so in most cases with some regard to the parties' availability, which is important in terms of costs, continuity and client care.

PARTIES

9.11 The first defendant in a planning statutory review will be a minister; very often the Secretary of State for Housing, Communities and Local Government. If the decision-making department is the Department of Transport or Business Enterprise and Industrial Strategy, then the corresponding Secretary of State will be the first defendant.

9.12 If the claimant is the appellant, then the local planning authority(LPA) will be the second defendant. It is a matter for the LPA whether it participates in the proceedings. An LPA is not obliged to participate though it may wish to file evidence and make submissions of its own either in support of the first defendant's case or distinct and separate from it.

9.13 The claimant may be the LPA which seeks to challenge the Secretary of State's decision to allow an appeal. This is clear from TCPA 1990, s 288(2) which relates to the 'authority directly concerned'.[6] In those circumstances, the appellant would be an interested party. Similar considerations arise for an interested party to those of a second defendant: an interested party is not obliged to participate though it may wish to file evidence and make submissions of its own.

9.14 The claimant might not be a main party to the appeal. Planning statutory reviews are typically concerned with 'persons aggrieved'. The term has been given a wide meaning. A person who has taken part in the application or appeal process is highly likely to have the necessary standing to bring a claim as a person aggrieved. A mere busybody interfering in things which do not concern him would be much less well-placed, but an identified public interest may nevertheless suffice.[7] In this regard, it is foreseeable that if a proposal causes concern to a body or interest group, it is a potential claimant. Typically, such interest groups have taken points arising for heritage, nature conservation, landscape and safety issues.

COSTS

9.15 Unlike the costs position in respect of planning appeals, the starting point in High Court litigation is that costs follow the event: the party which succeeds recovers its reasonable costs from the other party or parties.[8] Orders as to costs are highly case-specific, but there are principles of general application which assist in providing orientation at an early stage as to the nature of the costs position at the end of a Planning Court case:

- One or more parties may obtain a protective costs order which limits the liabilities in costs in advance of the result.[9] In the case of an individual, the order might limit that individual's adverse costs liability to £5,000 and limit that individual's ability to recover costs from other parties to £35,000. Higher limits may apply to individuals and bodies with greater means. Like all features of litigation in the Administrative Court, the detailed provisions and case law on costs protection are extensive and it is a legal topic of its own.

---

[6] 'Without prejudice to subsection (1) or 1A, if the authority directly concerned with any order to which this section applies, or with any action on the part of the Secretary of State or the Welsh Ministers to which this section applies, or with any relevant costs order, wish to question the validity of that order or action on any of the grounds mentioned in subsection (1) or (1A) (as the case may be), the authority may make an application to the High Court under this section.'

[7] *Walton v Scottish Ministers* [2013] PTSR 51, especially the judgment of Lord Reed at [87] onwards.

[8] CPR r 44.2.

[9] See CPR r 45.43 as to Aarhus Convention claims.

9.15 *Applications and appeals against Secretary of State decisions*

- Where permission to proceed is refused, a claimant will be likely to be ordered to pay the reasonable costs of the acknowledgement of service of more than one party.[10]
- After a substantive hearing, if there is more than one party on the successful side of the case, only one set of costs will be awarded, absent good reason for a different course being taken.[11] One good reason is if an interested party can show that it has covered a separate issue, not dealt with by the first defendant.

---

[10] *Campaign to Protect Rural England – Kent Branch v Secretary of State for Communities and Local Government* [2019] EWCA Civ 1230, [2020] 1 WLR 352 at [8] and [17].
[11] *Bolton MDC v Secretary of State for the Environment* [1995] 1 WLR 1176.

Chapter 10

Next?

10.01 The system of planning appeals is long established, with its own practices, approaches and standards. Nevertheless, significant degrees of change are being driven both by the available technology, and timescales. Such change might bear upon:

- full use of digital documentation;
- proportionate and careful use of telephone and video;
- integration and transparency of procedure and guidance; and
- better use of the parties' professional teams.

FULL USE OF DIGITAL DOCUMENTATION

10.02 The Secretary of State has stated the general direction and scale of change via his Written Ministerial Statement of 13 May 2020:[1]

> 'Local planning authorities and the Planning Inspectorate drive the planning process forward and should ensure that it continues to operate effectively to support economic recovery. Moving to digital events and processes will be critical. This means adapting to working virtually, including virtual hearings and events (such as using video-conferencing and/or telephone) and making documents available for inspection online. The Government expects everyone involved in the planning process to engage proactively.'

That statement of intent is likely to remain the position regardless of the effects of Covid-19. Rather, Covid-19 has been an accelerant of change. This is so for most types of dispute resolution in courts and in tribunals. The principles and common sense guidance are the same for all and it is to be expected that planning appeals will follow suit, and in some respects, should lead. There are two distinct, but inter-related, aspects: use of digital rather than paper documents; and virtual hearings and events.

10.03 In respect of digital documentation, there are no particular barriers and considerable potential advantages to all participants, subject to proportionate use and control. One risk is in proliferation of material, and consequent loss of transparency. In part, this is because the provision of and reliance on electronic material is free. There is no cost limitation which arises from copying. It is easier to send the whole 500-page document rather than to spend the time extracting just the cover-page and the salient material. That task then falls on the other parties and the Inspector.

---

[1] https://www.parliament.uk/business/publications/written-questions-answers-statements/written-statement/Commons/2020-05-13/HCWS235/.

10.04 *Next?*

10.04 The potential for a loss of transparency lies in so much material being available that interested parties have neither the time nor the desire to engage with it. So, the other side of the digital coin is co-operation and control of the extent of materials, and the intelligent use of core bundles of the truly important materials. Further, there is real advantage in the inquiry procedure because of its requirement for either short or summary proofs of evidence. A collection of the summary proofs provides an easy overview for the interested person. Hence, the risks associated with reliance on digital documentation can be easily managed via case management directions and the promotion of existing tools such as the statement of common ground: that which is common ground does not need to be rehearsed.

10.05 The use of digital documents is primarily a change of working method for the user of the document. It requires different skills, habits and working knowledge. But the documents do not change. The approach to the planning merits does not change because the text is on screen, and not on paper. However, there is no reason to expect the future use of digital materials to be limited to text, drawings, plans and photographs. Provision of models, graphics and geographical information systems is the next step to introducing technology to the appeals system in the same way that it is being introduced at application stage for large schemes. That will lead to substantive change in decision-making because new, different or deeper insight into the substantive planning issues might be provided. It is now commonplace to produce a video representation of traffic conditions which allows the observer to visualise those conditions as they change during a peak period. A local plan may be supplemented by a digital plan which allows the interactions of constraints to be seen in combination from the specific perspective of a development proposal.[2] In turn, that will present new challenges in proving and testing, for example, the algorithm which produces the geospatial data model which is relied upon.

PROPORTIONATE AND CAREFUL USE OF TELEPHONE AND VIDEO

10.06 For the same reasons that digital documentation will increase in its use, so too will the use of remote methods of interacting with Inspectors. The optimum outcome would be:

- building on the use of telephone case management conferences to improve effectiveness and timeliness;
- web-casting events in which there is substantial public interest in order to enhance community participation; and
- minimising the use of video for active participants.

The first two points are rather self-evident. Telephone case management is a long-standing feature of civil litigation and it is unsurprising that it has had a positive effect in those appeals to which it has been applied. Its further potential is clear, as is the potential for use of video-linked case management hearings which improve interaction and understanding in comparison to telephone hearings. Short hearings which are not concerned with the substantive merits are well suited to remote means. There is little third-party interest in the procedural aspects, no evidence is given, the range of documents required is small, and the general pattern of the hearing is consistent and predictable.

---

[2] See the fast-evolving projects at https://futurecities.catapult.org.uk.

10.07 The effort and resources required to webcast an appeal event are substantial for those venues which do not have a permanent installation for that purpose. Some local authority venues are equipped to webcast meetings and other events, but the extent of provision is variable. When such provision is available, it may enhance participation by interested parties who wish to observe.

10.08 The use of video for active participants arises strongly in the context of social distancing. The extent to which it is a suitable means for providing an opportunity to be heard is evolving. It is evolving in many more contexts than planning appeals. The key limitation is in the hearing of evidence and the interactions which are lost without gathering in a place and a room. Key themes include:

- Before a hearing or inquiry commences, and during it, witnesses and representatives 'sort things out' which have not been resolved before they met together. Misunderstandings are resolved, weaknesses are acknowledged and solutions are identified.
- 'The overarching criterion is that whatever mechanism is used to conduct a hearing must be in the interests of justice, that issue being assessed by reference to the unusual circumstances that prevail and the unhappy alternative if a hearing is adjourned. Every hearing we conduct in whatever form must provide a fair hearing.'[3]
- Where the decision is of lasting importance, it is important that the issues are fully and openly tested and the parties are provided with the opportunity to persuade the decision-maker, in person.
- Courts and Tribunals 'will expect a high level of cooperation between parties and between their professional representatives'.[4]
- Cases involving a large number of witnesses and significant disputes of fact or opinion which in normal circumstances would be determined at a hearing with oral evidence and cross examination may not be practical.
- Evidence to be given on oath on matters of fact is particularly ill-suited to video-linked hearings at inquiry, in the absence of the types of controls which are more routinely adopted in court proceedings.

10.09 Absent the limitations arising from social distancing, video-linked events will no doubt find their niche and role, the decision in respect of which is necessarily highly fact- and case-specific. If the benefits of giving and seeing evidence as set out in Chapter 5 are to be retained, then the use of video is to be avoided, if possible, where those features of the evidence make a difference.

INTEGRATION AND TRANSPARENCY

10.10 Is it necessary to amend the procedure rules and guidance in order to give effect to changes in culture, timeliness and use of technology? No, it is not necessary, but it is desirable.

---

[3] Lord Chief Justice of England and Wales, Master of the Rolls and President of the Family Division: https://www.judiciary.uk/wp-content/uploads/2020/04/Message-to-CJJ-and-DJJ-9-April-2020.pdf.

[4] Guidance from the President of the Upper Tribunal (Lands Chamber) at para 17: https://www.judiciary.uk/wp-content/uploads/2020/05/Presidential-Guidance-on-the-Conduct-of-Proceedings-in-the-Lands-Chamber-Upper-Tribunal.pdf.

10.11 *Next?*

10.11 What emerges from Chapters 2 to 5 is, first, a lack of integration. In England, there are eight different sets of procedural rules for planning appeals. There are still further sets of rules which are specific to infrastructure schemes and orders, such as in respect of compulsory purchase. To these rules are to be added the various sources of guidance which also tell the parties how they should act. The National Planning Practice Guidance (NPPG) in respect of planning appeals extends to 63 paragraphs, which, when printed, amount to some 40 pages of material. The Planning Inspectorate (PINS) Procedural Guide[5] contains a further 101 pages of guidance.

10.12 Given the degree of commonality of the preparatory stages and the essential similarity between the appeal events which take place, regardless of the type of case or ultimate decision-maker, why are eight sets of procedural rules desirable? It appears doubtful that the real differences between the way in which the rules frame the fair preparation and conduct of an appeal actually justify separation and division of the rules. This is because the essence of preparing all planning appeals is simple:

- timely statement of the case to be advanced;
- identification of what is agreed and not agreed; and
- ensuring compliance with a procedural timetable.

10.13 Likewise, hearings and inquiries follow similar structures with a limited number of variations such as the difference in the order of calling evidence as between enforcement and non-enforcement appeals. The current array of rules is unnecessary, as is shown by the amendments which have resulted in one set of regulations in Wales.

10.14 An example of a lack of integration with a resultant lack of transparency is in trying to understand the difference between a 'statement of case' and a 'hearing statement'. A hearing statement is one thing for an appeal determined by a hearing, but a statement of case is another thing for an appeal determined by inquiry. But they are defined in precisely the same way. Therefore, the rules provide that they are the same thing, whereas they clearly are not.

10.15 This is more than a semantic point in that it causes delay and confusion if an appeal is made on the basis that an inquiry is sought, but the Planning Inspectorate disagrees and decides that the case should proceed by way of hearing. The 'statement of case' prepared in support of an appeal by way of inquiry will very rarely suffice for a hearing because the appellant will have expected to prepare proofs of evidence. Typically, this results in a delay of weeks or months in issue of a start date letter and the commencement of real progress being made in determining the appeal. That problem would remain, to a degree, even if it were clarified that a 'hearing statement' is required to include all of the evidence whereas a 'statement of case' must state the case clearly, but not contain the evidence. However, it would be much clearer to parties, and to the Planning Inspectorate's case officers, if the rules were consolidated and the definitions made to be workable and relate to the reality. Further flexibility in switching between modes of determination has been established via the Rosewell Review. It will be further enabled by amendment to s 319A(2) of the Town and Country Planning Act 1990, prompting a real re-think of how these features of the system interact.

---

[5] Procedural Guide *Planning Appeals – England* July 2020.

Integration and transparency **10.19**

10.16 Consolidation of the procedural rules would still leave a lack of integration and transparency in the guidance. The guidance is to be found primarily in the NPPG and in procedural guides published by the Planning Inspectorate. Their authorship and intended audiences are mixed. The result is a lack of clarity of the status of the two documents. The procedural guides are a half-way house between: (i) a practical summary of the procedure rules to assist those who are unfamiliar with the process, and; (ii) statements of policy. For example, a really very important policy statement is only to be found buried in an Annex to the procedural guide, namely the criteria for determining the mode of appeal.[6] Are these criteria produced by the Planning Inspectorate, or do they have a ministerial origin? Why are they not in the NPPG given that their existence is a statutory requirement and are the minister's criteria, not the Planning Inspectorate's criteria. The distinction and the respective roles of the Planning Inspectorate and the minister and his appointed inspectors has become less clear cut. In consequence, the relative status of the Procedural Guide and the NPPG is less clear.

10.17 It would aid transparency and produce a more coherent body of guidance if the respective documents fulfilled a clear scope, did not overlap and did not appear to each incorporate the other by reference. The PINS guidance does and plainly ought to provide assistance to participants by re-stating the procedure rules in accessible language, explaining what to expect at an appeal event and provide practical and logistical information which is necessary for efficient participation. In fact, the procedural guidance repeats and *'is to be read alongside'* the NPPG. In this way, the same point is often made twice in slightly different ways. The first ten paragraphs of the Procedural Guide are all concerned with matters which are fully articulated in the NPPG: the need to discuss a scheme with the planning authority before appeal; the need for a sound justification for refusal; the basis on which a costs award may be made.

10.18 The point can be made by way of practical example. Any planning appeal will require the consideration of planning conditions and so the Inspector and the parties will direct their minds to how they should be drafted. The Procedural Guide provides:

> '2.6.1 The appellant and local planning authority should look at the planning practice guidance on the use of planning conditions; and Appendix A – "Suggested Models of Acceptable Conditions for Use in Appropriate Circumstances" (which is still in existence) to Circular 11/95: Use of conditions in planning permission (which has been cancelled).'

10.19 The Inspector and parties to the appeal therefore have to understand that:

- there was formerly a series of ministerial circulars, most of which were cancelled in 2012 and 2014, but an Appendix to a circular on conditions was not cancelled;

- there is now an online body of Planning Practice Guidance, which does not suggest model conditions, nor provide any model conditions; but

---

[6] From Annex K of the Procedural Guide *Planning Appeals – England* February 2020 (https://assets.publishing.service.gov.uk/government/uploads/system/uploads/attachment_data/file/864777/Procedural_Guide_Planning_appeals_version_8_.pdf); Appendix 1 to the Procedural Guide – Wales is in materially identical terms (https://gov.wales/sites/default/files/publications/2019-01/procedural-guide-wales.pdf).

10.20 *Next?*

- the Procedural Guide and the Planning Practice Guidance contains a hyperlink to the Appendix to the cancelled circular.

10.20 A culture of procedural co-operation, to reach decisions and resolve disputes both effectively and efficiently is promoted by documents which are clear in their scope and no more numerous or lengthy than is necessary. A well-integrated set of rules and a clear, succinct, scope of guidance would both assist the users and operators of the appeals system, including professional teams.

PROFESSIONAL TEAMS

10.21 Planning appeals routinely benefit from combined experience and expertise which is very valuable. The legal members of those teams have two important and relevant professional obligations in the context of making an appeal run efficiently: (i) to advance their client's case without fear, and; (2) to assist the tribunal. An active invitation from Inspectors to provide that assistance would promote a culture of co-operation in the preparation of appeals. If this were not forthcoming, the use of the costs regime has a potential in this regard which has not yet been harnessed.

10.22 The changes recommended by the Rosewell Review were not changes to rules. In large measure, they were changes to culture, applying rules and practice which already exist, in a timely way. As a culture of co-operation on the effective running of appeals takes hold, the professions will be doing more of the work so that the decision-maker's task is as straightforward as possible.

10.23 When properly undertaken, it will be evident that focused calling of evidence and equally focused questions from the parties are both the most efficient and the most effective means of determining very many issues. Where it is not, the professions will say so. This applies to schemes over a wide range of scales and general importance. The benefit to the effectiveness of decision-making is not necessarily determined by the scale or importance of the development. In other words, it does not follow that an appeal for a small scheme should be dealt with by the inquisitorial method of the hearing, whereas a large scheme should be determined with the assistance of advocates. On the contrary, the question is not about the scheme but about the nature of the issue. For example, consistency of a party's position with other material or with another decision is an issue that can arise in any appeal and is always best dealt with by calling evidence to address that issue.

10.24 For the reasons given in Chapter 4, once the decision has been made to determine an appeal by way of inquiry, then the parties have a right to call evidence and to cross examine. It is not a right which is presently in the Inspector's discretion, per the rule. However, it is assumed at case management conferences in Rosewell cases that the Inspector may decide how the evidence is to be heard. The professions will know whether it is better to hear the evidence in one way or another so this ought not to be a real issue – if a party wishes to exercise the right to ask questions, then the relevant, proportionate and courteous questions should be asked.

10.25 This is a part of the driver behind the Rosewell Review. It has been effective to date and it appears that the culture and approach will grow and be grafted and transplanted elsewhere in the appeals system.

Appendix 1

Town and Country Planning Act 1990, ss 70, 77 and 78 (as amended)

PART III   CONTROL OVER DEVELOPMENT

Determination of applications

70   Determination of applications: general considerations.

(1) Where an application is made to a local planning authority for planning permission—

  (a) subject to section 62D(5) and sections 91 and 92, they may grant planning permission, either unconditionally or subject to such conditions as they think fit; or

  (b) they may refuse planning permission.

(1A) Where an application is made to a local planning authority for permission in principle—

  (a) they may grant permission in principle; or

  (b) they may refuse permission in principle.

(2) In dealing with an application for planning permission or permission in principle the authority shall have regard to—

  (a) the provisions of the development plan, so far as material to the application,

  (aza) a post-examination draft neighbourhood development plan, so far as material to the application,

  (aa) any considerations relating to the use of the Welsh language, so far as material to the application;

  (b) any local finance considerations, so far as material to the application, and

  (c) any other material considerations.

(2ZZA) The authority must determine an application for technical details consent in accordance with the relevant permission in principle.

  This is subject to subsection (2ZZC).

(2ZZB) An application for technical details consent is an application for planning permission that—

Appendix 1

  (a) relates to land in respect of which permission in principle is in force,

  (b) proposes development all of which falls within the terms of the permission in principle, and

  (c) particularises all matters necessary to enable planning permission to be granted without any reservations of the kind referred to in section 92.

(2ZZC) Subsection (2ZZA) does not apply where—

  (a) the permission in principle has been in force for longer than a prescribed period, and

  (b) there has been a material change of circumstances since the permission came into force.

  'Prescribed' means prescribed for the purposes of this subsection in a development order.

(2ZA) Subsection (2)(aa) applies only in relation to Wales.

(2A) Subsections (1A), (2)(b) and (2ZZA) to (2ZZC) do not apply in relation to Wales.

(3) Subsection (1) has effect subject to section 65 and to the following provisions of this Act, to sections 66, 67, 72 and 73 of the Planning (Listed Buildings and Conservation Areas) Act 1990 and to section 15 of the Health Services Act 1976.

(3B) For the purposes of subsection (2)(aza) (but subject to subsections (3D) and (3E)) a draft neighbourhood development plan is a 'post-examination draft neighbourhood development plan' if—

  (a) a local planning authority have made a decision under paragraph 12(4) of Schedule 4B with the effect that a referendum or referendums are to be held on the draft plan under that Schedule,

  (b) the Secretary of State has directed under paragraph 13B(2)(a) of that Schedule that a referendum or referendums are to be held on the draft plan under that Schedule,

  (c) an examiner has recommended under paragraph 13(2)(a) of Schedule A2 to the Planning and Compulsory Purchase Act 2004 (examination of modified plan) that a local planning authority should make the draft plan, or

  (d) an examiner has recommended under paragraph 13(2)(b) of that Schedule that a local planning authority should make the draft plan with modifications.

(3C) In the application of subsection (2)(aza) in relation to a post-examination draft neighbourhood development plan within subsection (3B)(d), the local planning authority must take the plan into account as it would be if modified in accordance with the recommendations.

(3D) A draft neighbourhood development plan within subsection (3B)(a) or (b) ceases to be a post-examination draft neighbourhood development plan for the purposes of subsection (2)(aza) if—

  (a) section 38A(4)(a) (duty to make plan) or (6) (cases in which duty does not apply) of the Planning and Compulsory Purchase Act 2004 applies in relation to the plan,

Town and Country Planning Act 1990, ss 70, 77 and 78 (as amended)

- (b) section 38A(5) (power to make plan) of that Act applies in relation to the plan and the plan is made by the local planning authority,
- (c) section 38A(5) of that Act applies in relation to the plan and the local planning authority decide not to make the plan,
- (d) a single referendum is held on the plan and half or fewer of those voting in the referendum vote in favour of the plan, or
- (e) two referendums are held on the plan and half or fewer of those voting in each of the referendums vote in favour of the plan.

(3E) A draft neighbourhood development plan within subsection (3B)(c) or (d) ceases to be a post-examination draft neighbourhood development plan for the purposes of subsection (2)(aza) if—

- (a) the local planning authority make the draft plan (with or without modifications), or
- (b) the local planning authority decide not to make the draft plan.

(3F) The references in subsection (3B) to Schedule 4B are to that Schedule as applied to neighbourhood development plans by section 38A(3) of the Planning and Compulsory Purchase Act 2004.

(4) In this section—

'local finance consideration' means—

- (a) a grant or other financial assistance that has been, or will or could be, provided to a relevant authority by a Minister of the Crown, or
- (b) sums that a relevant authority has received, or will or could receive, in payment of Community Infrastructure Levy;

'Minister of the Crown' has the same meaning as in the Ministers of the Crown Act 1975;

'relevant authority' means—

- (a) a district council;
- (b) a county council in England;
- (c) the Mayor of London;
- (d) the council of a London borough;
- (e) a Mayoral development corporation;
- (f) an urban development corporation;
- (g) a housing action trust;
- (h) the Council of the Isles of Scilly;
- (i) the Broads Authority;
- (j) a National Park authority in England;
- (k) the Homes and Communities Agency; or
- (l) a joint committee established under section 29 of the Planning and Compulsory Purchase Act 2004.

Appendix 1

Secretary of State's powers as respects planning applications and decisions

77 Reference of applications to Secretary of State.

(1) The Secretary of State may give directions requiring applications for planning permission or permission in principle, or for the approval of any local planning authority required under a development order, a local development order or a neighbourhood development order, to be referred to him instead of being dealt with by local planning authorities.

(2) A direction under this section—

   (a) may be given either to a particular local planning authority or to local planning authorities generally; and

   (b) may relate either to a particular application or to applications of a class specified in the direction.

(3) Any application in respect of which a direction under this section has effect shall be referred to the Secretary of State accordingly.

(4) Subject to subsection (5)—

   (a) where an application for planning permission is referred to the Secretary of State under this section, sections 70, 72(1) and (5), 73 and 73A shall apply, with any necessary modifications, as they apply to such an application which falls to be determined by the local planning authority;

   (b) where an application for permission in principle is referred to the Secretary of State under this section, section 70 shall apply, with any necessary modifications, as it applies to such an application which falls to be determined by the local planning authority;

and a development order may apply, with or without modifications, to an application so referred any requirements imposed by such an order by virtue of section 65 or 71.

(5) Before determining an application referred to him under this section, the Secretary of State shall, if either the applicant or the local planning authority wish, give each of them an opportunity of appearing before, and being heard by, a person appointed by the Secretary of State for the purpose.

(6) Subsection (5) does not apply to an application for planning permission referred to a Planning Inquiry Commission under section 101.

(6A) Subsection (5) does not apply to an application referred to the Welsh Ministers under this section instead of being dealt with by a local planning authority in Wales.

(7) The decision of the Secretary of State on any application referred to him under this section shall be final.

78 Right to appeal against planning decisions and failure to take such decisions.

(1) Where a local planning authority—

   (a) refuse an application for planning permission or grant it subject to conditions;

Town and Country Planning Act 1990, ss 70, 77 and 78 (as amended)

    (aa)   refuse an application for permission in principle;

    (b)   refuse an application for any consent, agreement or approval of that authority required by a condition imposed on a grant of planning permission or grant it subject to conditions; or

    (c)   refuse an application for any approval of that authority required under a development order, a local development order or a neighbourhood development order or grant it subject to conditions,

the applicant may by notice appeal to the Secretary of State.

(2) A person who has made such an application to the local planning authority may also appeal to the Secretary of State if the local planning authority have done none of the following—

    (a)   given notice to the applicant of their decision on the application;

    (aa)   given notice to the applicant that they have exercised their power under section 70A or 70B or 70C to decline to determine the application;

    (b)   given notice to him that the application has been referred to the Secretary of State in accordance with directions given under section 77,

within such period as may be prescribed by the development order or within such extended period as may at any time be agreed upon in writing between the applicant and the authority.

(3) Any appeal under this section shall be made by notice served within such time and in such manner as may be prescribed by a development order.

An applicant who wishes to appeal under subsection (1) or (2) shall give notice of appeal to the Secretary of State by—

    (a)   serving on the Secretary of State within—

        (i)   8 weeks from the date of receipt of the local planning authority's decision, or, as the case may be, within 8 weeks from the expiry of the period mentioned in subsection (2); or

        (ii)   such longer period as the Secretary of State may, at any time, allow,

a completed appeal form, obtained from the Secretary of State; and

    (b)   serving on the local planning authority a copy of the completed appeal form mentioned in sub-paragraph (a) as soon as reasonably practicable.

(4) The time prescribed for the service of such a notice must not be less than—

    (a)   28 days from the date of notification of the decision; or

    (b)   in the case of an appeal under subsection (2), 28 days from the end of the period prescribed as mentioned in subsection (2) or, as the case may be, the extended period mentioned in that subsection.

(4A) A notice of appeal under this section must be accompanied by such information as may be prescribed by a development order.

(4AA) An appeal under this section may not be brought or continued against the refusal of an application for planning permission if—

    (a)   the land to which the application relates is in Wales,

Appendix 1

    (b)   granting the application would involve granting planning permission in respect of matters specified in an enforcement notice as constituting a breach of planning control, and

    (c)   on the determination of an appeal against that notice under section 174, planning permission for those matters was not granted under section 177.

(4AB) An appeal under this section may not be brought or continued against the grant of an application for planning permission subject to a condition, if—

    (a)   the land to which the application relates is in Wales,

    (b)   an appeal against an enforcement notice has been brought under section 174 on the ground that the condition ought to be discharged, and

    (c)   on the determination of that appeal, the condition was not discharged under section 177.

(4BA) Once notice of an appeal under this section to the Welsh Ministers has been served, the application to which it relates may not be varied, except in such circumstances as may be prescribed by a development order.

(4BB) A development order which makes provision under subsection (4BA) must provide for an application which is varied to be subject to such further consultation as the Welsh Ministers consider appropriate.

(5)   For the purposes of the application of sections 79(1) and (3), 253(2)(c), 266(1)(b), 288(10)(b), 319A(7)(b) and 319B(7)(b) in relation to an appeal under subsection (2), it shall be assumed that the authority decided to refuse the application in question.

Appendix 2

Town and Country Planning (Development Management Procedure) (England) Order 2015
SI 2015/595

PART 7 APPEALS

37 Appeals

(1) An applicant who wishes to appeal to the Secretary of State under section 78 of the 1990 Act must give notice of appeal to the Secretary of State by—

    (a) serving on the Secretary of State within—

        (i) the time limit specified in paragraph (2); or

        (ii) such longer period as the Secretary of State may, at any time, allow,

    a completed appeal form, obtained from the Secretary of State, together with such of the documents specified in paragraph (3) as are relevant to the appeal; and

    (b) serving on the local planning authority a copy of the completed appeal form mentioned in sub-paragraph (a), as soon as reasonably practicable, together with a copy of the documents mentioned in paragraph (3)(b)(viii) to (x) (where those paragraphs apply), and any relevant documents mentioned in paragraph (3)(a)(ii) or paragraph (3)(b)(v), as the case may be.

(2) The time limit mentioned in paragraph (1) is—

    (a) in the case of a householder or minor commercial appeal, other than a type A or a type B appeal, 12 weeks from the date of the notice of the decision or determination giving rise to the appeal;

    (b) in the case of a type A appeal, 28 days from—

        (i) the date of the notice of the decision or determination giving rise to the appeal; or

        (ii) the expiry of the specified period;

    (c) in the case of a type B appeal, 28 days from the date on which the enforcement notice is served;

Appendix 2

    (d)   in all other cases, 6 months from—

        (i)   the date of the notice of the decision or determination giving rise to the appeal;

        (ii)   in a case in which the authority have served a notice on the applicant in accordance with article 5(2) that they require further information, and the applicant has not provided the information, the date of service of that notice; or

        (iii)   in any other case, the expiry of the specified period.

(3)   The documents mentioned in paragraph (1) are—

    (a)   in the case of a householder or minor commercial appeal—

        (i)   a copy of the application which was sent to the local planning authority which has occasioned the appeal;

        (ii)   any other plans, documents or drawings relating to the application which were not sent to the authority, except any plans, documents or drawings relating to amendments to the application proposed after the authority have made their determination; and

        (iii)   the notice of the decision or determination;

    (b)   in all other cases—

        (i)   a copy of the application which was sent to the local planning authority which has occasioned the appeal;

        (ii)   all plans, drawings and documents sent to the authority in connection with the application;

        (iii)   all correspondence with the authority relating to the application;

        [(iiia)   where the application was an application for technical details consent, details of the relevant permission in principle;]

        (iv)   any certificate provided to the authority under article 14;

        (v)   any other plans, documents or drawings relating to the application which were not sent to the authority, except any plans, documents or drawings relating to amendments to the application proposed after the authority have made their determination;

        (vi)   the notice of the decision or determination, if any;

        (vii)   if the appeal relates to an application for approval of certain matters in accordance with a condition on a planning permission, the application for that permission, the plans submitted with that application and the planning permission granted;

        (viii)   subject to paragraph (4), the applicant's full statement of case (if they wish to make additional representations);

        (ix)   subject to paragraph (4), a statement of which procedure (written representations, a hearing or an inquiry) the applicant considers should be used to determine the appeal; and

        (x)   subject to paragraph (4), a draft statement of common ground if the applicant considers that the appeal should be determined through a hearing or an inquiry.

(4) The relevant documents required in paragraph (3)(b)(viii) to (x) are not required to accompany the notice under paragraph (1)—

   (a) where a direction is given by the Secretary of State under section 321(3) of the 1990 Act (matters related to national security);

   (b) where section 293A of the 1990 Act (urgent Crown development) applies; or

   (c) in relation to type A or type B appeals.

(5) The Secretary of State may refuse to accept a notice of appeal from an applicant if the completed appeal form required under paragraph (1)(a) and the documents required under paragraph (3) are not served on the Secretary of State within the time limit specified in paragraph (2).

(6) The Secretary of State may provide, or arrange for the provision of, a website for use for such purposes as the Secretary of State thinks fit which—

   (a) relate to appeals under section 78 of the 1990 Act and this article; and

   (b) are capable of being carried out electronically.

(7) Where a person gives notice of appeal to the Secretary of State using electronic communications, the person is taken to have agreed—

   (a) to the use of such communications for all purposes relating to the appeal which are capable of being carried out electronically;

   (b) that the person's address for the purpose of such communications is the address incorporated into, or otherwise logically associated with, the person's notice of appeal; and

   (c) that the person's deemed agreement under this paragraph subsists until notice is given in accordance with article 46 that the person wishes to revoke the agreement.

(8) In this article—

   'draft statement of common ground' means a written statement containing factual information about the proposal which is the subject of the appeal that the applicant reasonably considers will not be disputed by the local planning authority;

   'full statement of case' means, and is comprised of, a written statement which contains full particulars of the case which a person proposes to put forward and copies of any documents which that person intends to refer to or put in evidence;

   'householder appeal' means an appeal under section 78(1) of the 1990 Act in respect of a householder application, except an appeal against the grant of any planning permission, consent, agreement or approval which is granted subject to conditions;

   'minor commercial appeal' means an appeal under section 78(1) of the 1990 Act in relation to a minor commercial application, except an appeal against the grant of any planning permission, consent, agreement or approval which is granted subject to conditions;

   'specified period' means the period specified in article 27 or article 34, as the case may be;

Appendix 2

'type A appeal' means an appeal under section 78(1) or 78(2) of the 1990 Act in respect of an application relating to land and development which are the same or substantially the same as the land and development in respect of which an enforcement notice—

(a) has been served no earlier than 2 years before the application is made;

(b) has been served before—

    (i) the date of the notice of the decision or determination giving rise to the appeal; or

    (ii) the expiry of the specified period; and

(c) is not withdrawn before the expiry of the period of 28 days from the date specified in sub-paragraph (b); and

'type B appeal' means an appeal under section 78(1) or 78(2) of the 1990 Act in respect of an application relating to land and development which are the same or substantially the same as the land and development in respect of which an enforcement notice—

(a) is served on or after—

    (i) the date of the notice of the decision or determination giving rise to the appeal, or

    (ii) the expiry of the specified period;

(b) is served earlier than 28 days before the expiry of the time limit specified—

    (i) in the case of a householder or minor commercial appeal, in paragraph (2)(a); or

    (ii) in any other case, in paragraph (2)(d); and

(c) is not withdrawn before the expiry of the period of 28 days from the date on which the enforcement notice is served.

Appendix 3

Town and Country Planning Appeals (Determination by Inspectors) (Inquiries Procedure) (England) Rules 2000 (as amended) SI 2000/1625

1 Citation, commencement and extent

(1) These Rules may be cited as the Town and Country Planning Appeals (Determination by Inspectors) (Inquiries Procedure) (England) Rules 2000.

(2) These Rules shall come into force on 1st August 2000.

(3) These Rules extend to England only.

2 Interpretation

(1) In these Rules, unless the context otherwise requires—

'assessor' means a person appointed by the Secretary of State to sit with an inspector at an inquiry or re-opened inquiry to advise the inspector on such matters arising as the Secretary of State may specify;

'the Commission' means the Historic Buildings and Monuments Commission for England;

'development order' has the meaning given in section 59 of the Planning Act;

'document' includes a photograph, map or plan;

'draft statement of common ground' means the draft statement of common ground (if any) submitted in accordance with article 33 of the 2010 Order, article 5V of the 2017 Order or regulation 8 of the Listed Buildings Regulations;

'electronic communication' has the meaning given in section 15(1) of the Electronic Communications Act 2000;

'full statement of case'—

(a) means, in relation to the applicant, the full statement of case submitted with their notice of appeal under article 33 of the 2010 Order, article 5V of the 2017 Order or regulation 8 of the Listed Buildings Regulations; and

Appendix 3

    (b)   in relation to everyone else means, and is comprised of, a written statement which contains full particulars of the case which a person proposes to put forward and copies of any documents which that person intends to refer to or put in evidence;

'inquiry' means a local inquiry in relation to which these Rules apply;

'inspector' means a person appointed by the Secretary of State under Schedule 6 to the Planning Act or, as the case may be, Schedule 3 to the Listed Buildings Act to determine an appeal;

'land' means the land or building to which an inquiry relates;

'the Listed Buildings Act' means the Planning (Listed Buildings and Conservation Areas) Act 1990;

'the Listed Buildings Regulations' means the Planning (Listed Buildings and Conservation Areas) Regulations 1990;

'listed building consent' has the meaning given in section 8(7) of the Listed Buildings Act;

'local planning authority' means the body who were responsible for dealing with the application occasioning the appeal;

'the 2010 Order' means the Town and Country Planning (Development Management Procedure) (England) (Order) 2010;

'the 2017 Order' means the Town and Country Planning (Permission in Principle) Order 2017;

'the Planning Act' means the Town and Country Planning Act 1990;

'pre-inquiry meeting' means a meeting held before an inquiry to consider what may be done with a view to securing that the inquiry is conducted efficiently and expeditiously, and where two or more such meetings are held references to the conclusion of a pre-inquiry meeting are references to the conclusion of the final meeting;

'questionnaire' means a document in the form supplied by the Secretary of State to local planning authorities for the purpose of proceedings under these Rules, and for this purpose a form is taken to be supplied where the Secretary of State has published it on a website and has notified the local planning authority, in a manner for the time being agreed between the Secretary of State and the authority for that purpose, of—

    (i)   publication of the form on the website,

    (ii)   the address of the website, and

    (iii)   the place on the website where the form may be accessed, and how it may be accessed;

'the 1992 Rules' means the Town and Country Planning Appeals (Determination by Inspectors) (Inquiries Procedure) Rules 1992;

'starting date' means the date of the notice given by the Secretary of State;

'statement of common ground' means a written statement prepared jointly by the local planning authority and the appellant and which contains agreed factual information about the proposal which is the subject of the appeal;

'statutory party' means—

    (a) a person mentioned in paragraph (1)(b)(i) of article 19 of the Town and Country Planning (General Development Procedure) Order 1995 whose representations the inspector is required by paragraph (3) of that article to take into account in determining the appeal to which an inquiry relates, and such a person whose representations the local planning authority were required by paragraph (1) of that article to take into account in determining the application occasioning the appeal; and

    (b) a person whose representations the inspector is required by paragraphs (3)(b) and (5) of regulation 6 of the Planning (Listed Buildings and Conservation Areas) Regulations 1990 to take into account in determining the appeal to which an inquiry relates, and a person whose representations the local planning authority were required by paragraph (3)(b) of that regulation to take into account in determining the application occasioning the appeal.

(2) In these Rules, and in relation to the use of electronic communications for any purpose of these Rules which is capable of being carried out electronically—

    (a) the expression 'address' includes any number or address used for the purposes of such communications, except that where these Rules impose an obligation on any person to provide a name and address to any other person, the obligation shall not be fulfilled unless the person on whom it is imposed provides a postal address;

    (b) references to statements, notices or other documents, or to copies of such documents, include references to such documents or copies of them in electronic form.

(3) Paragraphs (4) to (8) apply where an electronic communication is used by a person for the purpose of fulfilling any requirement in these Rules to give or send any statement, notice or other document to any other person ('the recipient').

(4) The requirement shall be taken to be fulfilled where the document transmitted by means of the electronic communication is—

    (a) capable of being accessed by the recipient,

    (b) legible in all material respects, and

    (c) sufficiently permanent to be used for subsequent reference.

(5) In paragraph (4), 'legible in all material respects' means that the information contained in the document is available to the recipient to no lesser extent than it would be if sent or given by means of a document in printed form.

(6) Where the electronic communication is received by the recipient outside the recipient's business hours, it shall be taken to have been received on the next working day; and for this purpose, 'working day' means a day which is not a Saturday, Sunday, Bank Holiday or other public holiday.

(7) A requirement in these Rules that any document should be in writing is fulfilled where that document meets the criteria in paragraph (4), and 'written' and cognate expressions are to be construed accordingly.

Appendix 3

(8) A requirement in these Rules to send more than one copy of a statement or other document may be complied with by sending one copy only of the statement or other document in question.

3 Application of Rules

(1) These Rules apply in relation to any local inquiry held in England by an inspector before he determines—

   (a) an appeal to the Secretary of State in relation to an application for planning permission or permission in principle under section 78 of the Planning Act;

   (b) an appeal to the Secretary of State in relation to listed building consent under section 20 of the Listed Buildings Act,

(1A) These Rules apply in relation to any local inquiry held in England by an inspector before he determines an appeal under section 78 of the Planning Act (as applied by regulations made under section 220 of that Act) subject to the modifications in rule 24A.

(2) Where these Rules apply in relation to an appeal which at some time fell to be disposed of in accordance with the Town and Country Planning (Inquiries Procedure) (England) Rules 2000 or Rules superseded by those Rules, any step taken or thing done under those Rules which could have been done under any corresponding provision of these Rules shall have effect as if it had been taken or done under that corresponding provision.

3A Notice from the Secretary of State

(1) In the case of an appeal under section 78 of the Planning Act (including an appeal under section 78 of the Planning Act as applied by regulations made under section 220 of that Act), as soon as practicable after a determination has been made under section 319A of the Planning Act that the appeal is to proceed at an inquiry, the Secretary of State shall send a notice to this effect to the appellant and the local planning authority.

(2) In the case of any other appeal to which these Rules apply, the Secretary of State shall as soon as practicable after receipt of all the documents required to enable the appeal to proceed, send a notice to the appellant and the local planning authority, informing them that an inquiry is to be held.

4 Preliminary information to be supplied by local planning authority

(1) The local planning authority shall, on receipt of the notice under rule 3A, forthwith inform the Secretary of State and the appellant in writing of the name and address of any statutory party who has made representations to them; and the Secretary of State shall, as soon as practicable thereafter, inform the appellant and the local planning authority in writing of the name and address of any statutory party who has made representations to him.

(2) This paragraph applies where—

   (a) the Secretary of State has given to the local planning authority a direction restricting the grant of planning permission or permission in principle for which application was made; or

TCPA (Determination by Inspectors) (Inquiries Procedure) (England) Rules 2000

(b) in a case relating to listed building consent, the Commission has given a direction to the local planning authority pursuant to section 14(2) of the Listed Buildings Act as to how the application is to be determined; or

(c) the Secretary of State or any other Minister of the Crown or any government department, or any body falling within rule 11(1)(c), has expressed in writing to the local planning authority the view that the application should not be granted either wholly or in part, or should be granted only subject to conditions; or

(d) any person consulted in pursuance of a development order has made representations to the local planning authority about the application.

(3) Where paragraph (2) applies, the local planning authority shall forthwith after the starting date inform the person concerned of the inquiry and, unless they have already done so, that person shall thereupon give the local planning authority a written statement of the reasons for making the direction, expressing the view or making the representations, as the case may be.

(4) The local planning authority shall ensure that within 1 week of the starting date—

(a) the Secretary of State and the appellant have received a completed questionnaire and a copy of each of the documents referred to in it; and

(b) any—

(i) statutory party; and

(ii) other person who made representations to the local planning authority about the application occasioning the appeal,

have been notified in writing that an appeal has been made and of the address to which and of the period within which they may make representations to the Secretary of State.

5 Notification of name of inspector

(1) Subject to paragraph (2), the Secretary of State shall notify in writing the name of the inspector to every person entitled to appear at the inquiry.

(2) Where the Secretary of State appoints another inspector instead of the person previously appointed and it is not practicable to notify the new appointment before the inquiry is held, the inspector holding the inquiry shall, at its commencement, announce his name and the fact of his appointment.

6 Receipt of full statements of case etc.

(1) The local planning authority shall ensure that, within 5 weeks of the starting date, 2 copies of their full statement of case have been received by the Secretary of State; and a copy of their full statement of case has been received by any statutory party.

(2) The local planning authority shall—

(a) include in their full statement of case—

(i) details of the time and place where the opportunity to inspect and take copies described in paragraph (13) below shall be afforded

Appendix 3

    (including, in any case in which the local planning authority rely on paragraph (13A), the details mentioned in that paragraph); and

   (ii) where rule 4(2) applies, the terms of any direction given together with a statement of the reasons therefor together with any view expressed or representation made on which they intend to rely in their submissions at the inquiry; and

 (b) where rule 4(2) applies, within the period mentioned in paragraph (1) send a copy of their full statement of case to the person concerned.

(3) As soon as practicable after receiving the information in rule 4(1) (preliminary information to be supplied by local planning authority), the appellant shall ensure that a copy of their full statement of case has been received by any statutory party.

(4) The Secretary of State shall, as soon as practicable after receipt, send a copy of the local planning authority's full statement of case to the appellant.

(5) [*revoked by SI 2013/2137*]

(6) The Secretary of State may in writing require any other person who has notified him of an intention or a wish to appear at an inquiry, to send within 4 weeks of being so required—

 (a) 3 copies of their full statement of case to him; and

 (b) a copy of their full statement of case to any statutory party;

and the Secretary of State shall, as soon as practicable after receipt, send a copy of each such full statement of case to the local planning authority and the appellant.

(7) The Secretary of State shall, as soon as practicable—

 (a) send to any person from whom he requires a full statement of case in accordance with paragraph (6) a copy of the statements of case of the appellant and the local planning authority; and

 (b) inform that person of the name and address of every person to whom his full statement of case is required to be sent.

(8) The Secretary of State may in writing require any person who has sent a full statement of case in accordance with these Rules, article 33 of the 2010 Order, article 5V of the 2017 Order or regulation 8 of the Listed Buildings Regulations, to provide such further information about the matters contained in the full statement of case as he may specify and may specify the time within which the information shall be received by him.

(9) A local planning authority or appellant required to provide further information shall ensure that—

 (a) 2 copies of that information have been received by the Secretary of State within the specified time; and

 (b) a copy has been received by any statutory party within the specified time,

and the Secretary of State shall, as soon as practicable after receipt, send a copy of the further information received from the local planning authority to the appellant and a copy of the further information received from the appellant to the local planning authority.

TCPA (Determination by Inspectors) (Inquiries Procedure) (England) Rules 2000

(10) Any other person required to provide further information shall ensure that—

    (a) 3 copies of that information have been received by the Secretary of State within the specified time; and

    (b) a copy has been received by any statutory party within the specified time,

and the Secretary of State shall, as soon as practicable after receipt, send a copy of the further information to the local planning authority and the appellant.

(11) [*revoked by SI 2013/2137*]

(12) The Secretary of State shall, as soon as practicable after receipt, send to the inspector any full statement of case, document, further information sent to him in accordance with this rule, article 33 of the 2010 Order, article 5V of the 2017 Order or regulation 8 of the Listed Buildings Regulations, and received by him within the relevant period, if any, specified.

(13) The local planning authority shall afford to any person who so requests a reasonable opportunity to inspect and, where practicable, take copies of—

    (a) any full statement of case, information or other document a copy of which has been sent to the local planning authority in accordance with this rule, article 33 of the 2010 Order, article 5V of the 2017 Order or regulation 8 of the Listed Buildings Regulations,; and

    (b) the local planning authority's completed questionnaire, and full statement of case, and information or other documents sent by the local planning authority pursuant to this rule.

(13A) For the purposes of the previous paragraph an opportunity shall be taken to have been afforded to a person where the person is notified of—

    (a) publication on a website of the documents mentioned in that paragraph;

    (b) the address of the website;

    (c) the place on the website where the documents may be accessed, and how they may be accessed.

(14) [*revoked by SI 2009/455*]

(15) [*revoked by SI 2009/455*]

7 Statement of matters and pre-inquiry meetings

(1) An inspector may, within 10 weeks of the starting date, send to the appellant, the local planning authority and any statutory party a written statement of the matters about which he particularly wishes to be informed for the purposes of his consideration of the appeal.

(2) An inspector shall hold a pre-inquiry meeting—

    (a) if he expects an inquiry to last for 8 days or more, unless he considers it is unnecessary; or

    (b) in respect of shorter inquiries, if it appears to him necessary.

(3) An inspector shall give not less than 2 weeks written notice of a pre-inquiry meeting to—

Appendix 3

    (a)   the appellant;

    (b)   the local planning authority;

    (c)   any statutory party;

    (d)   any other person known to be entitled to appear at the inquiry; and

    (e)   any other person whose presence at the meeting appears to him to be desirable.

(4)   The inspector—

    (a)   shall preside at the pre-inquiry meeting;

    (b)   shall determine the matters to be discussed and the procedure to be followed;

    (c)   may require any person present at the pre-inquiry meeting who, in his opinion, is behaving in a disruptive manner to leave; and

    (d)   may refuse to permit that person to return or to attend any further pre-inquiry meeting, or may permit him to return or attend only on such conditions as he may specify.

(5)   If the inspector requests any further information from the appellant or the local planning authority at the pre-inquiry meeting, they shall ensure that 2 copies of it have been received by him and a copy has been received by any statutory party within 4 weeks of the conclusion of the pre-inquiry meeting and the inspector shall, as soon as practicable after receipt, send a copy of the further information received from the local planning authority to the appellant and a copy of the further information received from the appellant to the local planning authority.

8 Inquiry timetable

(1)   In respect of all inquiries that appear to the Secretary of State likely to last for 8 days or more, the inspector shall prepare a timetable for the proceedings.

(2)   In respect of shorter inquiries, the inspector may at any time prepare a timetable for the proceedings at, or at part of, an inquiry.

(3)   The inspector may, at any time, vary the timetable arranged under the preceding paragraphs.

(4)   The inspector may specify in a timetable arranged pursuant to this rule a date by which any proof of evidence and summary sent in accordance with rule 14(1) shall be received by him.

9 Notification of appointment of assessor

Where the Secretary of State appoints an assessor, he shall notify in writing every person entitled to appear at the inquiry of the name of the assessor and of the matters on which he is to advise the inspector.

10 Date and notification of inquiry

(1)   The date fixed by the Secretary of State for the holding of an inquiry shall be—

(a) not later than 16 weeks after the starting date unless he considers such a date impracticable; or

(b) the earliest date after that period which he considers to be practicable.

(2) Unless the Secretary of State agrees a lesser period of notice with the appellant and the local planning authority, he shall give not less than 4 weeks written notice of the date, time and place fixed by him for the holding of an inquiry to every person entitled to appear at the inquiry.

(2A) A written notice shall be taken to have been given by the Secretary of State for the purposes of paragraph (2) where he and any person entitled to appear at the inquiry have agreed that notice of the matters mentioned in that paragraph may instead be accessed by that person on a website, and —

(a) the notice is a notice to which that agreement applies;

(b) the Secretary of State has published that notice on a website;

(c) not less than 4 weeks before the date fixed by the Secretary of State for the holding of the inquiry, the person is notified of—

(i) the publication of the notice on a website,

(ii) the address of the website, and

(iii) the place on the website where the notice may be accessed, and how it may be accessed.

(3) The Secretary of State may vary the date fixed for the holding of an inquiry, whether or not the date as varied is within the period of 16 weeks mentioned in paragraph (1); and paragraphs (2) to (2A) shall apply to the variation of a date as it applied to the date originally fixed.

(4) The Secretary of State may vary the time or place for the holding of an inquiry and shall give such notice of any such variation as appears to him to be reasonable.

(5) The Secretary of State may in writing require the local planning authority to take one or more of the following steps—

(a) not less than 2 weeks before the date fixed for the holding of an inquiry, to publish a notice of the inquiry in one or more newspapers circulating in the locality in which the land is situated;

(b) to send a notice of the inquiry to such persons or classes of persons as he may specify, within such period as he may specify; or

(c) to post a notice of the inquiry in a conspicuous place near to the land, within such period as he may specify.

(6) Where the land is under the control of the appellant he shall—

(a) if so required in writing by the Secretary of State, affix a notice of the inquiry firmly to the land or to some object on or near the land, in such manner as to be readily visible to and legible by members of the public; and

(b) not remove the notice, or cause or permit it to be removed, for such period before the inquiry as the Secretary of State may specify.

Appendix 3

(7) Every notice of inquiry published, sent or posted pursuant to paragraph (5), or affixed pursuant to paragraph (6), shall contain—

    (a) a clear statement of the date, time and place of the inquiry and of the powers enabling the inspector to determine the appeal in question;

    (b) a written description of the land sufficient to identify approximately its location;

    (c) a brief description of the subject matter of the appeal; and

    (d) details of where and when copies of the local planning authority's completed questionnaire and any documents sent by and copied to the authority pursuant to rule 6, article 33 of the 2010 Order, article 5V of the 2017 Order or regulation 8 of the Listed Buildings Regulations, may be inspected.

11 Appearances at inquiry

(1) The persons entitled to appear at an inquiry are—

    (a) the appellant;

    (b) the local planning authority;

    (c) any of the following bodies if the land is situated in their area and they are not the local planning authority—

        (i) a county or district council;

        (ii) an enterprise zone authority designated under Schedule 32 to the Local Government, Planning and Land Act 1980;

        (iii) the Broads Authority, within the meaning of the Norfolk and Suffolk Broads Act 1988;

        (iv) a housing action trust specified in an order made under section 67(1) of the Housing Act 1988;

    (d) where the land is in an area previously designated as a new town, the Homes and Communities Agency;

    (e) any statutory party;

    (f) the council of the parish in which the land is situated, if that council made representations to the local planning authority in respect of the application in pursuance of a provision of a development order;

    (g) where the application was required to be notified to the Commission under section 14 of the Listed Buildings Act, the Commission;

    (h) any other person who has sent a full statement of case in accordance with rule 6(6).

(2) Nothing in paragraph (1) shall prevent the inspector from permitting any other person to appear at an inquiry, and such permission shall not be unreasonably withheld.

(3) Any person entitled or permitted to appear may do so on his own behalf or be represented by any other person.

TCPA (Determination by Inspectors) (Inquiries Procedure) (England) Rules 2000

12 Representatives of government departments and other authorities at inquiry

(1) Where—

    (a) the Secretary of State or the Commission has given a direction described in rule 4(2)(a) or (b); or

    (b) the Secretary of State or any other Minister of the Crown or any government department, or any body falling within rule 11(1)(c), has expressed a view described in rule 4(2)(c) and the local planning authority have included its terms in a statement served in accordance with rule 6(1),

the appellant, the local planning authority or a person entitled to appear may, not later than 4 weeks before the date of an inquiry, apply in writing to the Secretary of State for a representative of the Secretary of State or of the other Minister, department or body concerned to be made available at the inquiry.

(2) Where an application is made in accordance with paragraph (1), the Secretary of State shall make a representative available to attend the inquiry or, as the case may be, send the application to the other Minister, department or body concerned, who shall make a representative available to attend the inquiry.

(3) Any person attending an inquiry as a representative in pursuance of this rule shall state the reasons for the direction or expressed view and shall give evidence and be subject to cross-examination to the same extent as any other witness.

(4) Nothing in paragraph (3) shall require a representative of a Minister or a government department to answer any question which in the opinion of the inspector is directed to the merits of government policy.

13 Inspector may act in place of Secretary of State

An inspector may in place of the Secretary of State take such steps as the Secretary of State is required or enabled to take under or by virtue of rule 6(6) to (10), rule 10, rule 12(1), rule 12(2), rule 21 and rule 22; and where an inspector requires further information or copies pursuant to rules 6(8) or 22, that information or copies shall be sent to him.

14 Proofs of evidence

(1) Any person entitled to appear at an inquiry who proposes to give, or to call another person to give, evidence at the inquiry by reading a proof of evidence shall simultaneously send—

    (a) 2 copies of the proof of evidence, in the case of the local planning authority and the appellant, and 3 copies in the case of any other person, to the Secretary of State together with any written summary; and

    (b) one copy of these to any statutory party;

and the Secretary of State shall, as soon as practicable after receipt, send a copy of each proof of evidence together with any summary to the local planning authority and the appellant.

Appendix 3

(2) No written summary shall be required where the proof of evidence proposed to be read contains no more than 1500 words.

(3) The proof of evidence and any summary shall be received by the Secretary of State no later than—

    (a) 4 weeks before the date fixed for the holding of the inquiry, or

    (b) where a timetable has been arranged pursuant to rule 8, which specifies a date by which the proof of evidence and any summary shall be received by the Secretary of State, that date.

(4) The Secretary of State shall send to the inspector, as soon as practicable after receipt, any proof of evidence together with any summary sent to him in accordance with this rule and received by him within the relevant period, if any, specified in this rule.

(5) Where a written summary is provided in accordance with paragraph (1), only that summary shall be read at the inquiry, unless the inspector permits or requires otherwise.

(6) Any person required by this rule to send copies of a proof of evidence to the inspector shall send with them the same number of copies of the whole, or the relevant part, of any document referred to in the proof of evidence, unless a copy of the document or part of the document in question is already available for inspection pursuant to rule 6(13).

(7) The local planning authority shall afford to any person who so requests a reasonable opportunity to inspect and, where practicable, take copies of any document sent to or by them in accordance with this rule.

(8) For the purposes of the previous paragraph an opportunity shall be taken to have been afforded to a person where the person is notified, in a manner for the time being agreed between him and the local planning authority for that purpose, of—

    (a) publication of the relevant document on a website,

    (b) the address of the website,

    (c) the place on the website where the document may be accessed, and how it may be accessed.

15 Statement of common ground

(1) The local planning authority and the appellant shall—

    (a) together prepare an agreed statement of common ground; and

    (b) ensure that the Secretary of State and any statutory party receives a copy of it, within 5 weeks of the starting date.

(2) The local planning authority shall afford to any person, who so requests, a reasonable opportunity to inspect and, where practicable, take copies of the statement of common ground sent to the Secretary of State.

(3) For the purposes of the previous paragraph an opportunity shall be taken to have been afforded to a person where the person is notified, in a manner for the time being agreed between him and the local planning authority for that purpose, of—

(a) publication of the statement of common ground on a website,

(b) the address of the website,

(c) the place on the website where the document may be accessed, and how it may be accessed.

16 Procedure at inquiry

(1) Except as otherwise provided in these Rules, the inspector shall determine the procedure at an inquiry.

(2) At the start of the inquiry the inspector shall identify what are, in his opinion, the main issues to be considered at the inquiry and any matters on which he requires further explanation from the persons entitled or permitted to appear.

(3) Nothing in paragraph (2) shall preclude any person entitled or permitted to appear from referring to issues which they consider relevant to the consideration of the appeal but which were not issues identified by the inspector pursuant to that paragraph.

(4) Unless in any particular case the inspector otherwise determines, the local planning authority shall begin and the appellant shall have the right of final reply; and the other persons entitled or permitted to appear shall be heard in such order as the inspector may determine.

(5) A person entitled to appear at an inquiry shall be entitled to call evidence and the appellant, the local planning authority and any statutory party shall be entitled to cross-examine persons giving evidence, but, subject to the foregoing and paragraphs (6) and (9), the calling of evidence and the cross-examination of persons giving evidence shall otherwise be at the discretion of the inspector.

(6) The inspector may refuse to permit the—

(a) giving or production of evidence;

(b) cross-examination of persons giving evidence; or

(c) presentation of any other matter,

which he considers to be irrelevant or repetitious; but where he refuses to permit the giving of oral evidence, the person wishing to give the evidence may submit to him any evidence or other matter in writing before the close of the inquiry.

(7) Where a person gives evidence at an inquiry by reading a summary of his proof of evidence in accordance with rule 14(5)—

(a) the proof of evidence referred to in rule 14(1) shall be treated as tendered in evidence, unless the person required to provide the summary notifies the inspector that he now wishes to rely on the contents of the summary alone; and

(b) the person whose evidence the proof of evidence contains shall then be subject to cross-examination on it to the same extent as if it were evidence he had given orally.

(8) The inspector may direct that facilities shall be afforded to any person appearing at an inquiry to take or obtain copies of documentary evidence open to public inspection.

Appendix 3

(9) The inspector may—

    (a) require any person appearing or present at an inquiry who, in his opinion, is behaving in a disruptive manner to leave; and

    (b) refuse to permit that person to return; or

    (c) permit him to return only on such conditions as he may specify,

but any such person may submit to him any evidence or other matter in writing before the close of the inquiry.

(10) The inspector may allow any person to alter or add to a full statement of case received by the Secretary of State or him under rule 6, article 33 of the 2010 Order, article 5V of the 2017 Order or regulation 8 of the Listed Buildings Regulations, so far as may be necessary for the purposes of the inquiry; but he shall (if necessary by adjourning the inquiry) give every other person entitled to appear who is appearing at the inquiry an adequate opportunity of considering any fresh matter or document.

(11) The inspector may proceed with an inquiry in the absence of any person entitled to appear at it.

(12) The inspector may take into account any written representation or evidence or any other document received by him from any person before an inquiry opens or during the inquiry provided that he discloses it at the inquiry.

(13) The inspector may from time to time adjourn an inquiry and, if the date, time and place of the adjourned inquiry are announced before the adjournment, no further notice shall be required.

(14) In respect of any inquiry that the Secretary of State expects to last for 8 or more days, any person, who appears at the inquiry and makes closing submissions, shall by the close of the inquiry provide the inspector with a copy of their closing submissions in writing.

17 Site inspections

(1) The inspector may make an unaccompanied inspection of the land before or during an inquiry without giving notice of his intention to the persons entitled to appear at the inquiry.

(2) During an inquiry or after its close, the inspector—

    (a) may inspect the land in the company of the appellant, the local planning authority and any statutory party; and

    (b) shall make such an inspection if so requested by the appellant or the local planning authority before or during an inquiry.

(3) In all cases where the inspector intends to make an accompanied inspection he shall announce during the inquiry the date and time at which he proposes to make it.

(4) The inspector shall not be bound to defer an inspection of the kind referred to in paragraph (2) where any person mentioned in that paragraph is not present at the time appointed.

TCPA (Determination by Inspectors) (Inquiries Procedure) (England) Rules 2000

18 Procedure after inquiry

(1) Where an assessor has been appointed, he may, after the close of the inquiry make a report in writing to the inspector in respect of the matters on which he was appointed to advise, and where he does so the inspector shall state in his notification of his decision pursuant to rule 19 that such a report was made.

(2) When making his decision the inspector may disregard any written representations or evidence or any other document received after the close of the inquiry.

(3) If, after the close of an inquiry, an inspector proposes to take into consideration any new evidence or any new matter of fact (not being a matter of government policy) which was not raised at the inquiry and which he considers to be material to his decision, he shall not come to a decision without first—

   (a) notifying in writing the persons entitled to appear at the inquiry who appeared at it of the matter in question; and

   (b) affording them an opportunity of making written representations to him or of asking for the re-opening of the inquiry,

   and they shall ensure that such written representations or request to re-open the inquiry are received by the Secretary of State within 3 weeks of the date of the notification.

(4) An inspector may, as he thinks fit, cause an inquiry to be re-opened, and he shall do so if asked by the appellant or the local planning authority in the circumstances and within the period mentioned in paragraph (3); and where an inquiry is re-opened—

   (a) the inspector shall send to the persons entitled to appear at the inquiry who appeared at it a written statement of the matters with respect to which further evidence is invited; and

   (b) paragraphs (2) to (7) of rule 10 shall apply as if the references to an inquiry were references to a re-opened inquiry.

19 Notification of decision

(1) The inspector shall, as soon as practicable, notify his decision on an appeal, and his reasons for it, in writing to—

   (a) all persons entitled to appear at the inquiry who did appear, and

   (b) any other person who, having appeared at the inquiry, has asked to be notified of the decision.

(1A) Notification in writing of a decision and reasons shall be taken to have been given to a person for the purposes of this rule where—

   (a) the Secretary of State and the person have agreed that decisions and reasons required under this rule to be given in writing may instead be accessed by that person via a website;

   (b) the decision and reasons are a decision and reasons to which that agreement applies;

   (c) the Secretary of State has published the decision and reasons on a website;

Appendix 3

- (d) the person is notified, in a manner for the time being agreed between him and the Secretary of State, of—
    - (i) the publication of the decision and reasons on a website;
    - (ii) the address of the website;
    - (iii) the place on the website where the decision and reasons may be accessed, and how they may be accessed.

(2) Any person entitled to be notified of the inspector's decision under paragraph (1) may apply to the Secretary of State in writing for an opportunity to inspect any documents listed in the notification and any report made by an assessor and the Secretary of State shall afford him that opportunity.

(2A) For the purposes of the previous paragraph an opportunity shall be taken to have been afforded to a person where that person is notified of—

- (a) publication of the relevant documents on a website;
- (b) the address of the website;
- (c) the place on the website where the documents may be accessed, and how they may be accessed.

(3) Any application made pursuant to paragraph (2) shall be received by the Secretary of State within 6 weeks of the date of the decision.

20 Procedure following quashing of decision

(1) Where a decision of an inspector on an appeal in respect of which an inquiry has been held is quashed in proceedings before any court, the Secretary of State—

- (a) shall send to the persons entitled to appear at the inquiry who appeared at it a written statement of the matters with respect to which further representations are invited for the purposes of his further consideration of the appeal; and
- (b) shall afford to those persons the opportunity of making written representations to him in respect of those matters or of asking for the re-opening of the inquiry; and
- (c) may, as he thinks fit, cause the inquiry to be re-opened (whether by the same or a different inspector), and if he does so paragraphs (2) to (7) of rule 10 shall apply as if the references to an inquiry were references to a re-opened inquiry.

(2) Those persons making representations or asking for the inquiry to be re-opened under paragraph (1)(b) shall ensure that such representations or requests are received by the Secretary of State within 3 weeks of the date of the written statement sent under paragraph (1)(a).

21 Allowing further time

The Secretary of State may at any time in any particular case allow further time for the taking of any step which is required or enabled to be taken by virtue of these Rules, and references in these Rules to a day by which, or a period within which, any step is required or enabled to be taken shall be construed accordingly.

22 Additional copies

(1) The Secretary of State may at any time before the close of an inquiry request from any person entitled to appear additional copies of the following—

(a) a full statement of case sent in accordance with rule 6, article 33 of the 2010 Order, article 5V of the 2017 Order or regulation 8 of the Listed Buildings Regulations;

(b) a proof of evidence sent in accordance with rule 14; or

(c) any other document or information sent to the Secretary of State before or during an inquiry,

and may specify the time within which such copies should be received by him.

(2) Any person so requested shall ensure that the copies are received by the Secretary of State within the period specified.

23 Sending of notices etc.

Notices or documents required or authorised to be sent or supplied under these Rules may be sent or supplied—

(a) by post; or

(b) by using electronic communications to send or supply the notice or document (as the case may be) to a person at such address as may for the time being be specified by the person for that purpose.

23A Withdrawal of consent to use of electronic communications

Where a person is no longer willing to accept the use of electronic communications for any purpose which, under these Rules, is capable of being carried out using such communications, he shall give notice in writing—

(a) withdrawing any address notified to the Secretary of State or (as the case may be) to a local planning authority for that purpose, or

(b) revoking any agreement entered into with the Secretary of State or (as the case may be) with a local planning authority for that purpose,

and such withdrawal or revocation shall be final and shall take effect on a date specified by the person in the notice but not less than seven days after the date on which the notice is given.

24 Mayor of London

(1) In this rule 'the Mayor' means the Mayor of London.

(2) Where an inquiry is held into an appeal arising from an application in respect of which the Mayor has directed the local planning authority to refuse the application these Rules shall apply subject to the following modifications—

(a) in rule 3A—

(i) in paragraph (1), after 'the appellant' insert ', the Mayor';

(ii) in paragraph (2), after 'the appellant' insert ', the Mayor';

Appendix 3

(b) in rule 4—

   (i) in paragraph (1) after 'inform the Secretary of State' and after 'inform the appellant' insert ', the Mayor';

   (ii) in paragraph (2) after sub-paragraph (d) insert

'or

    (e) the Mayor has given to the local planning authority a direction to refuse the application for planning permission or permission in principle.';

   (iii) in paragraph (4)(a) after the 'Secretary of State' insert ', the Mayor';

(c) in rule 6—

   (i) in paragraph (1) after 'The local planning authority' insert 'and the Mayor' and for '2' substitute '3';

   (ii) in paragraph (3) insert 'and the Mayor, and that the Mayor has received a copy of their draft statement of common ground' after 'any statutory party';

   (iii) for paragraph (4) substitute—

'The Secretary of State shall, as soon as practicable after receipt, send—

    (a) copies of the full statement of case of the Mayor to the local planning authority;

    (b) copies of the full statement of case of the local planning authority to the Mayor; and

    (c) copies of the full statements of case of the local planning authority and the Mayor to the appellant.';

   (iv) . . .

   (v) in paragraph (6) for '3' substitute '4' and after 'the local planning authority' insert ', the Mayor';

   (vi) in paragraph (7)(a) after 'the appellant' insert ', the Mayor';

   (vii) in paragraph (9) after 'local planning authority' insert ', the Mayor', in sub-paragraph (a) for '2' substitute '3' and for 'send a copy of the further information received from the local planning authority to the appellant and a copy of the further information received from the appellant to the local planning authority' substitute—

'send—

    (a) copies of the further information received from the appellant and the local planning authority to the Mayor;

    (b) copies of the further information received from the appellant and the local planning authority to the Mayor; and

    (c) copies of the further information received from the local planning authority and the Mayor to the appellant.';

TCPA (Determination by Inspectors) (Inquiries Procedure) (England) Rules 2000

        (viii) in paragraph (10) for '3' substitute '4' and after 'the local planning authority' insert ', the Mayor';

        (ix) . . .

        (x) . . .

  (d) in rule 7—

        (i) in paragraph (1) after 'the local planning authority' insert ', the Mayor'; and

        (ii) in paragraph (5) after 'from the appellant' insert ', the Mayor', for '2' substitute '3' and delete all the words after 'receipt,' and substitute—

        'send—

          (a) copies of the further information received from the appellant and the Mayor to the local planning authority;

          (b) copies of the further information received from the appellant and the local planning authority to the Mayor; and

          (c) copies of the further information received from the local planning authority and the Mayor to the appellant';

  (e) in rule 10(2) after 'the appellant' insert ', the Mayor';

  (f) in rule 11 after paragraph (1)(h) insert—

    '(i) the Mayor in relation to an inquiry arising from an application in respect of which he has given to the local planning authority a direction to refuse the application for planning permission or permission in principle.';

  (g) in rule 12—

        (i) after paragraph (1)(b) insert—

        'or

          (c) the Mayor has given to the local planning authority a direction to refuse the application for planning permission or permission in principle,'; and

        (ii) after 'body concerned' insert 'or of the mayor';

  (h) in rule 14—

        (i) in paragraph (1)(a) after 'the local planning authority' insert ', the Mayor', for '2' substitute '3' and for '3' substitute '4'; and

        (ii) in paragraph (1) for 'summary to the local planning authority and the appellant' substitute 'summary to the local planning authority, the Mayor and the appellant';

  (i) in rule 15(1) after 'The local planning authority' insert ', the Mayor';

  (j) in rule 16(5) after 'the local planning authority' insert ', the Mayor'; and

  (k) in rule 18(4) after 'by the appellant' insert ', the Mayor'.

(3) Where an inquiry is held into an appeal arising from an application which the local planning authority was required to notify to the Mayor but which is not

Appendix 3

an appeal falling within paragraph (1), these Rules shall apply as if the Mayor were a statutory party.

24A Advertisement appeals

(1) Where an inquiry is held into an appeal under section 78 of the Planning Act, as applied by regulations made under section 220 of that Act, these Rules shall apply, subject to the modifications in this rule.

(2) In rule 2 (interpretation), after the definition of 'starting date', insert—

'"statement of case" means, and is comprised of, a written statement which contains full particulars of the case which a person proposes to put forward at an inquiry and a list of any documents which that person intends to refer to or put in evidence;'.

(3) In rule 4(4) (preliminary information to be supplied by local planning authority) for '1 week' substitute '2 weeks'.

(4) In rule 6 (receipt of full statements of case etc)—

(a) in the heading, omit the word 'full';

(b) for 'full statement of case' substitute 'statement of case' wherever it appears;

(c) in paragraph (1) for '5 weeks' substitute '6 weeks';

(d) for paragraph (3) substitute—

'(3) The appellant shall ensure that, within 6 weeks of the starting date, 2 copies of their statement of case have been received by the Secretary of State and a copy has been received by any statutory party.';

(e) in paragraph (4) after 'to the appellant' insert 'and a copy of the appellant's statement of case to the local planning authority';

(f) after paragraph (4) insert—

'(5) The appellant and the local planning authority may in writing each require the other to send them a copy of any document, or of the relevant part of any document, referred to in the list of documents comprised in their statement of case; and any such document or relevant part, shall be sent, as soon as practicable, to the party who required it.';

(g) after paragraph (10), insert—

'(11) Any person other than the appellant who sends a statement of case to the Secretary of State shall send with it a copy of—

(a) any document; or

(b) the relevant part of any document,

referred to in the list comprised in that statement, unless a copy of the document or part of the document in question is already available for inspection pursuant to paragraph (13).';

(h) in paragraph (12) after 'specified' insert 'in this rule'; and

TCPA (Determination by Inspectors) (Inquiries Procedure) (England) Rules 2000

      (i)   in paragraph (13)(b) after 'statement of case' insert 'together with a copy of any document, or of the relevant part of any document referred to in the list comprised in that statement'.

(5) In rule 7 (statement of matters and pre-inquiry meetings) for '10 weeks' substitute '12 weeks'.

(6) In rule 10 (date and notification of inquiry)—

    (a)   in paragraph (1)(a) for '16 weeks' substitute '20 weeks'; and

    (b)   in paragraph (3) for '16 weeks' substitute '20 weeks'.

(7) In rule 15 (statement of common ground) in paragraph (1)(b) for '5 weeks' substitute '6 weeks'.

(8) In rule 24(2)(c) (Mayor of London: modifications to rule 6)—

    (a)   for paragraph (ii) substitute—

        '(ii) in paragraph (3) for "2" substitute "3";';

    (b)   in paragraph (iii) in the substituted paragraph (4)—

        (i)   in sub-paragraph (a) for 'statement' substitute 'statements' and after 'of case of' insert 'the appellant and'; and

        (ii)   in sub-paragraph (b) for 'statement' substitute 'statements' and after 'of case of' insert 'the appellant and'; and

    (c)   after paragraph (iii) insert—

        '(iiia) in paragraph (5) for "The appellant and the local planning authority may in writing each require the other" substitute "Any party required to provide a statement of case pursuant to paragraph (1) or (3) may in writing require any other party so required";'

25 Revocation, savings and transitional provisions

(1) Subject to paragraph (2), the Town and Country Planning Appeals (Determination by Inspectors) (Inquiries Procedure) Rules 1992 are hereby revoked in relation to England.

(2) Subject to paragraph (3) any appeal to which the 1992 Rules applied which has not been determined on the date when these Rules come into force, shall be continued under the 1992 Rules.

(3) Where a decision of an inspector on an appeal to which the 1992 Rules applied is subsequently quashed in proceedings before any court, the decision shall be re-determined in accordance with the Town and Country Planning (Inquiries Procedure) (England) Rules 2000.

Appendix 4

Town and Country Planning (Hearings Procedure) (England) Rules 2000 (as amended) SI 2000/1626

1 Citation, commencement and extent

(1) These Rules may be cited as the Town and Country Planning (Hearings Procedure) (England) Rules 2000.

(2) These Rules shall come into force on 1st August 2000.

(3) These Rules extend to England only.

2 Interpretation

(1) In these Rules—

'electronic communication' has the meaning given in section 15(1) of the Electronic Communications Act 2000;

'full statement of case'—

(a) means, in relation to the appellant, the full statement of case submitted with their notice of appeal under article 33 of the 2010 Order, article 5V of the 2017 Order or regulation 8 of the Listed Buildings Regulations; and

(b) in relation to everyone else means, and is comprised of, a written statement which contains full particulars of the case which a person proposes to put forward and copies of any documents which that person intends to refer to or put in evidence;

'document' includes a photograph, map or plan;

'draft statement of common ground' means the draft statement of common ground (if any) submitted in accordance with article 33 of the 2010 Order, article 5V of the 2017 Order or regulation 8 of the Listed Buildings Regulations;

'hearing' means a hearing in relation to which these Rules apply;

'inquiry' means a local inquiry in relation to which the Town and Country Planning (Inquiries Procedure) (England) Rules 2000 or the Town and Country Planning Appeals (Determination by Inspectors) (Inquiries Procedure) (England) Rules 2000 apply;

TCP (Hearings Procedure) (England) Rules 2000 (as amended)

'inspector' means—

(a) in relation to a transferred appeal, a person appointed by the Secretary of State to determine an appeal;

(b) in relation to a non-transferred appeal, a person appointed by the Secretary of State to hold a hearing or a re-opened hearing;

'land' means the land or building to which a hearing relates;

'the Listed Buildings Act' means the Planning (Listed Buildings and Conservation Areas) Act 1990;

'the Listed Buildings Regulations' means the Planning (Listed Buildings and Conservation Areas) Regulations 1990;

'local planning authority' means the body who were responsible for dealing with the application occasioning the appeal;

'non-transferred appeal' means an appeal which falls to be determined by the Secretary of State, including an appeal which falls to be so determined by virtue of a direction under paragraph 3(1) of Schedule 6 to the Planning Act or paragraph 3(1) of Schedule 3 to the Listed Buildings Act;

'the 2010 Order' means the Town and Country Planning (Development Management Procedure) (England) (Order) 2010;

'the 2017 Order' means the Town and Country Planning (Permission in Principle) Order 2017;

'the Planning Act' means the Town and Country Planning Act 1990;

'questionnaire' means a document in the form supplied by the Secretary of State to local planning authorities for the purpose of proceedings under these Rules, and for this purpose a form is taken to be supplied where the Secretary of State has published it on a website and has notified the local planning authority of—

(i) publication of the form on the website,

(ii) the address of the website, and

(iii) the place on the website where the form may be accessed, and how it may be accessed;

'starting date' means the date of the notice given by the Secretary of State under rule 3A;

'statement of common ground' means a written statement prepared jointly by the local planning authority and the appellant, which contains agreed factual information about the proposal which is the subject of the appeal;

'statutory party' means—

(a) a person mentioned in paragraph (1)(b)(i) of article 19 of the Town and Country Planning (General Development Procedure) Order 1995 whose representations the Secretary of State is required by paragraph (3) of that article to take into account in determining the appeal to which a hearing relates; and such a person whose representations the local planning authority were required by paragraph (1) of that article to take into account in determining the application occasioning the appeal; and

Appendix 4

        (b)   a person whose representations the Secretary of State is required by paragraphs (3)(b) and (5) of regulation 6 of the Planning (Listed Buildings and Conservation Areas) Regulations 1990 to take into account in determining the appeal to which a hearing relates; and a person whose representations the local planning authority were required by paragraph (3)(b) of that regulation to take into account in determining the application occasioning the appeal; and

'transferred appeal' means an appeal which falls to be determined by a person appointed by the Secretary of State under Schedule 6 to the Planning Act or Schedule 3 to the Listed Buildings Act.

(2) In these Rules, and in relation to the use of electronic communications for any purpose of these Rules which is capable of being effected electronically—

    (a) the expression 'address' includes any number or address used for the purposes of such communications, except that where these Rules impose an obligation on any person to provide a name and address to any other person, the obligation shall not be fulfilled unless the person on whom it is imposed provides a postal address;

    (b) references to statements, notices, or other documents, or to copies of such documents, include references to such documents or copies of them in electronic form.

(3) Paragraphs (4) to (8) apply where an electronic communication is used by a person for the purpose of fulfilling any requirement in these Rules to give or send any statement, notice or other document to any other person ('the recipient').

(4) The requirement shall be taken to be fulfilled where the document transmitted by means of the electronic communication is—

    (a) capable of being accessed by the recipient,

    (b) legible in all material respects, and

    (c) sufficiently permanent to be used for subsequent reference.

(5) In paragraph (4), 'legible in all material respects' means that the information contained in the statement, notice or document is available to the recipient to no lesser extent than it would be if sent or given by means of a document in printed form.

(6) Where the electronic communication is received by the recipient outside the recipient's business hours, it shall be taken to have been received on the next working day; and for this purpose 'working day' means a day which is not a Saturday, Sunday, Bank Holiday or other public holiday.

(7) A requirement in these Rules that any document should be in writing is fulfilled where that document meets the criteria in paragraph (4), and "written" and cognate expressions are to be construed accordingly.

(8) A requirement in these Rules to send more than one copy of a statement or other document may be complied with by sending one copy only of the statement or other document in question.

3 Application of Rules

(1) These Rules apply in relation to any hearing held in England for the purposes of a non-transferred or a transferred appeal made on or after 1st August 2000 under—

TCP (Hearings Procedure) (England) Rules 2000 (as amended)

    (a)   section 78 of the Planning Act;

    (b)   section 20 of the Listed Buildings Act.

(1A)   These Rules apply in relation to any hearing held in England for the purposes of a non-transferred or a transferred appeal under section 78 of the Planning Act (as applied by regulations made under section 220 of that Act) subject to the modifications in rule 20A.

(2)   Where these Rules apply in relation to an appeal which at some time fell to be disposed of in accordance with the Town and Country Planning (Inquiries Procedure) (England) Rules 2000 or the Town and Country Planning Appeals (Determination by Inspectors) (Inquiries Procedure) (England) Rules 2000, any step taken or thing done under those Rules which could have been done under any corresponding provision of these Rules shall have effect as if it had been taken or done under that corresponding provision.

3A Notice from the Secretary of State

(1)   In the case of an appeal under section 78 of the Planning Act (including an appeal under section 78 of the Planning Act as applied by regulations made under section 220 of that Act) as soon as practicable after a determination has been made under section 319A of the Planning Act that the appeal is to proceed at a hearing, the Secretary of State shall send a notice to this effect to the appellant and the local planning authority.

(2)   In the case of any other appeal to which these Rules apply, the Secretary of State shall, as soon as practicable after receipt of all the documents required to enable the appeal to proceed, send a notice to the appellant and the local planning authority, informing them that a hearing is to be held.

4 Preliminary information to be supplied by local planning authority

(1)   The local planning authority shall, on receipt of the notice under rule 3A, forthwith inform the Secretary of State and the appellant in writing of the name and address of any statutory party who has made representations to them; and the Secretary of State shall, as soon as practicable thereafter, inform the appellant and the local planning authority in writing of the name and address of any statutory party who has made representations to him.

(2)   The local planning authority shall ensure that within 1 week of the starting date—

    (a)   the Secretary of State and the appellant have received a completed questionnaire and a copy of each of the documents referred to in it;

    (b)   any—

        (i)   statutory party; and

        (ii)   other person who made representations to the local planning authority about the application occasioning the appeal,

    has been notified in writing that an appeal has been made and of the address to which and of the period within which they may make representations to the Secretary of State.

Appendix 4

5 Notification of name of inspector

(1) This rule applies where a hearing is to be held for the purposes of a transferred appeal.

(2) Subject to paragraph (3), the Secretary of State shall notify in writing the name of the inspector to every person entitled to appear at the hearing.

(3) Where the Secretary of State appoints another inspector instead of the person previously appointed and it is not practicable to notify the new appointment before the hearing is held, the inspector holding the hearing shall, at its commencement, announce his name and the fact of his appointment.

6 Receipt of full statements of case etc.

(1) As soon as practicable after receiving the information in rule 4(1) (preliminary information to be supplied by local planning authority), the appellant shall ensure that a copy of their full statement of case has been received by any statutory party.

(1A) The local planning authority shall ensure that, within 5 weeks of the starting date, 2 copies of their full statement of case have been received by the Secretary of State, and that a copy has been received by any statutory party.

(2) The Secretary of State may in writing require the appellant and the local planning authority to provide such further information about the matters contained in their full statement of case as he may specify; such information shall be provided in writing and the appellant or the local planning authority, as the case may be, shall ensure that 2 copies are received by the Secretary of State and a copy is received by any statutory party within such period as the Secretary of State may reasonably require.

(3) Any statutory party, and any person who made representations to the local planning authority about the application occasioning the appeal or who was notified about the application occasioning the appeal, shall ensure that the Secretary of State has received 3 copies of any written comments they wish to make concerning the appeal within 5 weeks of the starting date.

(4) [*revoked*]

(5) The Secretary of State shall send, as soon as practicable after receipt, a copy of any—

   (a) full statement of case received by him pursuant to paragraph (1A) and, further information provided pursuant to paragraph (2) . . . from, in each case, the appellant or the local planning authority to the other of those two parties; and

   (b) written comments made by persons pursuant to paragraph (3), to the local planning authority and the appellant.

(6) The local planning authority shall afford to any person who so requests a reasonable opportunity to inspect, and where practicable, take copies of—

   (a) the local planning authority's completed questionnaire, full statement of case and any document copied to the authority under paragraph (5), article 33 of the 2010 Order, article 5V of the 2017 Order or regulation 8 of the Listed Buildings Regulations; and

TCP (Hearings Procedure) (England) Rules 2000 (as amended)

(b) further information provided by the authority under paragraph (2) . . .,

and shall specify in their full statement of case the time and place where such opportunity shall be afforded.

(6A) For the purposes of the previous paragraph an opportunity shall be taken to have been afforded to a person where the person is notified of—

    (a) publication on a website of any document mentioned in sub-paragraph (a) or (b) of the previous paragraph;

    (b) the address of the website;

    (c) the place on the website where the document may be accessed, and how it may be accessed.

(7) The Secretary of State shall send to the inspector, as soon as practicable after receipt, any full statement of case, document, part of any document or written comments received by the Secretary of State within the relevant period specified for receiving such documents pursuant to paragraphs (1A) to (3), article 33 of the 2010 Order, article 5V of the 2017 Order or regulation 8 of the Listed Buildings Regulations.

(8) In the case of a non-transferred appeal, the Secretary of State, and in the case of a transferred appeal, the inspector, may in determining the appeal disregard any comments made pursuant to paragraph (3) which are received after the relevant period specified for receipt.

6A Statement of common ground

(1) The local planning authority and the appellant shall—

    (a) together prepare an agreed statement of common ground; and

    (b) ensure that the Secretary of State receives it and that any statutory party receives a copy of it within 5 weeks of the starting date.

(2) The local planning authority shall afford to any person who so requests, a reasonable opportunity to inspect, and where practicable, take copies of the statement of common ground sent to the Secretary of State.

(3) For the purposes of the previous paragraph, an opportunity shall be taken to have been afforded to a person where the person is notified of—

    (a) publication of the statement of common ground on a website;

    (b) the address of the website; and

    (c) the place on the website where the document may be accessed and how it may be accessed.

7 Date and notification of hearing

(1) The date fixed by the Secretary of State for the holding of a hearing shall be—

    (a) not later than 10 weeks after the starting date, unless he considers such a date impracticable; or

    (b) the earliest date after that period which he considers to be practicable.

Appendix 4

(2) Unless the Secretary of State agrees a lesser period of notice with the appellant and the local planning authority, he shall give not less than 4 weeks written notice of the date, time and place fixed by him for the holding of a hearing to every person entitled to appear at the hearing.

(2A) A written notice shall be taken to have been given by the Secretary of State for the purposes of paragraph (2) where he and any person entitled to appear at the hearing have agreed that notice of the matters mentioned in that paragraph may instead be accessed by that person via a website, and—

    (a) the notice is a notice to which that agreement applies;

    (b) the Secretary of State has published the notice on a website;

    (c) not less than 4 weeks before the date fixed by the Secretary of State for the holding of the inquiry, the person is notified of—

        (i) the publication of the notice on a website,

        (ii) the address of the website, and

        (iii) the place on the website where the notice may be accessed, and how it may be accessed.

(3) The Secretary of State may vary the date fixed for the holding of a hearing, whether or not the date as varied is within the period of 10 weeks mentioned in paragraph (1); and paragraghs (2) and (2A) shall apply to a variation of a date as it applied to the date originally fixed.

(4) The Secretary of State may vary the time or place for the holding of a hearing and shall give such notice of any variation as appears to him to be reasonable.

(5) The Secretary of State may in writing require the local planning authority to take one or both of the following steps—

    (a) not less than 2 weeks before the date fixed for the holding of a hearing, to publish a notice of the hearing in one or more newspapers circulating in the locality in which the land is situated;

    (b) to send a notice of the hearing to such persons or classes of persons as he may specify, within such period as he may specify.

(6) Every notice of hearing published or sent pursuant to paragraph (5) shall contain—

    (a) a clear statement of the date, time and place of the hearing and of the powers enabling the Secretary of State or inspector to determine the appeal in question;

    (b) a written description of the land sufficient to identify approximately its location;

    (c) a brief description of the subject matter of the appeal; and

    (d) details of where and when copies of the local planning authority's completed questionnaire and documents sent by and copied to the authority pursuant to rule 6, article 33 of the 2010 Order, article 5V of the 2017 Order or regulation 8 of the Listed Buildings Regulations may be inspected.

8 Method of procedure

(1) Subject to paragraphs (3) and (4), if either the appellant or the local planning authority at any time before or during the hearing is of the opinion that the hearings procedure is inappropriate in determining the appeal and that the appeal should not proceed in this way then they may inform the Secretary of State in writing, before the hearing, or the inspector, during the hearing, of their opinion and the reasons for it, and—

   (a) the Secretary of State, before the hearing, shall, after consulting the other party who may inform the Secretary of State of his opinion in writing pursuant to this paragraph, decide whether an inquiry should be arranged instead; or

   (b) the inspector, during the hearing, shall, after consulting the other party who may inform the inspector of his opinion pursuant to this paragraph, decide whether the hearing should be closed and an inquiry held instead.

(2) Except in the case of an appeal under section 78 of the Planning Act (including an appeal under section 78 of the Planning Act as applied by regulations made under section 220 of that Act), if at any time during a hearing it appears to the inspector that the hearings procedure is inappropriate, he may, after consulting the appellant and the local planning authority, decide to close the proceedings and arrange for an inquiry to be held instead.

(3) In the case of an appeal under section 78 of the Planning Act (including an appeal under section 78 of the Planning Act as applied by regulations made under section 220 of that Act), if either the appellant or the local planning authority at any time before or during a hearing is of the opinion that the hearings procedure is inappropriate to determine the appeal and that the appeal should not proceed in this way then they may inform the Secretary of State in writing, before the hearing, or the inspector, during the hearing and the reasons for it.

(4) Where paragraph (3) applies, the Secretary of State shall consult the other party, who may inform the Secretary of State of their opinion in writing pursuant to this paragraph, before exercising the power in section 319A(4) of the Planning Act.

9 Appearances at hearing

(1) The persons entitled to appear at the hearing are—

   (a) the appellant;

   (b) the local planning authority; and

   (c) any statutory party.

(2) Nothing in paragraph (1) shall prevent the inspector from permitting any other person to appear at a hearing, and such permission shall not be unreasonably withheld.

(3) Any person entitled or permitted to appear may do so on his own behalf or be represented by any other person.

Appendix 4

10 Inspector may act in place of Secretary of State in respect of transferred appeals

(1) This rule applies where a hearing is to be held or has been held in respect of a transferred appeal.

(2) An inspector may in place of the Secretary of State take such steps as the Secretary of State is required or enabled to take under or by virtue of rules 6(2), 6(5), 7 and 18; and where an inspector requires further information or copies pursuant to rules 6(2) or 18(2) that information or copies shall be sent to him.

11 Procedure at hearing

(1) Except as otherwise provided in these Rules, the inspector shall determine the procedure at a hearing.

(2) A hearing shall take the form of a discussion led by the inspector and cross-examination shall not be permitted unless the inspector considers that cross-examination is required to ensure a thorough examination of the main issues.

(3) Where the inspector considers that cross-examination is required under paragraph (2) he shall consider, after consulting the appellant and the local planning authority, whether the hearing should be closed and an inquiry held instead.

(4) At the start of the hearing the inspector shall identify what are, in his opinion, the main issues to be considered at the hearing and any matters on which he requires further explanation from any person entitled or permitted to appear.

(5) Nothing in paragraph (4) shall preclude any person entitled or permitted to appear from referring to issues which they consider relevant to the consideration of the appeal but which were not issues identified by the inspector pursuant to that paragraph.

(6) A person entitled to appear at a hearing shall be entitled to call evidence but, subject to the foregoing and paragraphs (7) and (8), the calling of evidence shall otherwise be at the inspector's discretion.

(7) The inspector may refuse to permit the—

(a) giving or production of evidence; or

(b) presentation of any other matter,

which he considers to be irrelevant or repetitious; but where he refuses to permit the giving of oral evidence, the person wishing to give the evidence may submit to him any evidence or other matter in writing before the close of the hearing.

(8) The inspector may—

(a) require any person appearing or present at a hearing who, in his opinion, is behaving in a disruptive manner to leave; and

(b) refuse to permit that person to return; or

(c) permit him to return only on such conditions as he may specify,

but any such person may submit to him any evidence or other matter in writing before the close of the hearing.

TCP (Hearings Procedure) (England) Rules 2000 (as amended)

(9) The inspector may allow any person to alter or add to a full statement of case received under rule 6, article 33 of the 2010 Order, article 5V of the 2017 Order or regulation 8 of the Listed Buildings Regulations so far as may be necessary for the purposes of the hearing; but he shall (if necessary by adjourning the hearing) give every other person entitled to appear who is appearing at the hearing an adequate opportunity of considering any fresh matter or document.

(10) The inspector may proceed with a hearing in the absence of any person entitled to appear at it.

(11) The inspector may take into account any written representation or evidence or any other document received by him from any person before a hearing opens or during the hearing provided that he discloses it at the hearing.

(12) The inspector may from time to time adjourn a hearing and, if the date, time and place of the adjourned hearing are announced at the hearing before the adjournment, no further notice shall be required.

12 Site inspections

(1) Where it appears to the inspector that one or more matters would be more satisfactorily resolved by adjourning the hearing to the appeal site he may adjourn the hearing to that site and conclude the hearing there provided he is satisfied that—

    (a) the hearing would proceed satisfactorily and that no party would be placed at a disadvantage;

    (b) all parties present at the hearing would have the opportunity to attend the adjourned hearing; and

    (c) the local planning authority, the appellant or any statutory party has not raised reasonable objections to it being continued at the appeal site.

(2) Unless the hearing is to be adjourned to the appeal site pursuant to paragraph (1), the inspector—

    (a) may inspect the land during the hearing or after its close; and

    (b) shall inspect the land if requested to do so by the appellant or the local planning authority before or during the hearing.

(3) Where the inspector intends to make an inspection under paragraph (2), he shall ask the appellant and the local planning authority whether they wish to be present.

(4) Where the appellant or the local planning authority have indicated that they wish to be present the inspector shall announce the date and time at which he proposes to make the inspection during the hearing and shall make the inspection in the company of–

    (a) the appellant and the local planning authority; and

    (b) at the inspector's discretion, any other person entitled or permitted to appear at the hearing who is appearing or did appear at it.

(5) The inspector shall not be bound to defer an inspection of the kind referred to in paragraph (2) where any person mentioned in paragraph (4) is not present at the time appointed.

Appendix 4

13 Procedure after hearing—non-transferred appeals

(1) This rule applies where a hearing has been held for the purposes of a non-transferred appeal.

(2) After the close of the hearing, the inspector shall make a report in writing to the Secretary of State which shall include his conclusions and his recommendations or his reasons for not making any recommendations.

(3) When making his determination the Secretary of State may disregard any written representations, evidence or other document received after the hearing has closed.

(4) If, after the close of the hearing, the Secretary of State—

(a) differs from the inspector on any matter of fact mentioned in, or appearing to him to be material to, a conclusion reached by the inspector, or

(b) takes into consideration any new evidence or new matter of fact (not being a matter of government policy),

and is for that reason disposed to disagree with a recommendation made by the inspector, he shall not come to a decision which is at variance with that recommendation without first notifying in writing the persons entitled to appear at the hearing who appeared at it of his disagreement and the reasons for it; and affording them an opportunity of making written representations to him or (if the Secretary of State has taken into consideration any new evidence or new matter of fact, not being a matter of government policy) of asking for the re-opening of the hearing.

(5) Those making written representations or requesting the hearing to be re-opened pursuant to paragraph (4), shall ensure that such representations or request are received by the Secretary of State within 3 weeks of the date of the Secretary of State's notification under that paragraph.

(6) The Secretary of State may, as he thinks fit, cause a hearing to be re-opened, and he shall do so if asked by the appellant or the local planning authority in the circumstances mentioned in paragraph (4) and within the period mentioned in paragraph (5); and where a hearing is re-opened (whether by the same or a different inspector)–

(a) the Secretary of State shall send to the persons entitled to appear at the hearing who appeared at it a written statement of the matters with respect to which further evidence is invited; and

(b) paragraphs (2) to (6) of rule 7 shall apply as if the references to a hearing were references to a re-opened hearing.

14 Procedure after hearing—transferred appeals

(1) This rule applies where a hearing has been held for the purposes of a transferred appeal.

(2) When making his decision the inspector may disregard any written representations, or evidence or any other document received after the hearing has closed.

(3) If, after the close of the hearing, an inspector proposes to take into consideration any new evidence or any new matter of fact (not being a matter of government

TCP (Hearings Procedure) (England) Rules 2000 (as amended)

policy) which was not raised at the hearing and which he considers to be material to his decision, he shall not come to a decision without first—

(a) notifying in writing persons entitled to appear at the hearing who appeared at it of the matter in question; and

(b) affording them an opportunity of making written representations to him or of asking for the re-opening of the hearing,

and they shall ensure that such written representations or request to re-open the hearing are received by the Secretary of State within 3 weeks of the date of the notification.

(4) An inspector may, as he thinks fit, cause a hearing to be re-opened and he shall do so if asked by the appellant or the local planning authority in the circumstances and within the period mentioned in paragraph (3); and where a hearing is re-opened—

(a) the inspector shall send to the persons entitled to appear at the hearing who appeared at it a written statement of the matters with respect to which further evidence is invited; and

(b) paragraphs (2) to (6) of rule 7 shall apply as if the references to a hearing were references to a re-opened hearing.

15 Notification of decision—non-transferred appeals

(1) This rule applies where a hearing has been held for the purposes of a non-transferred appeal.

(2) The Secretary of State shall notify his decision on an appeal, and his reasons for it, in writing to—

(a) all persons entitled to appear at the hearing who did appear; and

(b) any other person who, having appeared at the hearing, has asked to be notified of the decision.

(2A) Notification in writing of a decision and reasons shall also be taken to have been given to a person for the purposes of this rule where—

(a) the Secretary of State and the person have agreed that decisions and reasons required under this rule to be given in writing may instead be accessed by that person on a website;

(b) the decision and reasons are a decision and reasons to which that agreement applies;

(c) the Secretary of State has published the decision and reasons on a website;

(d) the person is notified of—

(i) the publication of the decision and reasons on a website;

(ii) the address of the website;

(iii) the place on the website where the decision and reasons may be accessed, and how they may be accessed.

(3) Where a copy of the inspector's report is not sent with the notification of the decision, the notification shall be accompanied by a statement of his

Appendix 4

conclusions and of any recommendations made by him; and if a person entitled to be notified of the decision has not received a copy of that report, he shall be supplied with a copy of it on written application to the Secretary of State.

(4) In this rule 'report' does not include any documents appended to the inspector's report; but any person who has received a copy of the report may apply to the Secretary of State in writing for an opportunity of inspecting any such documents and the Secretary of State shall afford him that opportunity.

(4A) For the purposes of the previous paragraph an opportunity shall be taken to have been afforded to a person where that person is notified of—

    (a) publication of the relevant documents on a website;

    (b) the address of the website;

    (c) the place on the website where the documents may be accessed, and how they may be accessed.

(5) A person applying to the Secretary of State under—

    (a) paragraph (3) shall ensure that his application is received by the Secretary of State within 4 weeks;

    (b) paragraph (4) shall ensure that his application is received by the Secretary of State within 6 weeks,

of the date of the Secretary of State's decision.

16 Notification of decision—transferred appeals

(1) This rules applies where a hearing has been held for the purposes of a transferred appeal.

(2) An inspector shall notify his decision on an appeal, and his reason for it, in writing to—

    (a) all persons entitled to appear at the hearing who did appear; and

    (b) any other person who, having appeared at the hearing, has asked to be notified of the decision.

(3) Any person entitled to be notified of the inspector's decision under paragraph (2) may apply to the Secretary of State in writing, for an opportunity of inspecting any documents listed in the notification and the Secretary of State shall afford him that opportunity.

(4A) For the purposes of the previous paragraph an opportunity shall be taken to have been afforded to a person where that person is notified of—

    (a) publication of the relevant documents on a website;

    (b) the address of the website;

    (c) the place on the website where the documents may be accessed, and how they may be accessed.

(4) Any person making an application under paragraph (3) shall ensure that it is received by the Secretary of State within 6 weeks of the date of the inspector's decision.

TCP (Hearings Procedure) (England) Rules 2000 (as amended)

17 Procedure following quashing of decision

(1) Where a decision of the Secretary of State or an inspector on an appeal in respect of which a hearing has been held is quashed in proceedings before any court, the Secretary of State—

- (a) shall send to the persons entitled to appear at the hearing who appeared at it a written statement of the matters with respect to which further representations are invited for the purposes of his further consideration of the appeal;
- (b) shall afford to those persons the opportunity of making written representations to him in respect of those matters or of asking for the re-opening of the hearing; and
- (c) may, as he thinks fit, cause the hearing to be re-opened or an inquiry held instead (whether by the same or a different inspector) and if he re-opens the hearing paragraphs (2) to (6) of rule 7 shall apply as if the references to a hearing were to a re-opened hearing.

(2) Those persons making representations or asking for the hearing to be re-opened under paragraph (1)(b) shall ensure that such representations or request are received by the Secretary of State within 3 weeks of the date of the written statement sent under paragraph (1)(a).

18 Further time and additional copies

(1) The Secretary of State may at any time in any particular case allow further time for the taking of any step which is required or enabled to be taken by virtue of these Rules, and references in these Rules to a day by which, or a period within which, any step is required or enabled to be taken shall be construed accordingly.

(2) The Secretary of State may at any time before the close of a hearing request from any person entitled to appear additional copies of the following—

- (a) a full statement of case or comments sent in accordance with rule 6, article 33 of the 2010 Order, article 5V of the 2017 Order or regulation 8 of the Listed Buildings Regulations; or
- (b) any other document or information sent to the Secretary of State before or during a hearing,

and may specify the time within which such copies should be received by him and any person so requested shall ensure that the copies are received within the period specified.

19 Sending of notices etc.

Notices or documents required or authorised to be sent or supplied under these Rules may be sent or supplied—

(a) by post; or

(b) by using electronic communications to send or supply the notice or document (as the case may be) to a person at such address as may for the time being be specified by the person for that purpose.

Appendix 4

19A Withdrawal of consent to use of electronic communications

Where a person is no longer willing to accept the use of electronic communications for any purpose under these Rules which is capable of being effected electronically, the person shall give notice in writing—

(a) withdrawing any address notified to the Secretary of State or to a local planning authority for that purpose, or

(b) revoking any agreement entered into with the Secretary of State or with a local planning authority for that purpose,

and such withdrawal or revocation shall be final and shall take effect on a date specified by the person in the notice but not less than seven days after the date on which the notice is given.

20 Mayor of London

(1) In this rule 'the Mayor' means the Mayor of London.

(2) Where a hearing is held into an appeal arising from an application in respect of which the Mayor has directed the local planning authority to refuse the application these Rules shall apply subject to the following modifications—

    (a) in rule 3A—

        (i) in paragraph (1), after 'the appellant' insert ', the Mayor';

        (ii) in paragraph (2), after 'the appellant' insert ', the Mayor';

    (b) in rule 4—

        (i) in paragraph (1), after 'inform the Secretary of State' and after 'inform the appellant' insert ', the Mayor';

        (ii) in paragraph (2)(a) after 'the Secretary of State' insert ', the Mayor';

        (iii) in paragraph (2)(b)(i), after 'statutory party' insert 'and the Mayor';

    (c) in rule 6—

        (i) in paragraph (1) insert 'and the Mayor, and that the Mayor has received a copy of their draft statement of common ground' after 'any statutory party';

        (ia) in paragraph (1A) insert 'and the Mayor' after 'The local planning authority' and substitute '3' for '2';

        (ii) in paragraph (2), after both references to 'the appellant' insert ', the Mayor' and for '2' substitute '3';

        (iii) in paragraph (3), for '3' substitute '4';

        (iv) . . .

        (v) in paragraph (5)(a), after 'the appellant' insert ', the Mayor' and for 'of those two parties' substitute 'parties required to provide such documents';

        (vi) in paragraph (5)(b), after 'the local planning authority' insert ', the Mayor'.

TCP (Hearings Procedure) (England) Rules 2000 (as amended)

- (ca) in rule 6A(1) after 'The local planning authority' insert ', the Mayor';
- (d) in rule 7(2) after 'the appellant' insert ', the Mayor';
- (e) in rule 8—
  - (i) in paragraph (1), for 'If either the appellant' substitute 'If the appellant, the Mayor', for each reference to 'party' substitute 'parties' and for each reference to 'his opinion' substitute 'their opinions';
  - (ii) in paragraph (2), after 'the appellant' insert ', the Mayor';
  - (iii) in paragraph (3), for 'if either the appellant' substitute 'if the appellant, the Mayor';
  - (iv) in paragraph (4), for 'party' substitute 'parties';
- (f) in rule 9(1)—
  - (i) at the end of sub-paragraph (b) delete 'and';
  - (ii) after sub-paragraph (c) add—

    'and

    (d) the Mayor.';
- (g) in rules 13(6) and 14(4), after 'the appellant' insert ', the Mayor'.

(3) Where a hearing is held into an appeal arising from an application which a local planning authority was required to notify to the Mayor but which is not an appeal falling within paragraph (2), these Rules shall apply as if the Mayor were a statutory party.

20A Advertisement appeals

(1) Where a hearing is held into an appeal under section 78 of the Planning Act as applied by regulations made under section 220 of that Act, these Rules apply subject to the modifications in this rule.

(2) In rule 2 (interpretation), after the definition of 'hearing', insert—

'"hearing statement" means, and is comprised of, a written statement which contains full particulars of the case which a person proposes to put forward at a hearing and a list of any documents which that person intends to refer to or put in evidence;'.

(3) In rule 4(2) (preliminary information to be supplied by local planning authority) for '1 week' substitute '2 weeks'.

(4) In rule 6 (receipt of hearing statements etc)—
- (a) in the heading, for 'full statement of case' substitute 'hearing statements';
- (b) for 'full statement of case' substitute 'hearing statement' wherever it appears;
- (c) for paragraphs (1) and (1A) substitute—

  '(1) The appellant and the local planning authority shall ensure that, within 6 weeks of the starting date, 2 copies of their hearing statement have been received by the Secretary of State and a copy has been received by any statutory party.';

Appendix 4

    (d)   in paragraph (3) for '5 weeks' substitute '6 weeks';

    (e)   in paragraph (5)(a) for 'paragraph (1A)' substitute 'paragraph (1)'; and

    (f)   in paragraph (7) for 'paragraphs (1A) to (3)' substitute 'paragraphs (1) to (3)'.

(5)   Omit rule 6A (statement of common ground).

(6)   In rule 7 (date and notification of hearing)—

    (a)   in paragraph (1)(a) for '10 weeks' substitute '12 weeks'; and

    (b)   in paragraph (3) for '10 weeks' substitute '12 weeks'.

(8)   In rule 11(9) (procedure at hearing) for 'full statement of case' substitute 'hearing statement'.

(9)   In rule 18(2)(a) (further time and additional copies) for 'full statement of case' substitute 'hearing statement'.

(10) In rule 20(2)(c) (Mayor of London: modifications to rule 6), for paragraphs (i) and (ia) substitute—

    '(i)   in paragraph (1), after "The appellant" insert ", the Mayor" and for "2" substitute "3";'.

(11) Omit rule 20(2)(ca).

Appendix 5

Town and Country Planning (Enforcement) (Determination by Inspectors) (Inquiries Procedure) (England) Rules 2002 (as amended) SI 2002/2685

1 Citation, commencement and extent

(1) These Rules may be cited as the Town and Country Planning (Enforcement) (Determination by Inspectors) (Inquiries Procedure) (England) Rules 2002 and shall come into force on 23rd December 2002.

(2) These Rules extend to England only.

2 Interpretation

(1) In these Rules—

'assessor' means a person appointed by the Secretary of State to sit with an inspector at an inquiry or re-opened inquiry to advise the inspector on such matters arising as the Secretary of State may specify;

'certificate of lawful use or development' means a certificate under section 191 or 192 of the Planning Act;

'document' includes a photograph, map or plan;

'electronic communication' has the meaning given in section 15(1) of the Electronic Communications Act 2000;

'enforcement appeal' means an appeal against an enforcement notice;

'enforcement notice' means a notice under section 172 of the Planning Act or under section 38 of the Listed Buildings Act;

'inquiry' means a local inquiry to which these Rules apply;

'inspector' means a person appointed by the Secretary of State under Schedule 6 to the Planning Act or, as the case may be, Schedule 3 to the Listed Buildings Act to determine an appeal;

'land' means the land or building to which an inquiry relates;

'Listed Buildings Act' means the Planning (Listed Buildings and Conservation Areas) Act 1990;

Appendix 5

'Listed Buildings Act certificate of lawfulness' means a certificate under section 26H of the Listed Buildings Act;

'local planning authority' means in relation to—

(a) an enforcement appeal, the body who issued the relevant enforcement notice;

(b) an appeal against the refusal or non-determination of an application for a certificate of lawful use or development, the body to whom the application was made;

(c) an appeal against the refusal or non-determination of an application for a Listed Buildings Act certificate of lawfulness, the body to whom that application was made;

'outline statement' means a written statement of the principal submissions which a person proposes to put forward at an inquiry;

'Planning Act' means the Town and Country Planning Act 1990;

'pre-inquiry meeting' means a meeting held before an inquiry to consider what may be done with a view to securing that the inquiry is conducted efficiently and expeditiously, and where two or more such meetings are held references to the conclusion of a pre-inquiry meeting are references to the conclusion of the final meeting;

'questionnaire' means a document in the form supplied by the Secretary of State to local planning authorities for the purpose of proceedings under these Rules, and for this purpose a form is taken to be supplied where the Secretary of State has published it on a website and has notified the local planning authority, in a manner for the time being agreed between the Secretary of State and the authority for that purpose, of—

(i) publication of the form on the website,

(ii) the address of the website, and

(iii) the place on the website where the form may be accessed, and how it may be accessed;

'relevant notice' means the Secretary of State's written notice under rule 4(1), informing the appellant and the local planning authority that an inquiry is to be held;

'starting date' means the date of the—

(a) Secretary of State's written notice to the appellant and the local planning authority that he has received all the documents required to enable him to entertain the appeal pursuant to regulation 10 of the Town and Country Planning (Enforcement Notices and Appeals) (England) Regulations 2002; or

(b) relevant notice,

whichever is the later;

'statement of case' means, and is comprised of, a written statement which contains full particulars of the case which a person proposes to put forward at an inquiry, and a list of any documents which that person intends to refer to or put in evidence;

TCP (Enforcement) (Determination by Inspectors) (Inquiries Procedure) (Eng) R 2002

'statement of common ground' means a written statement prepared jointly by the local planning authority and the appellant, which contains agreed factual information about the development, breach of condition or works which are the subject of the appeal.

(2) In these Rules, and in relation to the use of electronic communications for any purpose of these Rules which is capable of being carried out electronically—

(a) the expression 'address' includes any number or address used for the purposes of such communications, except that where these Rules impose an obligation on any person to provide a name and address to any other person, the obligation shall not be fulfilled unless the person on whom it is imposed provides a postal address;

(b) references to statements, notices, applications, or other documents, or to copies of such documents include references to such documents or copies of them in electronic form.

(3) Paragraphs (4) to (8) apply where an electronic communication is used by a person for the purpose of fulfilling any requirement in these Rules that a statement or other document should be sent or given to any other person ('the recipient').

(4) The requirement shall be taken to be fulfilled where the statement or other document which is transmitted by means of the electronic communication is—

(a) capable of being accessed by the recipient,

(b) legible in all material respects, and

(c) sufficiently permanent to be used for subsequent reference.

(5) In paragraph (4), 'legible in all material respects' means that the information contained in the notice or document is available to the recipient to no lesser extent than it would be if sent or given by means of a notice or document in printed form.

(6) Where the electronic communication is received by the recipient outside the recipient's business hours, it shall be taken to have been received on the next working day; and for this purpose 'working day' means a day which is not a Saturday, Sunday, Bank Holiday or other public holiday.

(7) A requirement in these Rules that any notice or document should be in writing is fulfilled where that document meets the criteria in paragraph (4), and 'written' and cognate expressions are to be construed accordingly.

(8) A requirement in these Rules to send more than one copy of a statement or other document may be complied with by sending one copy only of the statement or document in question.

3 Application of the Rules

(1) These Rules apply in relation to any local inquiry held in England by an inspector before he determines an appeal made on or after 23rd December 2002 under—

(a) section 174 of the Planning Act (appeal against enforcement notice);

(b) section 195 of the Planning Act (appeal against refusal or non-determination of an application for a certificate of lawful use or development);

Appendix 5

    (ba)   section 26K of the Listed Buildings Act (appeal against a refusal or failure to give a decision on an application for a Listed Buildings Act certificate of lawfulness);

    (c)   section 39 of the Listed Buildings Act (appeal against listed building enforcement notice),

but do not apply to any local inquiry by reason of the application of any provision mentioned in this rule by or under any other enactment.

(2)   Where these Rules apply in relation to an appeal which at some time fell to be disposed of in accordance with—

    (a)   the Town and Country Planning (Enforcement) (Inquiries Procedure) (England) Rules 2002; or

    (b)   the Town and Country Planning (Enforcement)(Inquiries Procedure) Rules 1992,

any step taken or thing done under those Rules which could have been done under any corresponding provision of these Rules shall have effect as if it had been taken or done under that corresponding provision.

4 Preliminary information to be supplied by local planning authority

(1)   The Secretary of State shall, as soon as practicable after it is determined to hold an inquiry under these Rules, inform the appellant and the local planning authority in writing that an inquiry is to be held.

(2)   The local planning authority shall within 2 weeks of the starting date—

    (a)   send to the Secretary of State and the appellant a completed questionnaire and a copy of each of the documents referred to in it;

    (b)   in the case of an enforcement appeal, notify any—

        (i)   person on whom a copy of the enforcement notice has been served;

        (ii)   occupier of property in the locality in which the land to which the enforcement notice relates is situated; and

        (iii)   other person who in the opinion of the local planning authority is affected by the breach of planning control or contravention of listed building . . . control which is alleged in the enforcement notice,

that an appeal has been made and of the address to which and of the period within which they may make representations to the Secretary of State.

5 Notification of name of inspector

(1)   The Secretary of State shall, subject to paragraph (2), notify the name of the inspector to every person entitled to appear at the inquiry.

(2)   Where the Secretary of State appoints another inspector instead of the person previously appointed and it is not practicable to notify the new appointment before the inquiry is held, the inspector holding the inquiry shall, at its commencement, announce his name and the fact of his appointment.

6 Service of statements of case etc.

(1) The local planning authority shall, within 6 weeks of the starting date, serve 2 copies of their statement of case on the Secretary of State and, in the case of an enforcement appeal, a copy on any person on whom a copy of the enforcement notice has been served.

(2) The local planning authority shall include in their statement of case details of the time and place where the opportunity will be given to inspect and take copies described in paragraph (13) (and including, in any case in which the local planning authority rely on paragraph (13A), the details mentioned in that paragraph).

(3) The appellant shall, within 6 weeks of the starting date, serve 2 copies of his statement of case on the Secretary of State and, in the case of an enforcement appeal, a copy on any person on whom a copy of the enforcement notice has been served.

(4) The Secretary of State shall, as soon as practicable after receipt, send a copy of the local planning authority's statement of case to the appellant and a copy of the appellant's statement of case to the local planning authority.

(5) The appellant and the local planning authority may in writing each require the other to send them a copy of any document, or the relevant part of any document, referred to in the list of documents comprised in that party's statement of case; and any such document, or relevant part, shall be sent, as soon as practicable, to the party who required it.

(6) The Secretary of State may in writing require any other person who has notified him of an intention or a wish to appear at the inquiry, to serve—

  (a) 3 copies of their statement of case on him within 4 weeks of being so required; and

  (b) in the case of an enforcement appeal, simultaneously, a copy of their statement of case on any person specified by the Secretary of State,

and the Secretary of State shall, as soon as practicable after receipt, send a copy of each such statement of case to the local planning authority and to the appellant.

(7) The Secretary of State shall, as soon as practicable—

  (a) send to any person from whom he requires a statement of case in accordance with paragraph (6) a copy of the statements of case of the appellant and the local planning authority; and

  (b) inform that person of the name and address of every person to whom his statement of case is required to be sent.

(8) The Secretary of State may in writing require any person, who has served on him a statement of case in accordance with this rule, to provide such further information about the matters contained in the statement of case as he may specify and may specify the time within which the information shall be sent to him.

(9) A local planning authority or appellant required to provide further information, shall send within the time specified—

Appendix 5

    (a)   2 copies of that information in writing to the Secretary of State; and

    (b)   in the case of an enforcement appeal, a copy to any person on whom a copy of the enforcement notice has been served,

and the Secretary of State shall, as soon as practicable after receipt, send a copy of the further information received from the local planning authority to the appellant and a copy of the further information received from the appellant to the local planning authority.

(10) Any other person required to provide further information shall send within the time specified—

    (a)   3 copies of that information in writing to the Secretary of State; and

    (b)   in the case of an enforcement appeal, a copy to any person on whom a copy of the enforcement notice has been served,

and the Secretary of State shall, as soon as practicable after receipt, send a copy of the further information to the local planning authority and the appellant.

(11) Any person other than the appellant who serves a statement of case on the Secretary of State shall send with it a copy of—

    (a)   any document; or

    (b)   the relevant part of any document,

referred to in the list comprised in that statement, unless a copy of the document or part of the document in question is already available for inspection pursuant to paragraph (13).

(12) The Secretary of State shall, as soon as practicable after receipt, send to the inspector any statement of case, document, further information and written comments sent to him in accordance with this rule and received by him within the relevant period, if any, specified in this rule.

(13) The local planning authority shall give any person who so requests a reasonable opportunity to inspect and, where practicable, take copies of—

    (a)   any statement of case, written comments, further information or other document a copy of which has been sent to the local planning authority in accordance with this rule; and

    (b)   the local planning authority's completed questionnaire and statement of case together with a copy of any document, or of the relevant part of any document, referred to in the list comprised in that statement, and any written comments, information or other document sent by the local planning authority pursuant to this rule.

(13A) For the purposes of the previous paragraph an opportunity is to be taken to have been given to a person where the person is notified of—

    (a)   publication on a website of the documents mentioned in that paragraph;

    (b)   the address of the website;

    (c)   the place on the website where the documents may be accessed, and how they may be accessed.

(14) If the local planning authority or the appellant wish to comment on another person's statement of case, they shall send within 9 weeks of the starting date—

TCP (Enforcement) (Determination by Inspectors) (Inquiries Procedure) (Eng) R 2002

    (a)   2 copies of their written comments to the Secretary of State; and

    (b)   in the case of an enforcement appeal, a copy of their written comments to any person on whom a copy of the enforcement notice has been served,

and the Secretary of State shall, as soon as practicable after receipt, send a copy of the written comments received from the appellant to the local planning authority and a copy of the written comments received from the local planning authority to the appellant.

(15)   Any person, other than the local planning authority or the appellant, who serves a statement of case on the Secretary of State under this rule and who wishes to comment on another person's statement of case, shall send, not less than 4 weeks before the date fixed for the holding of the inquiry—

    (a)   3 copies of their written comments to the Secretary of State; and

    (b)   in the case of an enforcement appeal, a copy of their written comments to any person on whom a copy of the enforcement notice has been served,

and the Secretary of State shall, as soon as practicable after receipt, send a copy of the written comments to the local planning authority and to the appellant.

7 Statement of matters and pre-inquiry meetings

(1)   An inspector may, within 12 weeks of the starting date, send to the appellant, the local planning authority and, in the case of an enforcement appeal, any person on whom a copy of the enforcement notice has been served, a written statement of the matters about which he particularly wishes to be informed for the purposes of his consideration of the appeal.

(2)   An inspector shall hold a pre-inquiry meeting—

    (a)   if he expects an inquiry to last for 4 days or more, unless he considers it is unnecessary; or

    (b)   for shorter inquiries, if it appears to him necessary.

(3)   An inspector shall give not less than 2 weeks' written notice of a pre-inquiry meeting to—

    (a)   the appellant;

    (b)   the local planning authority;

    (c)   any other person known to be entitled to appear at the inquiry; and

    (d)   any other person whose presence at the pre-inquiry meeting appears to him to be desirable.

(4)   The inspector—

    (a)   shall preside at the pre-inquiry meeting;

    (b)   shall determine the matters to be discussed and the procedure to be followed;

    (c)   may require any person present at the pre-inquiry meeting who, in his opinion, is behaving in a disruptive manner to leave; and

    (d)   may refuse to permit that person to return or to attend any further pre-inquiry meeting, or may permit him to return or attend only on such conditions as he may specify.

Appendix 5

(5) An inspector may request any further information from the appellant or the local planning authority at the pre-inquiry meeting.

(6) The appellant and the local planning authority shall—

    (a) send 2 copies of any further information requested under paragraph (5) to the inspector; and

    (b) in the case of an enforcement notice appeal, send a copy to any person on whom a copy of the enforcement notice has been served,

within 4 weeks of the conclusion of the pre-inquiry meeting.

(7) The inspector shall, as soon as practicable after receipt, send a copy of the further information received from the local planning authority to the appellant and a copy of any further information received from the appellant to the local planning authority.

8 Inquiry timetable

(1) In respect of inquiries that appear to the Secretary of State likely to last for 4 days or more, the inspector shall prepare a timetable for the proceedings.

(2) In respect of shorter inquiries, the inspector may at any time prepare a timetable for the proceedings at, or at part of, an inquiry.

(3) The inspector may, at any time, vary the timetable prepared under the preceding paragraphs.

(4) The inspector may specify in a timetable prepared pursuant to this rule a date by which any proof of evidence and summary sent in accordance with rule 15(1) shall be sent to him.

9 Date and notification of inquiry

(1) The date fixed by the Secretary of State for the holding of an inquiry shall be—

    (a) not later than 20 weeks after the starting date unless he considers such a date impracticable; or

    (b) the earliest date after that period which he considers to be practicable.

(2) Unless the Secretary of State agrees a lesser period of notice with the appellant and the local planning authority, he shall give not less than 4 weeks written notice of the date, time and place fixed by him for the holding of an inquiry to every person entitled to appear at the inquiry.

(3) The Secretary of State may vary the date fixed for the holding of an inquiry, whether or not the date as varied is within the period of 20 weeks mentioned in paragraph (1); and paragraph (2) shall apply to a variation of a date as it applied to the date originally fixed.

(3A) A written notice shall be taken to have been given by the Secretary of State for the purposes of paragraph (3) where he and any person entitled to appear at the inquiry have agreed that notice of the matters mentioned in that paragraph may instead be accessed by that person via a website, and—

    (a) the notice is a notice to which that agreement applies;

(b) the Secretary of State has published that notice on the website;

(c) not less than 4 weeks before the date fixed by the Secretary of State for the holding of the inquiry, the person is notified of—

　(i) the publication of the notice on a website,

　(ii) the address of the website, and

　(iii) the place on the website where the notice may be accessed, and how it may be accessed.

(4) The Secretary of State may vary the time or place for the holding of an inquiry and shall give such notice as appears to him to be reasonable.

(5) The Secretary of State may in writing require the local planning authority to take one or more of the following steps—

(a) not less than 2 weeks before the date fixed for the holding of an inquiry, to publish a notice of the inquiry in one or more newspapers circulating in the locality in which the land is situated;

(b) to send a notice of the inquiry to such persons or classes of persons as he may specify, within such period as he may specify; or

(c) to post a notice of the inquiry in a conspicuous place near to the land, within such period as he may specify.

(6) Where the land is under the control of the appellant, he shall—

(a) if so required in writing by the Secretary of State, affix a notice of the inquiry firmly to the land or to some object on or near the land, in such manner as to be readily visible to and legible by members of the public; and

(b) not remove the notice, or cause or permit it to be removed, for such period before the inquiry as the Secretary of State may specify.

(7) Every notice of inquiry published, sent or posted pursuant to paragraph (5), or affixed pursuant to paragraph (6), shall contain—

(a) a clear statement of the date, time and place of the inquiry and of the powers enabling the inspector to determine the appeal in question;

(b) a written description of the land sufficient to identify approximately its location;

(c) a brief description of the subject matter of the appeal; and

(d) details of where and when copies of the local planning authority's completed questionnaire and any document sent by and copied to the authority pursuant to rule 6 may be inspected.

10 Notification of appointment of assessor

Where the Secretary of State appoints an assessor he shall notify every person entitled to appear at the inquiry of the name of the assessor and of the matters on which he is to advise the inspector.

Appendix 5

11 Appearances at inquiry

(1) The persons entitled to appear at the inquiry are—

   (a) the appellant;

   (b) the local planning authority;

   (c) any of the following bodies if the land is situated in their area and they are not the local planning authority—

   (i) a county or a district council;

   (ii) an enterprise zone authority designated under Schedule 32 to the Local Government, Planning and Land Act 1980;

   (iii) the Broads Authority, within the meaning of the Norfolk and Suffolk Broads Act 1988;

   (iv) a housing action trust specified in an order made under section 67(1) of the Housing Act 1988;

   (d) where the land is in an area previously designated as a new town, the Homes and Communities Agency;

   (e) in the case of an enforcement appeal, any person on whom a copy of the enforcement notice has been served;

   (f) in the case of an appeal under section 195 of the Planning Act or an appeal under section 26K of the Listed Building Act, any person having an interest in the land;

   (g) the Historic Buildings and Monuments Commission for England where—

   (i) the inquiry relates to an enforcement notice under section 38 of the Listed Buildings Act;

   (ii) the listed building is in Greater London; and

   (iii) if an application for listed building consent had been made for the works set out in the enforcement notice, the Commission would have been notified of the application under a direction given under section 15(5) of the Listed Buildings Act;

   (h) any other person who has served a statement of case in accordance with rule 6(6).

(2) Nothing in paragraph (1) shall prevent the inspector from permitting any other person to appear at an inquiry and such permission shall not be unreasonably withheld.

(3) Any person entitled or permitted to appear may do so on his own behalf or be represented by any other person.

TCP (Enforcement) (Determination by Inspectors) (Inquiries Procedure) (Eng) R 2002

12 Information to be provided by all parties

Any person entitled or permitted to appear at the inquiry, who proposes to give, or call another person to give evidence at the inquiry, shall send in writing to the Secretary of State no later than 4 weeks before the inquiry—

(a) an estimate of the time required to present all their evidence; and

(b) the number of witnesses that they intend to call to give evidence.

13 Representatives of government departments at inquiry

(1) Where the Secretary of State or any other Minister of the Crown or any government department has expressed in writing to the local planning authority a view on an appeal and the authority refer to that view in a statement prepared pursuant to rule 6(1), the appellant may, not later than 4 weeks before the date of an inquiry, apply in writing to the Secretary of State for a representative of the Secretary of State or of the other Minister or department concerned to be made available at the inquiry.

(2) Where an application is made in accordance with paragraph (1), the Secretary of State shall make a representative available to attend the inquiry or, as the case may be, send the application to the other Minister or department concerned, who shall make a representative available to attend the inquiry.

(3) A person attending an inquiry as a representative pursuant to this rule shall state the reasons for the expressed view and shall give evidence and be subject to cross-examination to the same extent as any other witness.

(4) Nothing in paragraph (3) shall require a representative of a Minister or government department to answer any question, which in the opinion of the inspector, is directed to the merits of government policy.

14 Inspector may act in place of Secretary of State

An inspector may in place of the Secretary of State take such steps as the Secretary of State is required or enabled to take under or by virtue of rule 6(6) to (10), (14) and (15), rules 9, 22 and 23; and where an inspector requires further information or copies pursuant to rules 6(8) or 23, that information or copies shall be sent to him.

15 Proofs of evidence

(1) Any person entitled to appear at an inquiry who proposes to give, or to call another person to give, evidence at the inquiry by reading a proof of evidence shall—

  (a) subject to paragraph (2), send 2 copies, in the case of the local planning authority and the appellant, or 3 copies in the case of any other person, of the proof of evidence together with a written summary to the Secretary of State; and

  (b) in the case of an enforcement appeal, simultaneously send copies of these to any person on whom a copy of the enforcement notice has been served,

Appendix 5

and the Secretary of State shall, as soon as practicable after receipt, send a copy of each proof of evidence together with any summary to the local planning authority and the appellant.

(2) No written summary shall be required where the proof of evidence proposed to be read contains no more than 1500 words.

(3) The proof of evidence and any summary shall be sent to the Secretary of State no later than—

   (a) 4 weeks before the date fixed for the holding of the inquiry, or

   (b) where a timetable has been prepared pursuant to rule 8 which specifies a date by which the proof of evidence and any summary shall be sent to the Secretary of State, that date.

(4) The Secretary of State shall send to the inspector, as soon as practicable after receipt, any proof of evidence together with any summary sent to him in accordance with this rule within the relevant period, specified in this rule.

(5) Where a written summary is provided in accordance with paragraph (1), only that summary shall be read at the inquiry, unless the inspector permits or requires otherwise.

(6) Any person, required by this rule to send copies of a proof of evidence to the Secretary of State, or any other person, shall send with them the same number of copies of the whole, or the relevant part, of any document referred to in the proof of evidence, unless a copy of the document or part of the document in question is already available for inspection pursuant to rule 6(13).

(7) The local planning authority shall give any person who so requests a reasonable opportunity to inspect and, where practicable, take copies of any document sent to or by them in accordance with this rule.

(8) For the purposes of the previous paragraph an opportunity shall be taken to have been given to a person where the person is notified of—

   (a) publication of the relevant document on a website,

   (b) the address of the website,

   (c) the place on the website where the document may be accessed, and how it may be accessed.

16 Statement of common ground

(1) The local planning authority and the appellant shall together prepare an agreed statement of common ground and shall send it to—

   (a) the Secretary of State; and

   (b) in the case of an enforcement appeal, any person on whom a copy of the enforcement notice has been served,

   not less than 4 weeks before the date fixed for the holding of the inquiry.

(2) The local planning authority shall give any person who asks, a reasonable opportunity to inspect, and where practicable, take copies of the statement of common ground sent to the Secretary of State.

TCP (Enforcement) (Determination by Inspectors) (Inquiries Procedure) (Eng) R 2002

(3) For the purposes of the previous paragraph an opportunity shall be taken to have been given to a person where the person is notified of—

   (a) publication of the statement of common ground on a website,

   (b) the address of the website,

   (c) the place on the website where the document may be accessed, and how it may be accessed.

17 Procedure at inquiry

(1) Except as otherwise provided in these Rules, the inspector shall determine the procedure at an inquiry.

(2) At the start of the inquiry the inspector shall identify what are, in his opinion, the main issues to be considered at the inquiry and any matters on which he requires further explanation from the persons entitled or permitted to appear.

(3) Nothing in paragraph (2) shall preclude any person entitled or permitted to appear from referring to issues which they consider relevant to the consideration of the appeal but which were not issues identified by the inspector pursuant to that paragraph.

(4) Unless the inspector otherwise determines, the appellant shall begin and shall have the right of final reply; and the other persons entitled or permitted to appear shall be heard in such order as the inspector may determine.

(5) A person entitled to appear at an inquiry shall be entitled to call evidence and the appellant, the local planning authority and, in the case of an enforcement appeal, any person on whom a copy of the enforcement notice has been served shall be entitled to cross-examine persons giving evidence, but, subject to the foregoing and paragraphs (6) and (7), the calling of evidence and the cross-examination of persons giving evidence shall otherwise be at the discretion of the inspector.

(6) The inspector may refuse to permit the—

   (a) giving or production of evidence;

   (b) cross-examination of persons giving evidence; or

   (c) presentation of any matter,

   which he considers to be irrelevant or repetitious; but where he refuses to permit the giving of oral evidence, the person wishing to give the evidence may submit to him any evidence or other matter in writing before the close of the inquiry.

(7) Where a person gives evidence at an inquiry by reading a summary of his proof of evidence in accordance with rule 15(5)—

   (a) the proof of evidence referred to in rule 15(1) shall be treated as tendered in evidence, unless the person required to provide the summary notifies the inspector that he now wishes to rely on the contents of that summary alone; and

Appendix 5

(b) the person whose evidence the proof contains shall then be subject to cross-examination on it to the same extent as if it were evidence he had given orally.

(8) The inspector may direct that facilities shall be made available to any person appearing at an inquiry to take or obtain copies of documentary evidence open to public inspection.

(9) The inspector may—

(a) require any person appearing or present at an inquiry who, in his opinion, is behaving in a disruptive manner to leave; and

(b) refuse to permit that person to return; or

(c) permit him to return only on such conditions as he may specify,

but any such person may submit to him any evidence or other matter in writing before the close of the inquiry.

(10) The inspector may allow any person to alter or add to a statement of case served under rule 6 so far as may be necessary for the purposes of the inquiry; but he shall (if necessary by adjourning the inquiry) give every other person entitled to appear who is appearing at the inquiry an adequate opportunity of considering any fresh matter or document.

(11) The inspector may proceed with an inquiry in the absence of any person entitled to appear at it.

(12) The inspector may take into account any written representation or evidence or other document received by him from any person before an inquiry opens or during the inquiry provided that he discloses it at the inquiry.

(13) The inspector may from time to time adjourn an inquiry and, if the date, time and place of the adjourned inquiry are announced at the inquiry before the adjournment, no further notice shall be required.

(14) Where the Secretary of State expects an inquiry to last for 4 days or more, any person who appears at the inquiry and makes closing submissions, shall before the close of the inquiry, provide the inspector with a copy of their closing submissions in writing.

18 Site inspections

(1) The inspector may make an unaccompanied inspection of the land before or during an inquiry without giving notice of his intention to the persons entitled to appear at the inquiry.

(2) During an inquiry or after its close, the inspector—

(a) may inspect the land in the company of the appellant, the local planning authority, any person with an interest in the land and, in the case of an enforcement appeal, any other person on whom a copy of the enforcement notice has been served; and

(b) shall make such an inspection if so requested by the appellant or the local planning authority before or during an inquiry.

(3) In all cases where the inspector intends to make an accompanied site inspection he shall announce during the inquiry the date and time at which he proposes to make it.

(4) The inspector shall not be bound to defer an inspection of the kind referred to in paragraph (2) where any person mentioned in that paragraph is not present at the time appointed.

19 Procedure after inquiry

(1) Where an assessor has been appointed, he may, after the close of the inquiry make a report in writing to the inspector in respect of the matters on which he was appointed to advise, and where he does so the inspector shall state in his notification of his decision pursuant to rule 20 that such a report was made.

(2) When making his decision the inspector may disregard any written representations or evidence or any other document received after the close of the inquiry.

(3) If, after the close of the inquiry, an inspector proposes to take into consideration any new evidence or any new matter of fact (not being a matter of government policy) which was not raised at the inquiry and which he considers to be material to his decision, he shall not come to a decision without first—

   (a) notifying the persons entitled to appear at the inquiry who appeared at it of the matter in question; and

   (b) giving them an opportunity of making written representations to him or of asking for the re-opening of the inquiry,

and they shall send such written representations or request to re-open the inquiry to the Secretary of State within 3 weeks of the date of the notification.

(4) An inspector may, as he thinks fit, cause an inquiry to be re-opened, and he shall do so if asked by the appellant or the local planning authority in the circumstances and within the period mentioned in paragraph (3); and where an inquiry is re-opened—

   (a) the inspector shall send to the persons entitled to appear at the inquiry who appeared at it a written statement of the matters with respect to which further evidence is invited; and

   (b) paragraphs (2) to (7) of rule 9 shall apply as if references to an inquiry were references to a re-opened inquiry.

20 Notification of decision

(1) The inspector shall, as soon as practicable after reaching his decision, notify his decision on an appeal, and his reasons for it in writing to—

   (a) the appellant and the local planning authority;

   (b) all other persons entitled to appear at the inquiry who did appear; and

   (c) any other person who, having appeared at the inquiry, has asked to be notified of the decision.

(1A) Notification in writing of a decision and reasons shall be taken to have been given to a person for the purposes of this rule where—

Appendix 5

- (a) the Secretary of State and the person have agreed that decisions, reasons, and copies of reports required under this rule to be given in writing may instead be accessed by that person on a website;
- (b) the decision and reasons are a decision and reasons to which that agreement applies;
- (c) the Secretary of State has published the decision and reasons on a website;
- (d) the person is notified, in a manner for the time being agreed between him and the Secretary of State, of—
    - (i) the publication of the decision and reasons on a website;
    - (ii) the address of the website;
    - (iii) the place on the website where the decision and reasons may be accessed, and how they may be accessed.

(2) Any person entitled to be notified of the inspector's decision under paragraph (1) may apply to the Secretary of State in writing for an opportunity to inspect any documents listed in the notification and any report made by an assessor and the Secretary of State shall give him that opportunity.

(2A) For the purposes of the previous paragraph an opportunity shall be taken to have been given to a person where that person is notified of—
- (a) publication of the relevant documents on a website;
- (b) the address of the website;
- (c) the place on the website where the documents may be accessed, and how they may be accessed.

(3) Any application made pursuant to paragraph (2) shall be sent to the Secretary of State within 6 weeks of the date of the decision.

21 Procedure following remitting of appeal

(1) Where a decision of an inspector on an appeal for which an inquiry has been held is remitted by any court to the Secretary of State for rehearing and redetermination, the Secretary of State—
- (a) shall send to the persons entitled to appear at the inquiry who appeared at it a written statement of the matters on which further representations are invited in order for him to consider the appeal further;
- (b) shall give those persons the opportunity of making written representations to him about those matters or asking for the re-opening of the inquiry; and
- (c) may, as he thinks fit, cause the inquiry to be re-opened (whether by the same or a different inspector) and if he does so paragraphs (2) to (8) of rule 9 shall apply as if the references to an inquiry were references to a re-opened inquiry.

(2) Those persons making representations or asking for the inquiry to be re-opened under paragraph (1)(b) shall send such representations or requests to the Secretary of State within 3 weeks of the date of the written statement sent under paragraph (1)(a).

TCP (Enforcement) (Determination by Inspectors) (Inquiries Procedure) (Eng) R 2002

22 Allowing further time

The Secretary of State may at any time in any particular case allow further time for the taking of any step which is required or enabled to be taken by virtue of these Rules, and references in these Rules to a day by which, or period within which, any step is required or enabled to be taken shall be construed accordingly.

23 Additional copies

(1) The Secretary of State may at any time before the close of the inquiry request from any person entitled to appear additional copies of the following—

    (a) a statement of case sent in accordance with rule 6;

    (b) a proof of evidence sent in accordance with rule 15;

    (c) any other document or information sent to the Secretary of State before or during an inquiry,

and may specify the time within which such copies should be sent to him.

(2) Any person so requested shall send the copies to the Secretary of State within the period specified.

24 Sending of notices etc.

Notices or documents required or authorised to be served, sent or supplied under these Rules may be served, sent or supplied—

(a) by post; or

(b) by using electronic communications to serve, send or supply the notice or document (as the case may be) to a person at such address as may for the time being be specified by the person for that purpose.

24A Withdrawal of consent to use of electronic communications

Where a person is no longer willing to accept the use of electronic communications for any purpose of these Rules which is capable of being carried out electronically, he shall give notice in writing—

(a) withdrawing any address notified to the Secretary of State or to a local planning authority for that purpose, or

(b) revoking any agreement entered into with the Secretary of State or with a local planning authority for that purpose,

and such withdrawal or revocation shall be final and shall take effect on a date specified by the person in the notice but not less than seven days after the date on which the notice is given.

25 Revocation and savings

(1) Subject to paragraph (2), the Town and Country Planning (Enforcement) (Inquiries Procedure) Rules 1992 ('the 1992 Rules') shall continue to apply to any local inquiry in England held for the purposes of—

Appendix 5

       (a)   an enforcement appeal; or

       (b)   an appeal under section 195 of the Planning Act,

       which was made before 23rd December 2002.

(2)   Where a decision of an inspector on an appeal to which the 1992 Rules applied is subsequently remitted by any court to the Secretary of State for rehearing and redetermination, the matter shall be redetermined in accordance with these Rules or the Town and Country Planning (Enforcement) (Inquiries Procedure) (England) Rules 2002.

Appendix 6

Town and Country Planning (Referred Applications and Appeals Procedure) (Wales) Regulations 2017
SI 2017/544

PART 1   GENERAL

1 Title and commencement

The title of these Regulations is the Town and Country Planning (Referred Applications and Appeals Procedure) (Wales) Regulations 2017 and they come into force on the 5 May 2017.

2 Application

(1)   These Regulations apply in Wales in relation to—

   (a)   the applications listed in paragraph (2) made on or after the date on which these Regulations come into force; and

   (b)   the appeals listed in paragraph (2) where—

      (i)   the application which is the subject of the appeal is made on or after the date on which these Regulations come into force; or

      (ii)   the enforcement notice which is the subject of the appeal was issued on or after the date on which these Regulations come into force.

(2)   The applications and appeals referred to in paragraph (1) are—

   (a)   an application for planning permission referred to the Welsh Ministers under section 77 of the Planning Act (reference of applications to the Secretary of State);

   (b)   an appeal under section 78 of the Planning Act (right to appeal against planning decisions and failure to take such decisions) or under that section—

      (i)   as applied by section 198(3)(c) and (4) of that Act (tree preservation orders); and

      (ii)   as applied by regulations made under section 220 of the Planning Act (regulations controlling display of advertisements);

Appendix 6

(c) an appeal under section 174 of the Planning Act (appeal against enforcement notice) or under that section as applied by regulation 16 of, and Part 1 of Schedule 4 to, the 2015 Regulations (appeals against hazardous substances contravention notices);

(d) an appeal under section 195 of the Planning Act (appeals against refusal or failure to give decision on application for a certificate of lawfulness of existing or proposed use or development);

(e) an appeal under section 208 of the Planning Act (appeals against tree replacement notices);

(f) an appeal under section 217 of the Planning Act (appeal against a notice requiring the maintenance of land);

(g) an application for listed building consent referred to the Welsh Ministers under section 12, or for variation or discharge of conditions referred to them under that section as applied by section 19, or an appeal to them under section 20, of the Listed Buildings Act;

(h) an application for conservation area consent referred to the Welsh Ministers under section 12 (including an application to which that section is applied by section 19), or an appeal to them under section 20, of the Listed Buildings Act as those sections are applied by section 74(3) of that Act;

(i) an appeal under section 39 of the Listed Buildings Act (appeal against listed buildings enforcement notice) or under that section as applied by section 74(3) of that Act (appeal against conservation area enforcement notice);

(j) an application for hazardous substances consent referred to the Welsh Ministers under section 20 of the Hazardous Substances Act (reference of applications to Secretary of State);

(k) an appeal under section 21 of the Hazardous Substances Act (appeals against decisions or failure to take decisions relating to hazardous substances).

3 Interpretation

(1) In these Regulations—

'the Hazardous Substances Act' ('y Ddeddf Sylweddau Peryglus') means the Planning (Hazardous Substances) Act 1990;

'the Listed Buildings Act' ('y Ddeddf Adeiladau Rhestredig') means the Planning (Listed Buildings and Conservation Areas) Act 1990;

'the Planning Act' ('y Ddeddf Gynllunio') means the Town and Country Planning Act 1990;

'the 2015 Act' ('Deddf 2015') means the Planning (Wales) Act 2015;

'the 2012 Order' ('Gorchymyn 2012') means the Town and Country Planning (Development Management Procedure) (Wales) Order 2012;

'the 2012 Regulations' ('Rheoliadau 2012') means the Planning (Listed Buildings and Conservation Areas) (Wales) Regulations 2012;

'the 2015 Regulations' ('Rheoliadau 2015') means the Planning (Hazardous Substances) (Wales) Regulations 2015;

'appointed person' ('person penodedig') means a person appointed by the Welsh Ministers to determine an appeal or to report to the Welsh Ministers;

'advertisement application' ('cais i arddangos hysbyseb') means an application for express consent to display an advertisement made under Part 3 of the Town and Country Planning (Control of Advertisements) Regulations 1992;

'advertisement consent appeal' ('apêl ynghylch caniatâd >i arddangos >hysbyseb') means an appeal under section 78(1) of the Planning Act (as applied by regulations made under section 220 of the Planning Act) in relation to an advertisement application, except an appeal against the grant of any consent which is granted subject to conditions;

'appeal' ('apêl') means—

(a) the determination of a referred application; and

(b) an appeal made under sections 78, 174, 195, 208 or 217 of the Planning Act, sections 20 or 39 of the Listed Buildings Act or section 21 of the Hazardous Substances Act;

'appellant' ('apelydd') means, in the case of—

(a) an application referred to the Welsh Ministers under section 77 of the Planning Act, section 12 or 19 of the Listed Buildings Act or section 20 of the Hazardous Substances Act, the person who made that application to the local planning authority;

(b) an appeal under section 78 of the Planning Act, section 20 of the Listed Buildings Act or section 21 of the Hazardous Substances Act, the person whose application was refused, granted subject to conditions (other than advertisement consent appeals, householder appeals and minor commercial appeals) or not determined, by the local planning authority;

(c) an appeal under section 174 of the Planning Act, the person who has given notice of appeal to the Welsh Ministers under that section;

(d) an appeal under section 195 of the Planning Act, the person whose application under section 191 of that Act was refused;

(e) an appeal under section 208 of the Planning Act, the person who has given notice of appeal to the Welsh Ministers under that section;

(f) an appeal under section 217 of the Planning Act, the person who has given notice of appeal to the Welsh Ministers under that section;

(g) an appeal under section 39 of the Listed Buildings Act, the person who has given notice of appeal to the Welsh Ministers under that section;

'combined proceedings' ('achosion cyfunol') means proceedings which combine two or more of the following—

Appendix 6

- (a) written representations;
- (b) a hearing;
- (c) an inquiry.

'discontinuance notice' ('hysbysiad peidio â pharhau') means a notice under regulation 8 of the Town and Country Planning (Control of Advertisements) Regulations 1992;

'document' ('dogfen') includes a photograph, map or plan;

'dwellinghouse' ('tŷ anedd') does not include a building containing one or more flats, or a flat contained within such a building;

'electronic communication' ('cyfathrebiad electronig') has the meaning given in section 15(1) of the Electronic Communications Act 2000;

'enforcement appeal' ('apêl gorfodi') means an appeal against an enforcement notice;

'enforcement notice' ('hysbysiad gorfodi') means a notice under—

- (a) section 172(1) of the Planning Act;
- (b) section 182(1) of the Planning Act;
- (c) section 38(1) of the Listed Buildings Act or under that section as applied by section 74(3) of that Act;
- (d) section 46(1) of the Listed Buildings Act;
- (e) section 24(1) of the Hazardous Substances Act;
- (f) section 207(1) of the Planning Act;
- (g) section 215(1) of the Planning Act;

'full statement of case' ('datganiad achos llawn')—

- (a) in relation to appeals other than enforcement appeals, has the meaning given in—
    - (i) article 2 of the 2012 Order;
    - (ii) regulation 2 of the 2012 Regulations;
    - (iii) regulation 2 of the 2015 Regulations;
    - (iv) section 78 of the Planning Act as modified by regulation 15 of, and Part III of Schedule 4 to, the Town and Country Planning (Control of Advertisements) Regulations 1992;
    - (v) section 78 of the Planning Act as modified by regulation 15 of, and Part V of Schedule 4 to, the Town and Country Planning (Control of Advertisements) Regulations 1992;
    - (vi) section 78 of the Planning Act as modified by article 7 of, and Part I of Schedule 2 to, the Schedule (Form of Tree Preservation Order) to the Town and Country Planning (Trees) Regulations 1999;
- (b) in relation to enforcement appeals—

TCP (Referred Applicaitons and Appeals Procedure) (Wales) Regulations 2017

(i) in the case of an appeal against a notice under section 24(1) of the Hazardous Substances Act, has the meaning given in section 174 of the Planning Act as modified by regulation 16 of, and Part 1 of Schedule 4 to, the 2015 Regulations;

(ii) in all other cases, means the full statement of case submitted by the appellant under regulations 8, 9 or 10 of the Town and Country Planning (Enforcement Notices and Appeals) (Wales) Regulations 2017;

(c) means and is comprised of, in relation to appeals other than enforcement appeals—

(i) a written statement by the local planning authority containing full particulars of the case the local planning authority proposes to put forward in relation to the appeal; and

(ii) copies of any documents the local planning authority proposes to refer to or put in evidence;

(d) means and is comprised of, in relation to enforcement appeals—

(i) a written statement by the local planning authority containing—

(aa) a response to each ground of appeal pleaded by the appellant;

(bb) an indication of whether the local planning authority would be prepared to grant—

(bba) planning permission for the matters alleged in the enforcement notice to constitute a breach of planning control;

(bbb) listed building consent or conservation area consent for the works to which the listed building enforcement notice or conservation area enforcement notice relates, as the case may be;

(bbc) hazardous substances consent for the presence on, over or under the land of any quantity of hazardous substances to which the hazardous substances contravention notice relates;

(cc) particulars of the conditions, if any, they would wish to impose on any permission or consent they would be prepared to grant;

(dd) full particulars of the case the local planning authority proposes to put forward in relation to the appeal; and

(ii) copies of any documents the local planning authority proposes to refer to or put in evidence;

'householder appeal' ('apêl deiliad tŷ') means an appeal under section 78(1)(a) of the Planning Act in relation to a householder application but does not include—

Appendix 6

    (a)   an appeal against the grant of any planning permission which is granted subject to conditions; or

    (b)   an appeal which is accompanied by an appeal under section 174 of the Planning Act or under section 20 of the Listed Buildings Act;

'householder application' ('cais deiliad tŷ') means an application for—

    (a)   planning permission for the enlargement, improvement or other alteration of a dwellinghouse, or development within the curtilage of such a dwellinghouse, or

    (b)   change of use to enlarge the curtilage of a dwellinghouse,

for any purpose incidental to the enjoyment of the dwellinghouse but does not include—

    (i)   any other application for change of use,

    (ii)   an application for erection of a dwellinghouse, or

    (iii)   an application to change the number of dwellings in a building;

'interested persons' ('personau â buddiant') means—

    (a)   in relation to appeals other than enforcement appeals—

        (i)   any person notified or consulted in accordance with the Planning Act, Listed Buildings Act, Hazardous Substances Act, a development order or regulations, as the case may be, about the application; and

        (ii)   any other person who made representations to the local planning authority about that application;

    (b)   in relation to enforcement appeals and discontinuance notices, occupiers of properties in the locality of the site to which the enforcement notice or discontinuance notice relates; and

    (c)   in relation to enforcement appeals other than appeals against tree replacement notices, any person (other than the recipient of the enforcement notice) who, in the opinion of the local planning authority or hazardous substances authority, is affected by the matters alleged in the enforcement notice.

'by local advertisement' ('drwy hysbyseb lleol') means by publication of the notice in a newspaper circulating in the locality in which the land to which the appeal relates is situated;

'local planning authority' ('awdurdod cynllunio lleol') means in relation to—

    (a)   a referred application, the body which would have dealt with the application had it not been referred to the Welsh Ministers;

    (b)   an appeal under section 78 or section 195 of the Planning Act, section 20 of the Listed Buildings Act or section 21 of the Hazardous Substances Act, the body which was responsible for determining the application occasioning the appeal;

    (c)   an appeal under section 174, section 208 or section 217 of the Planning Act or section 39 of the Listed Buildings Act, the body which issued the notice occasioning the appeal;

'minor commercial appeal' ('apêl fasnachol fach') means an appeal under section 78(1)(a) of the Planning Act in relation to a minor commercial application but does not include—

(a) an appeal against the grant of any planning permission which is granted subject to conditions; or

(b) an appeal which is accompanied by an appeal under section 174 of the Planning Act or under section 20 of the Listed Buildings Act;

'minor commercial application' ('cais masnachol bach') means an application for planning permission for the enlargement, improvement or other alteration of an existing building of no more than 250 square metres gross external floor space at ground floor level, or part of that building, currently in use for any of the purposes set out in Schedule 1 to these Regulations which is an application for—

(a) the change of use from any of the purposes set out at paragraph 1 in Schedule 1 to these Regulations to any of the purposes set out in either paragraph 2 or paragraph 3 of that Schedule;

(b) the change of use from any of the purposes set out at paragraph 2 in Schedule 1 to these Regulations to any of the purposes set out in paragraph 3 of that Schedule; or

(c) the carrying out of building or other operations to a shop front;

'questionnaire' ('holiadur') means a document in the form supplied by the Welsh Ministers to a local planning authority for the purpose of any proceedings under these Regulations, and for this purpose a form is taken to be supplied where the Welsh Ministers have published it on a website and have notified the local planning authority of—

(a) publication of the form on the website;

(b) the address of the website; and

(c) the place on the website where the form may be accessed and how it may be accessed;

'referred application' ('cais atgyfeiriedig') means in relation to section 77 of the Planning Act, section 12 or 19 of the Listed Buildings Act and section 20 of the Hazardous Substances Act, the application which has been referred to the Welsh Ministers but does not include an application which is deemed to have been referred to the Welsh Ministers by virtue of regulation 9(3) of the 2012 Regulations;

'relevant time limits' ('terfynau amser perthnasol') means the time limits prescribed by these Regulations, or where the Welsh Ministers have exercised the power under regulation 7, any later time limit;

'representation' ('sylw') includes evidence, explanation, information and comments;

the 'representation period' ('cyfnod sylwadau') is the period of 6 weeks beginning with the starting date;

the 'starting date' ('dyddiad dechrau') means the date specified in the notice given by the Welsh Ministers under regulation 15 (notification of receipt of appeal);

Appendix 6

'working day' ('diwrnod gwaith') means a day which is not a Saturday, Sunday, Bank Holiday or other public holiday in Wales; and

'written representations' ('sylwadau >ysgrifenedig') includes supporting documents.

(2) In relation to the use of electronic communications for any purpose of these Regulations which is capable of being effected electronically—

(a) the expression 'address' ('cyfeiriad') includes any number or address used for the purposes of electronic communications;

(b) references to notices, representations or other documents, or to copies of such documents, include references to such documents or copies of them in electronic form.

4 Use of electronic communications

(1) Paragraphs (2) to (7) of this regulation apply where an electronic communication is used by a person for the purpose of fulfilling any requirement in these Regulations to give or send any notice or other document to any other person ('the recipient').

(2) The requirement will be taken to be fulfilled where the notice or other document transmitted by means of the electronic communication is—

(a) capable of being accessed by the recipient;

(b) legible in all material respects; and

(c) sufficiently permanent to be used for subsequent reference.

(3) In paragraph (2) 'legible in all material respects' ('darllenadwy ym mhob modd perthnasol') means that the information contained in the notice or other document is available to the recipient to no lesser extent than it would be if sent or given by means of a document in printed form.

(4) Where the electronic communication is received by the recipient outside the recipient's business hours, it will be taken to have been received on the next working day.

(5) A requirement in these Regulations that any document should be in writing is fulfilled where that document meets the criteria in paragraph (2), and 'written' ('ysgrifenedig') and cognate expressions are to be construed accordingly.

(6) Where an appellant, local planning authority or an interested party send any notice or other document to the Welsh Ministers using electronic communications, they will be taken to have agreed—

(a) to the use of such communications for all purposes relating to the appeal which are capable of being carried out electronically;

(b) that their address for the purposes of such communications is the address incorporated into, or otherwise logically associated with, the notice or document;

(c) that the deemed agreement of the appellant, local planning authority or an interested party under this paragraph will subsist until the appellant, local planning authority or interested party, as the case may be, gives notice in accordance with regulation 6 of a wish to revoke the agreement.

(7) Where an appellant, local planning authority or an interested party are taken to have agreed to the use of electronic communications under paragraph (6) they will also be taken to have agreed to the provision of a direct link to the notice or document on a website.

(8) A requirement in these Regulations to send more than one copy of a statement or other document is complied with by sending one copy only of the statement or other document in electronic form.

5 Transmission of documents

Notices or documents required to be sent or supplied under these Regulations may be sent or supplied by—

(a) post;

(b) using electronic communications to transmit the notice or document to a person at such address as may for the time being be specified by that person for such purpose; or

(c) providing a direct link to the notice or document to a person at such address as may for the time being be specified by that person for such purpose.

6 Withdrawal of consent to use of electronic communications

(1) Where a person is no longer willing to accept the use of electronic communications for any purpose of these Regulations which is capable of being effected electronically, the person must give notice in writing—

   (a) withdrawing any address notified to the Welsh Ministers or to a local planning authority for that purpose; or

   (b) revoking any agreement entered into with the Welsh Ministers or with a local planning authority for that purpose.

(2) Withdrawal or revocation under paragraph (1) is final and takes effect on the later of—

   (a) the date specified by the person in the notice but that date must not be less than 1 week after the date on which the notice is given; or

   (b) the expiry of the period of 1 week beginning with the date on which the notice is given.

7 Allowing further time

The Welsh Ministers may in any particular case give directions which extend the time limits prescribed by these Regulations.

8 Site inspections

(1) The Welsh Ministers may inspect the land to which the appeal relates.

(2) Where the Welsh Ministers intend to make an inspection under paragraph (1), they may notify the appellant and any other person as to the date and time of the inspection.

Appendix 6

(3) The Welsh Ministers are not required to defer an inspection where any person (including the appellant) is not present at the time appointed.

9 Further information

(1) The Welsh Ministers may request further representations from—

   (a) the appellant;

   (b) the local planning authority;

   (c) any interested person who made representations in relation to the appeal within 4 weeks of the starting date.

(2) In particular, the Welsh Ministers may in writing request—

   (a) from the person making any representation, a specified number of additional copies of that representation;

   (b) responses to questions posed by the Welsh Ministers about the matters contained in any representation.

(3) Each representation on any particular matter submitted following a request must not exceed 3,000 words and must be submitted in the time and manner specified by the Welsh Ministers.

(4) The Welsh Ministers may disregard any representation which—

   (a) is received out of time or in a manner other than that specified;

   (b) exceeds 3,000 words;

   (c) they regard as vexatious or frivolous; or

   (d) relates to the merits of policy set out in a development plan or any relevant policy statement made or published by the Welsh Ministers.

(5) In the event that a written representation exceeds 3,000 words, the Welsh Ministers may return the representation to the person submitting it with a request that the representation is re-submitted so that it does not exceed 3,000 words and within such time as the Welsh Ministers may specify when returning the representation.

(6) The Welsh Ministers may increase the number of words in paragraph (3) in any particular case and accordingly references to a maximum number of words are to such increased number.

(7) Where the Welsh Ministers exercise their discretion under paragraph (6) the written representation must be accompanied by a written summary containing no more than 1,500 words.

(8) The Welsh Ministers must make all written representations, and written responses to questions, received by them available in such manner as the Welsh Ministers think appropriate as soon as reasonably practicable.

10 Inspection of documents

(1) The local planning authority must give any person who so requests a reasonable opportunity to inspect and, where practicable, take copies of any document sent to or by it in accordance with these Regulations.

(2) For the purposes of paragraph (1), an opportunity will be taken to have been given to a person where the person is notified of—

 (a) publication on a website of the documents mentioned in that paragraph;

 (b) the address of the website;

 (c) the place on the website where the documents may be accessed and how they may be accessed.

11 Matters which may be raised in an appeal against decisions

(1) The appellant may not raise any matter which was not before the local planning authority at the time specified in paragraph (2) unless the appellant can demonstrate—

 (a) that the matter could not have been raised before that time, or

 (b) that its not being raised before that time was a consequence of exceptional circumstances.

(2) The time specified for the purposes of paragraph (1) is—

 (a) when the decision appealed against was made; or

 (b) when notice of appeal was given in relation to the local planning authority's failure to—

  (i) give notice to the appellant of their decision on the application;

  (ii) give notice to the appellant that they have exercised their power under section 70A or 70C of the Planning Act to decline to determine the application; or

  (iii) give notice that the application has been referred to the Welsh Ministers under section 77 of the Planning Act, section 12 of the Listed Buildings Act or section 20 of the Hazardous Substances Act.

(3) Nothing in paragraph (1) affects any requirement or entitlement to have regard to—

 (a) the provisions of the development plan, or

 (b) any other material circumstances.

12 Representations to be taken into account

In deciding an appeal the Welsh Ministers or the appointed person as the case may be, may disregard any representations, documents, evidence or information received after the relevant time limits.

13 Prescribed period

For the purposes of section 319B of the Planning Act, section 88E of the Listed Buildings Act and section 21B of the Hazardous Substances Act the prescribed period is 6 weeks from the starting date.

14 Determination of procedure

(1) The Welsh Ministers must in making their determination of procedure under section 319B(1) or section 217(7)(c) of the Planning Act, section 88E(1)

Appendix 6

of the Listed Buildings Act or section 21B(1) of the Hazardous Substances Act, identify which, if any, matters are to be considered at a hearing or an inquiry.

(2) Notice under section 319B(5), section 88E(5) or section 21B(5) must—

(a) identify the matters if any to be determined at a hearing or an inquiry;

(b) identify matters on which the Welsh Ministers require further representations;

(c) state whether such further representations are to be given in writing or at a hearing or inquiry; or

(d) contain a statement that the Welsh Ministers intend to determine the application on the basis of written representations.

(3) The Welsh Ministers must notify the appellant and the local planning authority within 6 weeks of the starting date of their determination of procedure under section 217(7)(c) which must set out the information specified in paragraph (2)(a) to (d).

(4) The provisions of regulation 9 apply if any further representations are requested by the Welsh Ministers.

PART 2 INITIAL PROCEDURE

15 Notification of receipt of appeal

(1) Paragraph (2) applies where—

(a) the Welsh Ministers have received all the documents they require to enable them to consider an appeal;

(b) the requisite fee (where applicable) has been paid in respect of the appeal; and

(c) in the case of a referred application, either the full statement of case and the application file have been received, or the period of 4 weeks beginning with the date on which the notice of reference is served has expired.

(2) The Welsh Ministers must, as soon as reasonably practicable advise the appellant and the local planning authority in writing—

(a) of the starting date;

(b) of the reference number allocated to the appeal;

(c) of the address to which written communications to the Welsh Ministers about the appeal are to be sent; and

(d) in the case of enforcement appeals, the grounds on which the appeal is being made.

(3) In the case of an appeal under section 208 of the Planning Act the Welsh Ministers must, as soon as reasonably practicable after receipt, send to the local planning authority a copy of the notice of appeal and full statement of case.

16 Questionnaire

(1) The local planning authority must send to the Welsh Ministers, and copy to the appellant, so as to be received within 5 working days of the starting date—

   (a) a completed questionnaire;

   (b) a copy of each of the documents referred to in it; and

   (c) in the case of enforcement appeals, a copy of the enforcement notice.

(2) Paragraph (1) does not apply to referred applications.

17 Notice to interested persons

(1) The local planning authority must give written notice of the appeal, so as to be received within 5 working days of the starting date, to interested persons.

(2) A notice under paragraph (1) must—

   (a) state the name of the appellant and the address of the site to which the appeal relates;

   (b) describe the subject matter of the appeal;

   (c) set out the matters notified to the appellant and the local planning authority under regulation 15(2);

   (d) state that copies of any representations made by interested persons to the local planning authority will be sent to the Welsh Ministers and the appellant;

   (e) state that any such representations will be considered by the Welsh Ministers when determining the appeal unless they are withdrawn within 4 weeks of the starting date;

   (f) state that in relation to appeals other than householder, advertisement consent and minor commercial appeals further representations may be sent to the Welsh Ministers so as to be received within 4 weeks of the starting date and that any representations must be accompanied by two copies.

PART 3 PROCEDURE FOR HOUSEHOLDER, ADVERTISEMENT CONSENT AND MINOR COMMERCIAL APPEALS

18 Application of Part 3

This Part only applies where—

(a) a householder, advertisement consent or minor commercial appeal is made in relation to an application; and

(b) the Welsh Ministers determine that it is a matter which is to be considered on the basis of written representations only.

19 Representations

(1) The appellant's representations in relation to the appeal (other than a referred application) will be deemed to comprise the notice of appeal and the documents accompanying it.

Appendix 6

(2) The appellant's representations in relation to a referred application will be deemed to comprise the application and its supporting documents.

(3) The local planning authority's representations in relation to the appeal will be deemed to comprise the completed questionnaire and the documents accompanying it.

(4) The Welsh Ministers must as soon as reasonably practicable after receipt, send a copy of the representations made by the local planning authority to the appellant and must send a copy of the representations made by the appellant to the local planning authority.

20 Transfer of appeal from Part 3

(1) At any time before an appeal is determined, the Welsh Ministers may determine that the procedures set out in this Part are no longer suitable for that appeal.

(2) Where such a determination is made the Welsh Ministers must notify the appellant and the local planning authority in writing that—

(a) the appeal is to be transferred from the procedures in this Part of these Regulations; and

(b) the appeal will proceed in accordance with Part 4 of these Regulations or by means of a hearing, inquiry or combined proceedings to such extent as the Welsh Ministers may specify having regard to any steps already taken in relation to those proceedings.

PART 4 WRITTEN REPRESENTATIONS

21 Application of Part 4

(1) This Part applies where—

(a) notice of appeal has been received; and

(b) the Welsh Ministers determine that the appeal is to be considered on the basis of written representations, a hearing, an inquiry or combined proceedings; or

(c) the appeal has been transferred from Part 3.

(2) This Part also applies where—

(a) the Welsh Ministers have made a determination that all or part of the appeal is to be considered on the basis of a hearing or inquiry, and

(b) they subsequently vary that determination such that the appeal or parts of the appeal is or are to be considered on the basis of written representations,

to such extent as the Welsh Ministers may specify having regard to any steps already taken in relation to the appeal.

22 Representations

(1) The appellant's representations in relation to the appeal (other than a referred application) will be deemed to comprise the notice of appeal, its accompanying documents (where applicable) and the full statement of case.

(2) The appellant's representations in relation to a referred application will be deemed to comprise the application, its supporting documents and, if the appellant so elects, a full statement of case.

(3) In relation to appeals, other than referred applications and enforcement appeals, the local planning authority may—

    (a) elect to treat the questionnaire, and the documents accompanying it, as their representations in relation to the appeal, and where they do so, they must notify the Welsh Ministers and the appellant accordingly when they send to the Welsh Ministers, and copy to the appellant, the questionnaire in accordance with regulation 16; or

    (b) submit a full statement of case to the Welsh Ministers which, together with the questionnaire and its accompanying documents, will be deemed to comprise the local planning authority's representations in relation to the appeal.

(4) In relation to a referred application, the local planning authority may elect to submit a full statement of case to the Welsh Ministers.

(5) In relation to enforcement appeals and discontinuance notices, the local planning authority must submit a full statement of case to the Welsh Ministers which, together with the questionnaire and its accompanying documents (where applicable), will be deemed to comprise the local planning authority's representations in relation to the appeal.

(6) The local planning authority must send two copies of their full statement of case under paragraphs (3)(b), (4) and (5) to the Welsh Ministers so as to be received within 4 weeks of the starting date.

(7) The Welsh Ministers must send a copy of the local planning authority's full statement of case—

    (a) to the appellant; and

    (b) in the case of an enforcement appeal, to any person on whom a copy of the enforcement notice has been served.

23 Interested persons' representations

(1) A person who has been notified under regulation 17 may send representations to the Welsh Ministers so as to be received by the Welsh Ministers within 4 weeks of the starting date.

(2) Interested persons must send three copies of any representations they make to the Welsh Ministers so as to be received within 4 weeks of the starting date.

(3) The Welsh Ministers must send a copy of any representations received from interested persons to the appellant and the local planning authority.

24 Further representations

(1) The appellant, the local planning authority, and interested persons may send written comments on each other's representations to the Welsh Ministers so as to be received within the representation period.

Appendix 6

(2) The appellant and the local planning authority must send two copies of any representations they make to the Welsh Ministers so as to be received within the representation period.

(3) Interested persons must send three copies of the any representations they make to the Welsh Ministers so as to be received within the representation period.

(4) The Welsh Ministers must send a copy of the written comments of each party to the other parties.

25 Written representations inappropriate

(1) At any time before an appeal is determined, the Welsh Ministers may determine that the procedures set out in this Part are no longer suitable for that appeal.

(2) Where such a determination is made the Welsh Ministers must notify the appellant and the local planning authority in writing that the appeal will proceed in accordance with Part 5 of these Regulations or by means of combined proceedings, to such extent as the Welsh Ministers may specify having regard to any steps already taken in relation to those proceedings.

PART 5 HEARINGS

26 Application of Part 5

(1) This Part applies where—

   (a) notice of appeal has been received; and

   (b) the Welsh Ministers determine that the appeal is to be considered in whole or in part on the basis of a hearing.

(2) This Part also applies where—

   (a) the Welsh Ministers have made a determination that all or part of the appeal is to be considered on the basis of written representations or inquiry; and

   (b) they subsequently vary that determination such that the appeal or parts of the appeal is or are to be considered on the basis of a hearing;

to such extent as the Welsh Ministers may specify having regard to any steps already taken in relation to the appeal.

27 Notification of name of appointed person

(1) The Welsh Ministers must notify the name of the appointed person to every person invited to take part in the hearing.

(2) Where the Welsh Ministers appoint another person instead of the person previously appointed and it is not practicable to notify the appointment before the hearing is held, the appointed person holding the hearing must, at its commencement, announce their name and the fact of their appointment.

28 Appointment of assessor

Where the Welsh Ministers appoint an assessor under paragraph 6 of Schedule 6 to the Planning Act, paragraph 6 of Schedule 3 to the Listed Buildings Act or paragraph 6

TCP (Referred Applicaitons and Appeals Procedure) (Wales) Regulations 2017

of the Schedule to the Hazardous Substances Act, they must notify the appellant, the local planning authority and any person invited to take part in the hearing of the name of the assessor and of the matters on which the assessor is to advise the appointed person.

29 Date, place and notification of hearing

(1) The Welsh Ministers must fix the date for the hearing which must be no later than 4 weeks after the end of the representation period.

(2) Where the Welsh Ministers consider it impracticable for the hearing to be held on a date fixed in accordance with paragraph (1), the date for the hearing must be the earliest date which the Welsh Ministers consider is practicable.

(3) Where the Welsh Ministers are satisfied, having regard to the nature of the appeal, that it is reasonable to do so, the Welsh Ministers may direct that different parts of a hearing are held at different locations.

(4) The Welsh Ministers must give at least 4 weeks' written notice of the date, time and place fixed for the hearing to—

(a) the appellant;

(b) the local planning authority; and

(c) any person invited to take part in the hearing.

(5) The written notice under paragraph (4) must identify the matters to be determined at the hearing and name the appointed person.

(6) The Welsh Ministers may vary the date fixed for the hearing, whether or not the date as varied is within the period of 4 weeks mentioned in paragraph (1), and paragraph (4) applies to a variation of a date as it applies to the date originally fixed.

(7) The Welsh Ministers may vary the time or place for the hearing and must give such notice of any variation as appears to them to be reasonable.

(8) Where an appeal is withdrawn after notice of the hearing has been given, the Welsh Ministers must give such notice of the cancellation of the hearing as appears to them to be reasonable.

30 Public notice of hearing

(1) The Welsh Ministers may require the local planning authority to take one or more of the following steps——

(a) not less than 2 weeks before the date fixed for the hearing, post and maintain a notice of the hearing—

(i) in a conspicuous place, or as close as is reasonably practicable to the land to which the appeal relates;

(ii) in one or more places where public notices are usually posted in the area in which the land to which the appeal relates is situated;

(b) not less than 2 weeks before the date fixed for the hearing, publish a notice of the hearing by local advertisement in the area in which the land to which the appeal relates is situated;

Appendix 6

   (c) send a notice of the hearing to such persons or classes of persons as they may specify, within such period as they may specify.

(2) Where a direction has been given under regulation 29(3), paragraph (1) has effect with the substitution—

   (a) for references to the hearing, with references to the part of the hearing which is to be held at a place specified in the direction; and

   (b) for references to the appeal, with references to that part of the appeal which is to be the subject of that part of the hearing.

(3) Any notice posted under paragraph (1)(a) must be readily visible to, and legible by, members of the public.

(4) Where, without any fault or intention of the local planning authority, the notice is removed, obscured or defaced before the commencement of the hearing, the local planning authority is not for that reason to be treated as having failed to comply with the requirements of paragraph (3) if the local planning authority has taken reasonable steps for the protection of the notice and, if need be, its replacement.

(5) A notice of a hearing posted, published or sent under paragraph (1) must contain—

   (a) a statement of the date, time and place of the hearing and of the powers enabling the Welsh Ministers to determine the appeal;

   (b) a written description of the land sufficient to identify approximately its location;

   (c) a brief description of the subject matter of the appeal; and

   (d) details of the place where and when copies of the application which is the subject of the appeal, the local planning authority's completed questionnaire and all other documents sent by and copied to the authority under these Regulations can be inspected.

31 Participation in a hearing

(1) The persons who may take part in a hearing are—

   (a) the appellant;

   (b) the local planning authority;

   (c) any person invited to take part by the Welsh Ministers.

(2) Nothing in paragraph (1) precludes the Welsh Ministers from permitting any other person to take part in a hearing.

(3) Any person who takes part may do so on their own behalf or be represented by any other person.

32 Absence, adjournment etc.

(1) The Welsh Ministers may proceed with a hearing in the absence of the appellant, the local planning authority and any person invited to take part.

(2) The Welsh Ministers may from time to time adjourn a hearing and, if the date, time and place of the adjourned hearing are announced at the hearing before the adjournment, no further notice is required.

33 Procedure at hearing

(1) The appointed person presides at any hearing and must determine the procedure at the hearing, subject to these Regulations.

(2) A hearing is to take the form of a discussion led by the appointed person and cross-examination is not to be permitted.

(3) Where the appointed person considers that cross-examination is required the appointed person must consider (after consulting the appellant) whether the hearing should be closed and an inquiry held instead.

(4) At the start of the hearing the appointed person must identify the matters on which the appointed person requires representations at the hearing.

(5) The appellant, the local planning authority and any person invited to take part in a hearing may call evidence.

(6) The appointed person may permit any other person to call evidence.

(7) The appointed person may refuse to permit the giving or production of evidence or presentation of any other matter which the appointed person considers to be irrelevant or repetitious.

(8) Where the appointed person refuses to permit the giving of oral evidence, the person wishing to give the evidence may submit to the appointed person representations in writing before the close of the hearing.

(9) The appointed person may—

   (a) require any person taking part in, or present at, a hearing who, in the appointed person's opinion, is behaving in a disruptive manner to leave; and

   (b) refuse to permit that person to return; or

   (c) permit that person to return only on such conditions as the appointed person may specify.

(10) Any person required to leave a hearing may submit to the appointed person representations in writing before the close of the hearing.

(11) The appointed person may take into account any written representation or any other document received by the appointed person from any person before a hearing opens or during the hearing provided the appointed person discloses it at the hearing.

(12) The appointed person may invite any person taking part in the hearing to make closing submissions and any person doing so must before the close of the hearing provide the appointed person with a copy of their closing submissions in writing.

(13) The appointed person may permit any person to make oral representations at the hearing.

(14) Any person entitled or permitted to make oral representations at a hearing may do so on their own behalf or be represented by another person.

34 Hearing inappropriate

(1) At any time before an appeal is determined, the Welsh Ministers may determine that the procedures set out in this Part are no longer suitable for that appeal.

Appendix 6

(2) Where such a determination is made the Welsh Ministers must notify the appellant and the local planning authority in writing that—

    (a) the appeal is to be transferred from the procedures in this Part of these Regulations; and

    (b) the appeal will proceed in accordance with Part 6 of these Regulations or by means of combined proceedings to such extent as the Welsh Ministers may specify having regard to any steps already taken in relation to those proceedings.

PART 6 INQUIRIES

35 Application of Part 6

(1) This Part applies where—

    (a) notice of appeal has been received; and

    (b) the Welsh Ministers determine that the appeal is to be considered in whole or in part on the basis of an inquiry.

(2) This Part also applies where—

    (a) the Welsh Ministers have made a determination that all or part of the appeal is to be considered on the basis of written representations or a hearing; and

    (b) they subsequently vary that determination such that the appeal or parts of the appeal is or are to be considered on the basis of an inquiry,

to such extent as the Welsh Ministers may specify having regard to any steps already taken in relation to the appeal.

36 Notification of name of appointed person

(1) The Welsh Ministers must notify the name of the appointed person to every person invited to take part in the inquiry.

(2) Where the Welsh Ministers appoint another person instead of the person previously appointed and it is not practicable to notify the appointment before the inquiry is held, the appointed person holding the inquiry must, at its commencement, announce their name and the fact of their appointment.

37 Appointment of assessor

Where the Welsh Ministers appoint an assessor under paragraph 6 of Schedule 6 to the Planning Act, paragraph 6 of Schedule 3 to the Listed Buildings Act or paragraph 6 of the Schedule to the Hazardous Substances Act, they must notify the appellant, the local planning authority and any person invited to take part in the inquiry of the name of the assessor and of the matters on which the assessor is to advise the appointed person.

38 Participation in an inquiry

(1) The persons who may take part in an inquiry are—

TCP (Referred Applicaitons and Appeals Procedure) (Wales) Regulations 2017

    (a)   the appellant;

    (b)   the local planning authority;

    (c)   any person invited to take part by the Welsh Ministers.

(2)   Nothing in paragraph (1) precludes the Welsh Ministers from permitting any other person to take part in an inquiry.

(3)   Any person who takes part may do so on their own behalf or be represented by any other person.

39 Absence, adjournment etc.

(1)   The Welsh Ministers may proceed with an inquiry in the absence of the appellant, the local planning authority and any persons invited to take part.

(2)   The Welsh Ministers may from time to time adjourn an inquiry and, if the date, time and place of the adjourned inquiry are announced at the inquiry before the adjournment, no further notice is required.

40 Pre-inquiry meetings

(1)   The appointed person may hold a pre-inquiry meeting prior to an inquiry to consider what may be done with a view to securing that the inquiry is conducted efficiently and expeditiously.

(2)   An appointed person must give not less than 2 weeks' written notice of a pre-inquiry meeting which the appointed person proposes to hold under paragraph (1) to—

    (a)   the appellant;

    (b)   the local planning authority;

    (c)   any person invited to take part at the pre-inquiry meeting.

(3)   Where a pre-inquiry meeting has been held under paragraph (1), the appointed person may hold a further pre-inquiry meeting and must arrange for such notice to be given of a further pre-inquiry meeting as appears necessary.

(4)   The appointed person—

    (a)   is to preside at any pre-inquiry meeting;

    (b)   is to determine the matters to be discussed and the procedure to be followed;

    (c)   may require any person present at the pre-inquiry meeting who, in the appointed person's opinion, is behaving in a disruptive manner to leave;

    (d)   may refuse to permit that person to return or to attend any further pre-inquiry meeting, or

    (e)   may permit that person to return or attend only on such conditions as the appointed person may specify.

41 Inquiry timetable

(1)   The appointed person may prepare a timetable for the proceedings in respect of inquiries and may do so at, or at part of, an inquiry.

Appendix 6

(2) The appointed person may, at any time, vary the timetable arranged under paragraph (1).

(3) The appointed person may specify in a timetable arranged under this regulation a date by which any written statement of evidence and summary sent in accordance with regulation 44 must be sent to the Welsh Ministers.

42 Date, place and notification of inquiry

(1) The Welsh Ministers must fix the date for the inquiry which must be no later than—

    (a) 12 weeks after the end of the representation period; or

    (b) (if later) in a case where a pre-inquiry meeting is held under regulation 40(1), 4 weeks after the conclusion of that meeting (or such shorter period after the conclusion of that meeting as the appellant, the local planning authority and the appointed person may agree).

(2) Where the Welsh Ministers consider it impracticable for the inquiry to be held on a date fixed in accordance with paragraph (1), the date for the inquiry must be the earliest date which the Welsh Ministers consider is practicable.

(3) Where the Welsh Ministers are satisfied, having regard to the nature of the application, that it is reasonable to do so, the Welsh Ministers may direct that different parts of an inquiry are held at different locations.

(4) The Welsh Ministers must give at least 4 weeks' written notice of the date, time and place fixed by them for the inquiry to—

    (a) the appellant;

    (b) the local planning authority; and

    (c) any person invited to take part in the inquiry.

(5) The written notice under paragraph (4) must identify the matters to be determined at the inquiry and name the appointed person.

(6) The Welsh Ministers may vary the date fixed for the inquiry, whether or not the date as varied is within the period of 12 weeks mentioned in paragraph (1), and paragraph (4) applies to a variation of a date as it applies to the date originally fixed.

(7) The Welsh Ministers may vary the time or place for the inquiry and must give such notice of any variation as appears to them to be reasonable.

(8) Where an appeal is withdrawn after notice of the inquiry has been given, the Welsh Ministers must give such notice of the cancellation of the inquiry as appears to them to be reasonable.

43 Public notice of inquiry

(1) The Welsh Ministers may require the local planning authority to take one or more of the following steps—

    (a) not less than 2 weeks before the date fixed for the inquiry, post and maintain a notice of the inquiry—

(i) in a conspicuous place, or as close as is reasonably practicable to the land to which the appeal relates;

(ii) in one or more places where public notices are usually posted in the area in which the land to which the appeal relates is situated;

(b) not less than 2 weeks before the date fixed for the inquiry, publish a notice of the inquiry by local advertisement in the area in which the land to which the appeal relates is situated;

(c) send a notice of the hearing to such persons or classes of persons as they may specify, within such period as they may specify.

(2) Where a direction has been given under regulation 42(3), paragraph (1) has effect with the substitution—

(a) for references to the inquiry, with references to the part of the inquiry which is to be held at a place specified in the direction; and

(b) for references to the appeal, with references to that part of the appeal which is to be the subject of that part of the inquiry.

(3) Any notice posted under paragraph (1)(a) must be readily visible to, and legible by, members of the public.

(4) Where, without any fault or intention of the local planning authority, the notice is removed, obscured or defaced before the commencement of the inquiry, the local planning authority is not for that reason to be treated as having failed to comply with the requirements of paragraph (3) if the local planning authority has taken reasonable steps for the protection of the notice and, if need be, its replacement.

(5) A notice of an inquiry posted, published or sent under paragraph (1) must contain—

(a) a statement of the date, time and place of the inquiry and of the powers enabling the Welsh Ministers to determine the appeal;

(b) a written description of the land sufficient to identify approximately its location;

(c) a brief description of the subject matter of the appeal; and

(d) details of the place where and when copies of the application which is the subject of the appeal, the local planning authority's completed questionnaire and all other documents sent by and copied to the authority under these Regulations can be inspected.

44 Written statements of evidence

(1) If the appellant, the local planning authority or any person invited to take part in the inquiry propose to give, or to call another person to give, evidence at the inquiry by reading a written statement—

(a) the appellant must send one copy of the statement, together with a written summary, to the local planning authority;

(b) the local planning authority must send one copy of the statement, together with a written summary, to the appellant;

Appendix 6

    (c)   the appellant and local planning authority must simultaneously send one copy of their statement, together with a written summary, to the Welsh Ministers;

    (d)   each person invited to take part in the inquiry must send one copy of their statement, together with a written summary, to the Welsh Ministers.

(2)   The Welsh Ministers must, as soon as reasonably practicable after receipt—

    (a)   send a copy of the written statement of evidence, together with any summary, of each person invited to take part in the inquiry to the local planning authority; and

    (b)   send a copy of each written statement of evidence, together with any summary, to each person invited to take part in the inquiry.

(3)   No written summary is required where the statement of evidence proposed to be read contains no more than 1,500 words.

(4)   The statement of evidence and any summary must be received by the Welsh Ministers no later than—

    (a)   4 weeks before the date fixed for the inquiry; or

    (b)   where a timetable has been arranged under regulation 41, the date specified in that timetable.

(5)   The Welsh Ministers must send to the appointed person, as soon as reasonably practicable after receipt, any statement of evidence together with any summary sent to them in accordance with this regulation and received by them within the relevant period, if any, specified in this regulation.

(6)   Where a written summary is provided in accordance with paragraph (1), only that summary is to be read at the inquiry unless the appointed person permits or requires otherwise.

(7)   Any person required by this regulation to send copies of a statement of evidence to the Welsh Ministers, must send with them the same number of copies of the whole, or the relevant part, of any document referred to in the statement, unless a copy of the document or relevant part of the document in question is already available for inspection under regulation 10.

45 Procedure at inquiry

(1)   The appointed person presides at the inquiry and must determine the procedure at the inquiry, subject to these Regulations.

(2)   At the start of the inquiry the appointed person must identify the matters on which the appointed person requires representations at the inquiry.

(3)   The appellant, the local planning authority and any person invited to take part in an inquiry may call evidence.

(4)   The appointed person may permit any other person to call evidence.

(5)   The appellant, local planning authority and any persons invited to take part in the inquiry are to be heard in such order as the appointed person may determine.

(6)   The appellant, local planning authority and any person invited to take part in an inquiry may cross examine persons giving evidence but, subject to the

TCP (Referred Applicaitons and Appeals Procedure) (Wales) Regulations 2017

foregoing and paragraphs (7) and (8), the calling of evidence and the cross examination of persons giving evidence are otherwise at the discretion of the appointed person.

(7) The appointed person may refuse to permit—

    (a) the giving or production of evidence;

    (b) the cross-examination of persons giving evidence; or

    (c) the presentation of any matter,

which the appointed person considers to be irrelevant or repetitious.

(8) Where a person gives evidence at an inquiry by reading a summary of their written statement of evidence in accordance with regulation 44(6)—

    (a) the written statement referred to in regulation 44(1) is to be treated as tendered in evidence unless the person required to provide the summary notifies the appointed person of a wish to rely on the contents of that summary alone; and

    (b) the person whose evidence the written statement contains is to be open to cross examination on it to the same extent as if it were evidence that had been given orally.

(9) Where the appointed person refuses to permit the giving of oral evidence, the person wishing to give the evidence may submit the evidence in writing to the appointed person before the close of the inquiry.

(10) The appointed person may—

    (a) require any person taking part in, or present at, an inquiry who, in the appointed person's opinion, is behaving in a disruptive manner to leave; and

    (b) refuse to permit that person to return; or

    (c) permit that person to return only on such conditions as the appointed person may specify.

(11) Any person required to leave an inquiry may submit to the appointed person representations in writing before the close of the inquiry.

(12) The appointed person may direct that facilities are afforded to any person taking part in an inquiry to take or obtain copies of documents that are open to public inspection.

(13) The appointed person may take into account any written representation or any other document received by the appointed person from any person before an inquiry opens or during the inquiry provided that the appointed person discloses it at the inquiry.

(14) The appointed person may invite any person taking part in the inquiry to make closing submissions.

(15) Any person who makes closing submissions must by the close of the inquiry provide the appointed person with a copy of those closing submissions in writing.

Appendix 6

46 Inquiry inappropriate

(1) At any time before an appeal is determined, the Welsh Ministers may determine that the procedures set out in this Part are no longer suitable for that appeal.

(2) Where such a determination is made the Welsh Ministers must notify the appellant and the local planning authority in writing that—

  (a) the appeal is to be transferred from the procedures in this Part of these Regulations; and

  (b) the appeal will proceed in accordance with Part 5 of these Regulations or by means of combined proceedings to such extent as the Welsh Ministers may specify having regard to any steps already taken in relation to those proceedings.

PART 7 PROCEDURE AFTER WRITTEN REPRESENTATIONS, HEARINGS, INQUIRES OR COMBINED PROCEEDINGS

Chapter 1 Appeals determined by appointed persons following written representations, hearings, inquiries or combined proceedings

47 Procedure after proceedings

(1) The appointed person must make a report in writing ('the appointed person's decision report')—

  (a) in relation to an appeal dealt with by means of written representations, when the appointed person has considered the written representations; or

  (b) after the close of the hearing, inquiry or combined proceedings.

(2) The appointed person's decision report must include the appointed person's conclusions and decision on the appeal.

(3) Where an assessor has been appointed, the assessor must, after the close of the hearing, inquiry or combined proceedings make a report in writing to the appointed person in respect of the matters on which the assessor was appointed to advise.

(4) Where an assessor makes a report in accordance with paragraph (3), the appointed person's decision report must state how far the appointed person agrees or disagrees with the assessor's report and, where the appointed person disagrees with the assessor, the reasons for that disagreement.

(5) When making the decision, the appointed person may disregard—

  (a) in relation to an appeal, or part of an appeal dealt with by means of written representations, any written representations received outside the relevant time limits;

  (b) any written representations, evidence or any other document received after the close of the hearing or inquiry.

(6) In relation to an appeal or part of an appeal dealt with by means of written representations, if after the relevant time limits, an appointed person proposes to take into consideration any new evidence or any new matter of fact (not being

a matter of Welsh Ministers' policy) which was not included in the written representations and which the appointed person considers to be material to the decision, the appointed person must not come to a decision without first—

(a) notifying the appellant, the local planning authority and interested persons who made written representations; and

(b) affording those notified under subparagraph (a) an opportunity of making written representations upon the new evidence or new matter of fact.

(7) If, after the close of the hearing or inquiry, an appointed person proposes to take into consideration any new evidence or any new matter of fact (not being a matter of Welsh Ministers' policy) which was not raised at the hearing or inquiry and which the appointed person considers to be material to the decision, the appointed person must not come to a decision without first—

(a) notifying the appellant, the local planning authority, the interested persons who made written representations and the persons who took part in the hearing or inquiry; and

(b) affording those notified under subparagraph (a) an opportunity of making written representations upon the new evidence or new matter of fact or of asking for the re-opening of the hearing or inquiry.

(8) The appellant, the local planning authority, the interested persons who made written representations and the persons who took part in the hearing or inquiry must ensure that written representations or requests to re-open the hearing or inquiry made under paragraphs (6) and (7) are received by the Welsh Ministers within the period specified in the Welsh Ministers' notification under those paragraphs.

(9) An appointed person may, as the appointed person thinks fit, cause a hearing or inquiry to be re-opened, and must do so if asked by the appellant or the local planning authority in the circumstances mentioned in paragraph (7) and within the period specified in the Welsh Ministers notification under paragraph (7).

(10) Where a hearing or inquiry is re-opened—

(a) the appointed person must send to the appellant, the local planning authority, the interested persons who made written representations and the persons who took part in the hearing or inquiry a written statement of the matters in respect of which further evidence is invited;

(b) further evidence submitted following a request must not exceed 3,000 words and must be submitted in the time and manner specified by the appointed person; and

(c) paragraphs (3) to (8) of regulation 29, regulation 30, paragraphs (3) to (8) of regulation 42 and regulation 43 apply as if the references to a hearing or an inquiry were references to a re-opened hearing or inquiry.

Chapter 2   Appeals determined by the Welsh Ministers following written representations, hearings, inquiries or combined proceedings

48 Procedure after proceedings

(1) The appointed person must make a report in writing to the Welsh Ministers—

Appendix 6

    (a)   in relation to an appeal dealt with by means of written representations, when the appointed person has considered the written representations; or

    (b)   after the close of the hearing, inquiry or combined proceedings.

(2)   The report must include the appointed person's conclusions and recommendations (or the appointed person's reasons for not making any recommendations).

(3)   Where an assessor has been appointed, the assessor must, after the close of the proceedings, make a report in writing to the appointed person in respect of the matters on which the assessor was appointed to advise.

(4)   Where an assessor makes a report in accordance with paragraph (3), the appointed person must append it to the appointed person's own report and must state in that report how far the appointed person agrees or disagrees with the assessor's report and, where the appointed person disagrees with the assessor, the reasons for that disagreement.

(5)   When making their decision the Welsh Minsters may disregard—

    (a)   in relation to an appeal or part of an appeal dealt with by means of written representations, any written representations received outside the relevant time limits;

    (b)   any written representations, evidence or any other document received after the close of the hearing or inquiry.

(6)   Paragraph (7) applies in relation to an appeal or part of an appeal dealt with by means of written representations, if the Welsh Ministers are disposed to disagree with a recommendation made by the appointed person because they—

    (a)   differ from the appointed person on any matter of fact mentioned in, or appearing to them to be material to, a conclusion reached by the appointed person; or

    (b)   propose to take into consideration any new evidence or any new matter of fact (not being a matter of Welsh Ministers' policy).

(7)   The Welsh Ministers must not come to a decision which is at variance with the recommendation made by the appointed person without first—

    (a)   notifying the appellant, the local planning authority and the interested persons who made written representations; and

    (b)   affording those notified under subparagraph (a) an opportunity of making written representations upon the new evidence or new matter of fact.

(8)   Paragraph (9) applies if, after the close of the hearing or inquiry, the Welsh Ministers are disposed to disagree with a recommendation made by the appointed person because they—

    (a)   differ from the appointed person on any matter of fact mentioned in, or appearing to them to be material to, a conclusion reached by the appointed person; or

    (b)   propose to take into consideration any new evidence or new matter of fact (not being a matter of Welsh Ministers' policy).

(9)   The Welsh Ministers must not come to a decision which is at variance with the recommendation made by the appointed person without first—

(a) notifying the appellant, the local planning authority, the interested persons who made written representations and the persons who took part in the hearing or inquiry of their disagreement and the reasons for it; and

(b) affording them an opportunity of making written representations upon the new evidence or new matter of fact to the Welsh Ministers or of asking for the re-opening of the hearing or inquiry.

(10) The appellant, the local planning authority, the interested persons who made written representations and the persons who took part in the hearing or inquiry must ensure that written representations or requests to re-open the hearing or inquiry made under paragraphs (7) and (9) are received by the Welsh Ministers within the period specified in the Welsh Ministers' notification under those paragraphs.

(11) The Welsh Ministers may, as they think fit, cause a hearing or inquiry to be re-opened, and they must do so if asked by the appellant or the local planning authority in the circumstances mentioned in paragraph (9) and within the period specified in the Welsh Ministers' notification under paragraph (9).

(12) Where a hearing or inquiry is re-opened (whether by the same or a different appointed person)—

(a) the Welsh Ministers must send to the appellant, the local planning authority, the interested persons who made written representations and the persons who took part in the hearing or inquiry a written statement of the matters in respect of which further evidence is invited;

(b) further evidence submitted following a request must not exceed 3,000 words and must be submitted in the time and manner specified by the Welsh Ministers; and

(c) paragraphs (3) to (8) of regulation 29, regulation 30, paragraphs (3) to (8) of regulation 42 and regulation 43 apply as if references to a hearing or an inquiry were references to a re-opened hearing or inquiry.

Chapter 3

49 Notice of decision

(1) The Welsh Ministers, or the appointed person as the case may be, must send the decision on an appeal, and their reasons for it in writing to—

(a) the appellant;

(b) the local planning authority;

(c) the persons who took part in the proceedings;

(d) any other person who asked to be notified of the decision and whom the Welsh Ministers consider it reasonable to notify.

(2) Where a copy of the appointed person's report is not sent with the notification of the decision, the notification must be accompanied by a statement of the appointed person's conclusions and of any recommendations made by the appointed person, and if a person entitled to be notified of the decision has not received a copy of that report, that person must be supplied with a copy of it on written application to the Welsh Ministers.

Appendix 6

(3) In this regulation 'report' ('adroddiad') does not include any documents appended to it; but any person who has received a copy of the report may apply to the Welsh Ministers in writing, within 6 weeks of the date of the Welsh Ministers decision, for an opportunity to inspect any such documents and the Welsh Ministers must afford that person that opportunity.

(4) Any person applying to the Welsh Ministers under paragraph (2) must ensure that the application is received by the Welsh Ministers within 4 weeks of the Welsh Ministers' determination.

PART 8 QUASHED DECISIONS

50 Procedure following quashing of decision

(1) Where a decision of the Welsh Ministers or an appointed person on an appeal is quashed in proceedings before any court, the Welsh Ministers—

    (a) must send to the persons who submitted written representations or who took part in the hearing or inquiry, a written statement of the matters in respect of which further representations are invited for the purposes of their further consideration of the appeal;

    (b) must afford to those persons the opportunity of making written representations to them in respect of those matters; and

    (c) may, as they think fit—

        (i) cause the hearing or inquiry to be re-opened;

        (ii) in the case of a hearing, cause an inquiry to be held instead (whether by the same or a different appointed person);

        (iii) in the case of an inquiry, cause a hearing to be held instead (whether by the same or a different appointed person);

        (iv) cause a hearing or inquiry to be held (where none was held previously); or

        (v) determine the matter on the basis of written representations.

(2) If the Welsh Ministers re-open the hearing or inquiry regulation 29 and regulation 42 apply as if the references to a hearing or inquiry are to a re-opened hearing or inquiry.

(3) Those persons making representations must ensure that such representations are received by the Welsh Ministers within the period specified in the Welsh Ministers' statement under paragraph (1)(a).

PART 9 NATIONAL SECURITY DIRECTIONS

51 Modifications where national security direction given

The modifications set out in Schedule 2 have effect where a direction is given by the Welsh Ministers under—

    (a) section 321(3) of the Planning Act (planning inquiries to be held in public subject to certain exceptions);

TCP (Referred Applicaitons and Appeals Procedure) (Wales) Regulations 2017

(b) paragraph 6(6) of Schedule 3 to the Listed Buildings Act (local inquiries and hearings); or

(c) paragraph 6(6) of the Schedule to the Hazardous Substances Act (local inquiries and hearings).

PART 10 ENFORCEMENT NOTICES ISSUED BY THE WELSH MINISTERS

52 Application of Regulations to enforcement notices issued by the Welsh Ministers

These Regulations apply to appeals against enforcement notices issued by the Welsh Ministers under section 182 of the Planning Act and to appeals against listed building enforcement notices issued by the Welsh Ministers under section 46 of the Listed Buildings Act, subject to the modifications set out in Schedule 3.

PART 11 REVOCATION AND CONSEQUENTIAL AMENDMENT

53 Revocation, transitional and saving provisions

(1) The instruments listed in column (1) of Schedule 4 are revoked in so far as they apply in relation to Wales to the extent indicated in column (3), subject to paragraphs (2) and (3).

(2) The instruments listed in column (1) of Schedule 4 continue to apply to appeals, other than enforcement appeals, where the appeal is made in relation to an application made before these Regulations come into force.

(3) The instruments listed in column (1) of Schedule 4 continue to apply to enforcement appeals where the appeal is made in relation to an enforcement notice issued before these Regulations come into force.

54 Consequential amendment

(1) The 2012 Order is amended as follows.

(2) In Schedule 2, in the Notice Under Article 10 of Application for Planning Permission, for 'Part 1 of the Town and Country Planning (Referrals and Appeals) (Written Representations Procedure) (Wales) Regulations 2015' substitute 'Part 3 of the Town and Country Planning (Referred Applications and Appeals Procedure) (Wales) Regulations 2017'.

SCHEDULE 1   MINOR COMMERCIAL DEVELOPMENT USES

Regulation 3

1 Shops

Use for all or any of the following purposes—

(a) for the retail sale of goods other than hot food,

Appendix 6

(b) as a post office,

(c) for the sale of tickets or as a travel agency,

(d) for the sale of sandwiches or other cold food for consumption off the premises,

(e) for hairdressing,

(f) for the direction of funerals,

(g) for the display of goods for sale,

(h) for the hiring out of domestic or personal goods or articles,

(i) for the washing or cleaning of clothes or fabrics on the premises,

(j) for the reception of goods to be washed, cleaned or repaired,

where the sale, display or service is to visiting members of the public.

2 Financial and professional services

Use for the provision of—

(a) financial services,

(b) professional services (other than health or medical services), or

(c) any other services (including use as a betting office) which it is appropriate to provide in a shopping area,

where the services are provided principally to visiting members of the public.

3 Food and drink

Use for the sale of food or drink for consumption on the premises or of hot food for consumption off the premises.

SCHEDULE 2   MODIFICATIONS WHERE NATIONAL SECURITY DIRECTION GIVEN

Regulation 51

Interpretation

1   Regulation 3 is read as if in the appropriate places there is inserted—

"'appointed representative' ("cynrychiolydd penodedig") means a person appointed under section 321(5) or (6) of the Planning Act, sections 22 and 40 of, and paragraph 6A of Schedule 3 to, the Listed Buildings Act and section 21 of, and paragraph 6A of the Schedule to, the Hazardous Substances Act;';

"'closed evidence' ("tystiolaeth gaeedig") means evidence which is subject to a security direction;';

"'security direction' ("cyfarwyddyd diogelwch") means a direction given by the Welsh Ministers or the Secretary of State under section 321(3) of the Planning Act, paragraph 6(6) of Schedule 3 to the Listed Buildings Act or paragraph 6(6) of the Schedule to the Hazardous Substances Act;'.

Site inspections

2 Regulation 8 is read as if—

    (a) at the end of paragraph (2) there is inserted 'and they must so notify any appointed representative';

    (b) after paragraph (2) there is inserted—

        '(2A) Where an inspection of a site involves the inspection of closed evidence, the Welsh Ministers may inspect the land in the company of the appellant and any appointed representative.'

Further information

3 Regulation 9 is read as if after paragraph (8) there is inserted—

    '(8A) Paragraph (8) does not apply where the representations and written responses received by the Welsh Ministers ("further representations") include or refer to closed evidence.

    (7B) Where further representations include or refer to closed evidence the Welsh Ministers must—

        (a) as soon as reasonably practicable after receipt, send the further representations to the appellant and any appointed representative; and

        (b) make the further representations (other than the closed evidence) available in such manner as the Welsh Ministers think appropriate as soon as reasonably practicable.'

Representations

4 Regulation 22 is read as if after paragraph (7) there is inserted—

    '(7A) Paragraph (7) does not apply where the full statement of case received by the Welsh Ministers ("the full statement of case") includes or refers to closed evidence.

    (7B) Where the full statement of case received includes or refers to closed evidence the Welsh Ministers must—

        (a) as soon as reasonably practicable after receipt, send the full statement of case to the appellant and any appointed representative; and

        (b) make the full statement of case (other than the closed evidence) available in such manner as the Welsh Ministers think appropriate as soon as reasonably practicable.'

Interested persons' representations

5 Regulation 23 is read as if after paragraph (3) there is inserted—

    '(3A) Paragraph (3) does not apply where the representations received by the Welsh Ministers from interested persons ("interested persons' representations") include or refer to closed evidence.

    (3B) Where the interested persons' representations include or refer to closed evidence the Welsh Ministers must—

Appendix 6

    (a) as soon as reasonably practicable after receipt, send the interested persons' representations to the appellant and any appointed representative; and

    (b) make the interested persons' representations (other than the closed evidence) available in such manner as the Welsh Ministers think appropriate as soon as reasonably practicable.'

Further representations

6 Regulation 24 is read as if after paragraph (4) there is inserted—

  '(4A) Paragraph (4) does not apply where the written comments received by the Welsh Ministers ("written comments") include or refer to closed evidence.

  (4B) Where the written comments include or refer to closed evidence the Welsh Ministers must—

    (a) as soon as reasonably practicable after receipt, send the written comments to the appellant and any appointed representative; and

    (b) make the written comments (other than the closed evidence) available in such manner as the Welsh Ministers think appropriate as soon as reasonably practicable.'

Appointment of assessor

7 Regulations 28 and 37 are read as if after 'the local planning authority' there is inserted ', any appointed representative'.

Date, place and notification of hearing and inquiry

8 Regulations 29 and 42 are read as if after paragraph (4)(b) there is inserted—

 '(ba) any appointed representative;'.

Participation in a hearing, participation in an inquiry

9 Regulations 31(1) and 38(1) are read as if after subparagraph (b) there is inserted—

 '(ba) any appointed representative;'.

Absence, adjournment etc.

10 Regulations 32(1) and 39(1) are read as if after 'local planning authority' there is inserted ', any appointed representative'.

Procedure at hearing

11 Regulation 33(5) is read as if after 'local planning authority' there is inserted ', any appointed representative'.

Pre-inquiry meetings

12 Regulation 40(2) is read as if after subparagraph (b) there is inserted—

 '(ba) any appointed representative;'.

TCP (Referred Applicaitons and Appeals Procedure) (Wales) Regulations 2017

Written statements of evidence

13   Regulation 44 is read as if—

   (a)   after paragraph (1) there is inserted—

   '(1A) Paragraph (1) does not apply where the written statement of evidence includes or refers to closed evidence.

   (1B) Where the written statement of evidence includes or refers to closed evidence—

   (a)   the appellant, the local planning authority and each person invited to take part in the inquiry who propose to give or call another person to give evidence at the inquiry by reading a written statement, must send to the Welsh Ministers—

   (i)   one copy of the written statement including closed evidence, together with a written summary;

   (ii)   one copy of the written statement excluding closed evidence ("the open statement"), together with a written summary;

   (b)   the appellant must send one copy of the open statement, together with a written summary, to the local planning authority;

   (c)   the local planning authority must send one copy of the open statement, together with a written summary, to the appellant.';

   (b)   after paragraph (2) there is inserted—

   '(2A) Paragraph (2) does not apply where the written statement of evidence includes or refers to closed evidence.

   (2B) Where the written statement of evidence includes or refers to closed evidence the Welsh Ministers must, as soon as reasonably practicable after receipt—

   (a)   send a copy of the open statement, together with any summary, of each person invited to take part in the inquiry to the local planning authority; and

   (b)   send a copy of each open statement, together with any summary, to each person invited to take part in the inquiry.'

Procedure at inquiry

14   Regulation 45 is read as if—

   (a)   in paragraphs (3), (5) and (6) after 'local planning authority' there is inserted ', any appointed representative';

   (b)   after paragraph (12) there is inserted—

   '(12A) Paragraph (12) does not apply if any written representation or any other document received by the appointed person ("further information") includes or refers to closed evidence.

   (12B) Where the further information includes or refers to closed evidence, the appointed person must—

Appendix 6

    (a)   disclose the further information to the appellant and any appointed representative;

    (b)   disclose the further information (other than the closed evidence) to the local planning authority and every person who takes part in the inquiry.'

Procedure after written representations, hearings, inquires or combined proceedings.

15   Regulation 47 is read as if after paragraph (4) there is inserted—

'(4A) Paragraph (4) does not apply where closed evidence was considered.

(4B) Where closed evidence was considered—

    (a)   the appointed person and assessor, where one has been appointed, must set out in a separate part ("the closed part") of their reports any description of that evidence together with any conclusions or recommendations in relation to that evidence; and

    (b)   where an assessor has been appointed, the appointed person must append the closed part of the assessor's report to the closed part of the appointed person's report and must state in the closed part of that report how far the appointed person agrees or disagrees with the closed part of the assessor's report and, where there is disagreement with the assessor, the reasons for that disagreement.'

16   Regulation 48 is read as if—

    (a)   after paragraph (4) there is inserted—

'(4A) Paragraph (4) does not apply where closed evidence was considered.

(4B) Where closed evidence was considered—

    (a)   the appointed person and assessor, where one has been appointed, must set out in a separate part ("the closed part") of their reports any description of that evidence together with any conclusions or recommendations in relation to that evidence; and

    (b)   where an assessor has been appointed, the appointed person must append the closed part of the assessor's report to the closed part of the appointed person's report and must state in the closed part of that report how far the appointed person agrees or disagrees with the closed part of the assessor's report and, where there is disagreement with the assessor, the reasons for that disagreement.';

    (b)   after paragraph (9) there is inserted—

'(9A) Paragraph (9) does not apply where the Welsh Ministers differ from the appointed person on any matter of fact mentioned in, or appearing to them to be material to, a conclusion reached by the appointed person in relation to a matter in respect of which closed evidence has been given.

TCP (Referred Applicaitons and Appeals Procedure) (Wales) Regulations 2017

(9B) Where the Welsh Ministers differ from the appointed person on any matter of fact mentioned in, or appearing to them to be material to, a conclusion reached by the appointed person in relation to a matter in respect of which closed evidence has been given, they must include the reasons for the Welsh Ministers disagreement unless—

    (a) the notification is addressed to a person who is neither the appointed representative nor any person specified, or of a description specified, in the security direction; and

    (b) the inclusion of the reasons would disclose any part of the closed evidence.'

Notification of decision

17 Regulation 49 is read as if—

(a) in paragraph (1), before 'The Welsh Ministers,' there is inserted 'Subject to paragraph (1A);

(b) after paragraph (1), there is inserted—

'(1A) Where the Welsh Ministers reasons for a decision relate to matters in respect of which closed evidence has been given, nothing in paragraph (1) requires the Welsh Ministers to notify those reasons to any person other than—

    (a) the appointed representative; or

    (b) a person specified, or of any description specified, in the security direction.';

(c) in paragraph (2), before 'Where a copy' there is inserted 'Subject to paragraph (3A)';

(d) after paragraph (3) there is inserted—

'(3A) Nothing in paragraphs (2) or (3) require the disclosure or inspection of the closed part of the appointed person's report, or of any documents comprising or containing closed evidence appended to the appointed person's report, to any person other than—

    (a) the appointed representative; or

    (b) a person specified, or of any description specified, in the security direction.'

Procedure following quashing of decision

18 Regulation 50(1) is read as if after subparagraph (a) there is inserted—

'(aa) subparagraph (a) does not apply where the matters referred to in subparagraph (a) will involve consideration of closed evidence;

(ab) where the matters referred to in subparagraph (a) will involve consideration of closed evidence, the Welsh Ministers will only send the written statement to—

    (i) the appointed representative; or

Appendix 6

> (ii) a person specified, or of any description specified, in the security direction;'.

Closed evidence not to be disclosed

19   After regulation 51 there is inserted—

'51A   Nothing in these Regulations is to be taken so as to require or permit closed evidence to be disclosed to any person other than—

> (a) the Welsh Ministers;
>
> (b) the appointed person; or
>
> (c) a person specified, or of any description specified, in the security direction.'

SCHEDULE 3   MODIFICATIONS WHERE ENFORCEMENT NOTICES ISSUED BY WELSH MINISTERS

Regulation 52

Interpretation

1   Regulation 3 is read as if in the definition of 'full statement of case', paragraph (d) provided—

'(d) means and is comprised of in relation to enforcement appeals—

> (i) a written statement by the Welsh Ministers containing—
>
> > (aa) a response to each ground of appeal pleaded by the appellant; and
> >
> > (bb) full particulars of the case the Welsh Ministers propose to put forward in relation to the appeal; and
>
> (ii) copies of any supporting documents the Welsh Ministers propose to refer to or put in evidence.'

Further information

2   Regulation 9 is read as if paragraph (1)(b) were omitted.

Inspection of documents

3   Regulation 10 does not apply.

Determination of procedure

4   Regulation 14(3) is read as if 'and the local planning authority' were omitted.

Notification of receipt of appeal

5   Regulation 15(2) is read as if, 'and the local planning authority' were omitted.

Questionnaire

6   Regulation 16 does not apply.

Notice to interested persons

7   Regulation 17 is read as if—

    (a)   in paragraph (1), 'local planning authority' read 'Welsh Ministers';

    (b)   in paragraph (2)(c), 'and the local planning authority' were omitted.

Representations

8   Regulation 22 is read as if—

    (a)   paragraph (5) read as if it provided—

        '(5) In relation to appeals against enforcement notices, the Welsh Ministers must send a full statement of case to the appellant and any person on whom a copy of the enforcement notice has been served, so as to be received within 4 weeks of the starting date.';

    (b)   paragraphs (6) and (7) were omitted.

Interested persons' representations

9   Regulation 23(3) is read as if 'and the local planning authority' were omitted.

Further representations

10   Regulation 24 is read as if—

    (a)   in paragraph (1), ', the local planning authority,' were omitted;

    (b)   in paragraph (2), 'and the local planning authority' were omitted.

Written representations inappropriate

11   Regulation 25(2) is read as if 'and the local planning authority' were omitted.

Appointment of assessor

12   Regulations 28 and 37 are read as if ', the local planning authority' were omitted.

Date, place and notification of hearing or inquiry

13   Regulations 29(4) and 42(4) are read as if subparagraphs (b) were omitted.

Public notice of hearing or inquiry

14   Regulations 30(5) and 43(5) are read as if subparagraphs (d) were omitted.

Participation in a hearing or inquiry

15   Regulations 31(1) and 38(1) are read as if subparagraphs (b) were omitted.

Absence and adjournment

16   Regulations 32(1) and 39(1) are read as if ', the local planning authority' were omitted.

Appendix 6

Procedure at hearing

17   Regulation 33(5) is read as if ', the local planning authority' were omitted.

Hearing inappropriate

18   Regulation 34(2) is read as if 'and the local planning authority' were omitted.

Pre-inquiry meetings

19   Regulation 40(2) is read as if subparagraph (b) were omitted.

Written statements of evidence

20   Regulation 44 is read as if—

(a)   in paragraph (1), ', the local planning authority' were omitted;

(b)   paragraphs (1)(a) and (b) were omitted;

(c)   paragraph (1)(c) read as if it provided—

'(c)   the appellant must send one copy of the appellant's statement, together with a written summary, to the Welsh Ministers;';

(d)   paragraph (2)(a) were omitted.

Procedure at inquiry

21   Regulation 45 is read as if in paragraphs (3), (5) and (6) ', the local planning authority' were omitted.

Inquiry inappropriate

22   Regulation 46(2) is read as if 'and the local planning authority' were omitted.

Procedure after proceedings

23   Regulation 47 is read as if—

(a)   in paragraphs (6)(a), (7)(a) and (8), ', the local planning authority' were omitted;

(b)   in paragraph (9), 'or the local planning authority' were omitted.

24   Regulation 48 is read as if—

(a)   in paragraphs (7)(a), (9)(a) and (10) ', the local planning authority' were omitted;

(b)   in paragraph (11), 'or the local planning authority' were omitted.

Notice of decision

25   Regulation 49(1) is read as if subparagraph (b) were omitted.

TCP (Referred Applicaitons and Appeals Procedure) (Wales) Regulations 2017

SCHEDULE 4 STATUTORY INSTRUMENTS REVOKED SO FAR AS THEY APPLY TO WALES

Regulation 53

Statutory Instruments revoked	References	Extent of revocation
Town and Country Planning (Enforcement) (Written Representations Procedure) (Wales) Regulations 2003	S.I. 2003/395 (W. 54)	The whole instrument
Town and Country Planning (Inquiries Procedure) (Wales) Rules 2003	S.I. 2003/1266	The whole instrument
Town and Country Planning Appeals (Determination by Inspectors) (Inquiries Procedure) (Wales) Rules 2003	S.I. 2003/1267	The whole instrument
Town and Country Planning (Enforcement) (Hearings Procedure) (Wales) Rules 2003	S.I. 2003/1268	The whole instrument
Town and Country Planning (Enforcement) (Inquiries Procedure) (Wales) Rules 2003	S.I. 2003/1269	The whole instrument
Town and Country Planning (Enforcement) (Determination by Inspectors) (Inquiries Procedure) (Wales) Rules 2003	S.I. 2003/1270	The whole instrument
Town and Country Planning (Hearings Procedure) (Wales) Rules 2003	S.I. 2003/1271	The whole instrument
Town and Country Planning (Electronic Communications) (Wales) (No. 2) Order 2004	S.I. 2004/3157 (W. 274)	Article 2 and Schedule 1 Paragraph (2) of article 3 and Schedule 3
Town and Country Planning (Electronic Communications) (Wales) (No. 3) Order 2004	S.I. 2004/3172	The whole instrument
Town and Country Planning (Application of Subordinate Legislation to the Crown) Order 2006	S.I. 2006/1282	Articles 35 and 37 to 43
Town and Country Planning (Amendment of Appeals Procedures) (Wales) Rules 2007	S.I. 2007/2285	The whole instrument
Town and Country Planning (Determination of Procedure) (Prescribed Period) (Wales) Regulations 2014	S.I. 2014/2775 (W. 281)	The whole instrument
The Planning (Listed Buildings and Conservation Areas) (Determination of Procedure) (Prescribed Period) (Wales) Regulations 2014	S.I. 2014/2776 (W. 282)	The whole instrument
Town and Country Planning (Referrals and Appeals) (Written Representations Procedure) (Wales) Regulations 2015	S.I. 2015/1331 (W. 124)	The whole instrument
Planning (Hazardous Substances) (Wales) Regulations 2015	S.I. 2015/1597 (W. 196)	Regulations 14, 17(2) and (3)

Appendix 7

Timescales – Rosewell

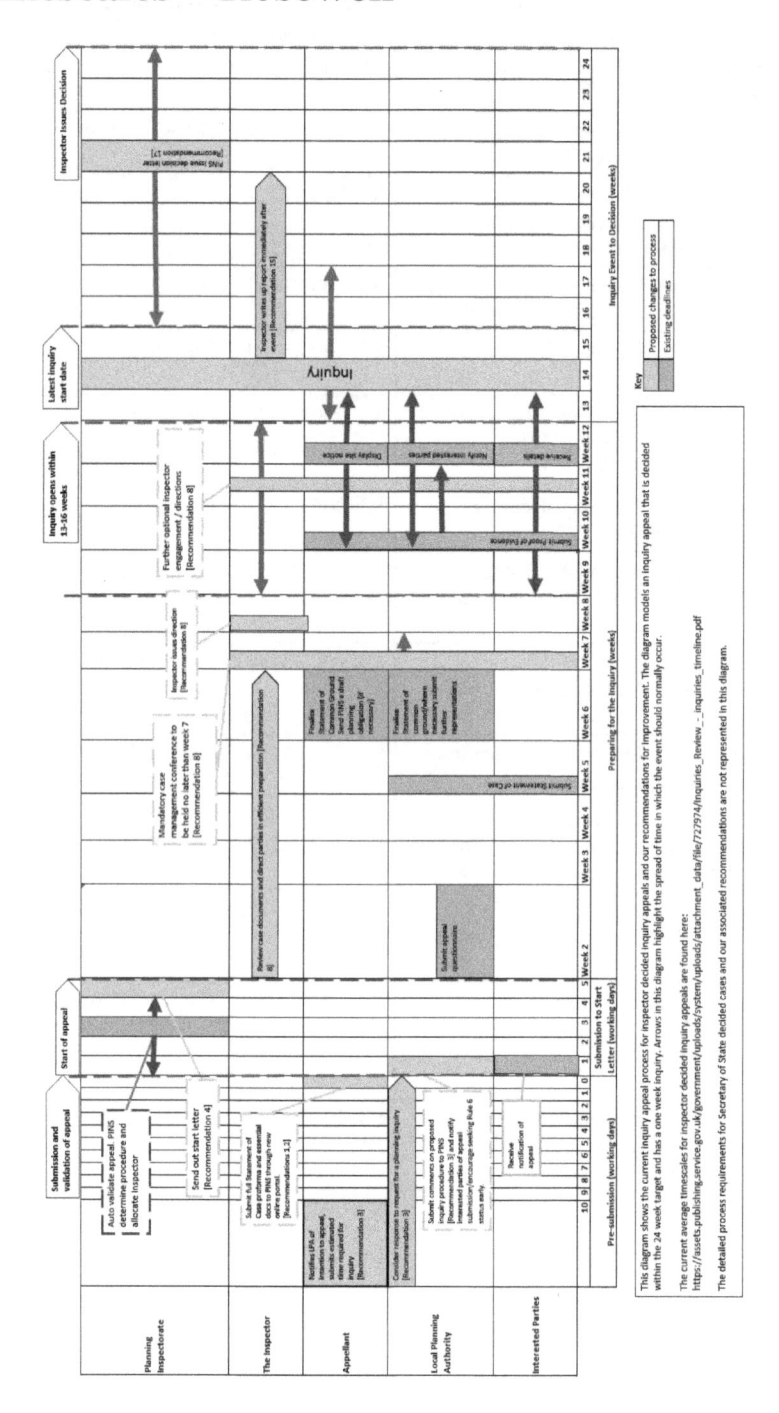

Appendix 8

Plan of an inquiry room

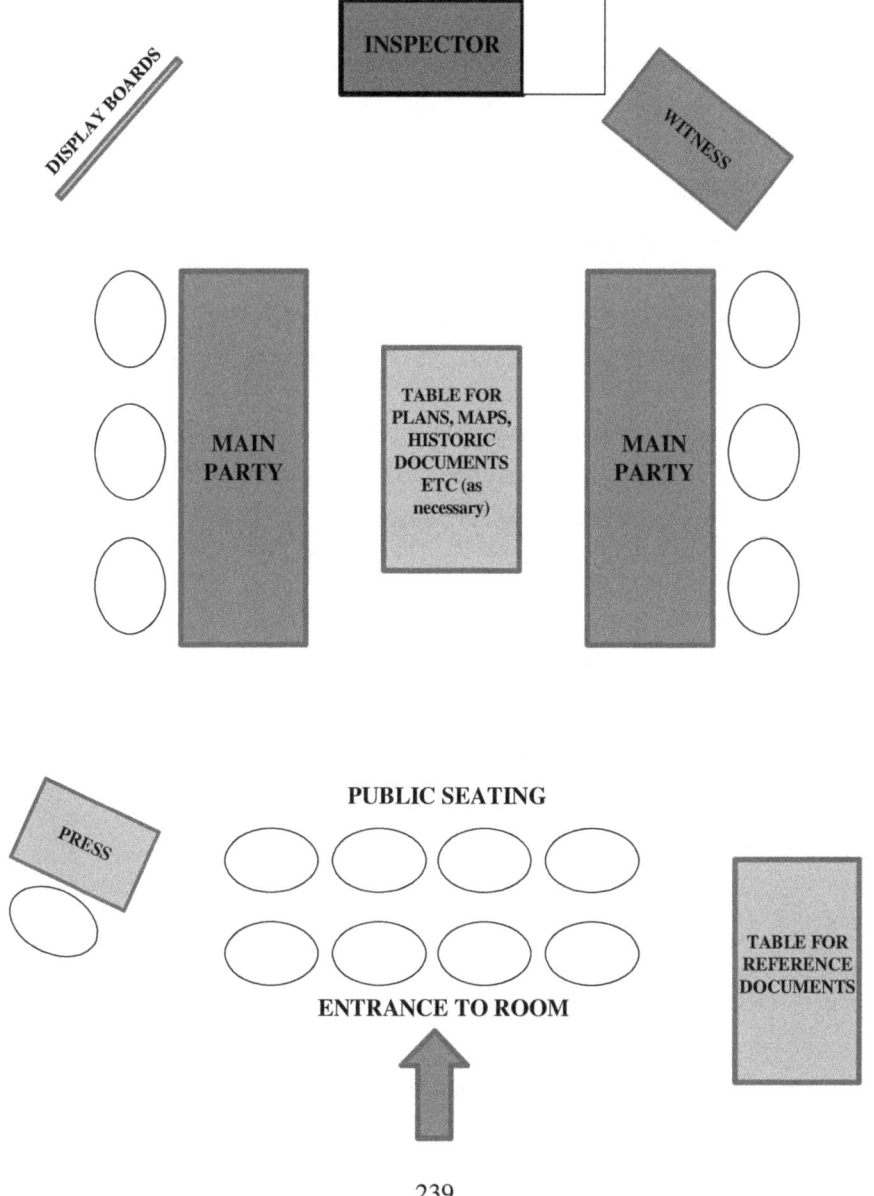

Appendix 9

Bar Council Code of Conduct – extracts

WITNESS PREPARATION GUIDANCE

Part 2 – B. The Core Duties

CD1 You must observe your duty to the court in the administration of justice [CD1].

CD2 You must act in the best interests of each client [CD2].

CD3 You must act with honesty, and with integrity [CD3].

CD4 You must maintain your independence [CD4].

CD5 You must not behave in a way which is likely to diminish the trust and confidence which the public places in you or in the profession [CD5].

CD6 You must keep the affairs of each client confidential [CD6].

CD7 You must provide a competent standard of work and service to each client [CD7].

CD8 You must not discriminate unlawfully against any person [CD8].

CD9 You must be open and co-operative with your regulators [CD9].

CD10 You must take reasonable steps to manage your practice, or carry out your role within your practice, competently and in such a way as to achieve compliance with your legal and regulatory obligations [CD10].

Part 2 – C. The Conduct Rules

C1. You and the court

Rules C3–C6

rC3

You owe a duty to the *court* to act with independence in the interests of justice. This duty overrides any inconsistent obligations which you may have (other than obligations under the criminal law). It includes the following specific obligations which apply whether you are acting as an advocate or are otherwise involved in the conduct of litigation in whatever role (with the exception of Rule C3.1 below, which applies when acting as an advocate):

.1   you must not knowingly or recklessly mislead or attempt to mislead the *court*;

.2   you must not abuse your role as an advocate;

.3   you must take reasonable steps to avoid wasting the *court's* time;

Bar Council Code of Conduct – extracts

.4 you must take reasonable steps to ensure that the *court* has before it all relevant decisions and legislative provisions;

.5 you must ensure that your ability to act independently is not compromised.

rC4

Your duty to act in the best interests of each *client* is subject to your duty to the *court*.

rC5

Your duty to the *court* does not require you to act in breach of your duty to keep the affairs of each *client* confidential.

Not misleading the court

rC6

Your duty not to mislead the *court* will include the following obligations:

.1 you must not:

    .a make submissions, representations or any other statement; or

    .b ask questions which suggest facts to witnesses

which you know, or are instructed, are untrue or misleading.

.2 you must not call witnesses to give evidence or put affidavits or witness statements to the *court* which you know, or are *instructed*, are untrue or misleading, unless you make clear to the *court* the true position as known by or instructed to you

Rule C7 – Not abusing your role as an advocate

rC7

Where you are acting as an advocate, your duty not to abuse your role includes the following obligations:

.1 you must not make statements or ask questions merely to insult, humiliate or annoy a witness or any other person;

.2 you must not make a serious allegation against a witness whom you have had an opportunity to cross-examine unless you have given that witness a chance to answer the allegation in cross-examination;

.3 you must not make a serious allegation against any person, or suggest that a person is guilty of a crime with which your *client* is charged unless:

    .a you have reasonable grounds for the allegation; and

    .b the allegation is relevant to your *client's* case or the credibility of a witness; and

    .c where the allegation relates to a third party, you avoid naming them in open *court* unless this is reasonably necessary.

.4 you must not put forward to the *court* a personal opinion of the facts or the law unless you are invited or required to do so by the *court* or by law

Appendix 9

C2. Behaving ethically

Rules C8–C9 – Honesty, integrity and independence

rC8

You must not do anything which could reasonably be seen by the public to undermine your honesty, integrity (CD3) and independence (CD4).

rC9

Your duty to act with honesty and with integrity under CD3 includes the following requirements:

- .1 you must not knowingly or recklessly mislead or attempt to mislead anyone;
- .2 you must not draft any statement of case, witness statement, affidavit or other document containing:
  - .a any statement of fact or contention which is not supported by your *client* or by your *instructions*;
  - .b any contention which you do not consider to be properly arguable;
  - .c any allegation of fraud, unless you have clear instructions to allege fraud and you have reasonably credible material which establishes an arguable case of fraud;
  - .d (in the case of a witness statement or affidavit) any statement of fact other than the evidence which you reasonably believe the witness would give if the witness were giving evidence orally;
- .3 you must not encourage a witness to give evidence which is misleading or untruthful;
- .4 you must not rehearse, practise with or coach a witness in respect of their evidence;
- .5 unless you have the permission of the representative for the opposing side or of the *court*, you must not communicate with any witness (including your *client*) about the case while the witness is giving evidence;
- .6 you must not make, or offer to make, payments to any witness which are contingent on their evidence or on the outcome of the case;
- .7 you must only propose, or accept, fee arrangements which are legal

C3. You and your client

Rules C15–C16 Best interests of each client, provision of a competent standard of work and confidentiality

rC15

Your duty to act in the best interests of each *client* (CD2), to provide a competent standard of work and service to each *client* (CD7) and to keep the affairs of each *client* confidential (CD6) includes the following obligations:

- .1 you must promote fearlessly and by all proper and lawful means the *client's* best interests;

Bar Council Code of Conduct – extracts

.2 you must do so without regard to your own interests or to any consequences to you (which may include, for the avoidance of doubt, you being required to take reasonable steps to mitigate the effects of any breach of this *Handbook*);

.3 you must do so without regard to the consequences to any other person (whether to your *professional client, employer* or any other person);

.4 you must not permit your *professional client, employer* or any other person to limit your discretion as to how the interests of the *client* can best be served; and

.5 you must protect the confidentiality of each *client's* affairs, except for such disclosures as are required or permitted by law or to which your *client* gives informed consent.

rC16

Your duty to act in the best interests of each *client* (CD2) is subject to your duty to the *court* (CD1) and to your obligations to act with honesty, and with integrity (CD3) and to maintain your independence (CD4).

rC17

Your duty to act in the best interests of each *client* (CD2) includes a duty to consider whether the *client's* best interests are served by different legal representation, and if so, to advise the *client* to that effect.

rC18

Your duty to provide a competent standard of work and service to each *client* (CD7) includes a duty to inform your *professional client*, or your *client* if instructed by a *client*, as far as reasonably possible in sufficient time to enable appropriate steps to be taken to protect the *client's* interests, if:

.1 it becomes apparent to you that you will not be able to carry out the *instructions* within the time requested, or within a reasonable time after receipt of *instructions*; or

.2 there is an appreciable risk that you may not be able to undertake the *instructions*

Rule C19 – Not misleading clients and potential clients

rC19

If you supply, or offer to supply, *legal services*, you must not mislead, or cause or permit to be misled, any person to whom you supply, or offer to supply, *legal services* about:

.1 the nature and scope of the *legal services* which you are offering or agreeing to supply;

.2 the terms on which the *legal services* will be supplied, who will carry out the work and the basis of charging;

.3 who is legally responsible for the provision of the services;

.4 whether you are entitled to supply those services and the extent to which you are regulated when providing those services and by whom; or

Appendix 9

.5 the extent to which you are covered by insurance against claims for professional negligence.

Rule C20 – Personal responsibility

rC20

Where you are a *BSB authorised individual*, you are personally responsible for your own conduct and for your professional work. You must use your own professional judgment in relation to those matters on which you are instructed and be able to justify your decisions and actions. You must do this notwithstanding the views of your *client, professional client, employer* or any other person.

Rule C21 – Accepting instructions

rC21

You must not accept *instructions* to act in a particular matter if:

.1 due to any existing or previous *instructions* you are not able to fulfil your obligation to act in the best interests of the prospective *client*; or

.2 there is a conflict of interest, or real risk of conflict of interest, between your own personal interests and the interests of the prospective *client* in respect of the particular matter; or

.3 there is a conflict of interest, or real risk of conflict of interest, between the prospective *client* and one or more of your former or existing *clients* in respect of the particular matter unless all of the *clients* who have an interest in the particular matter give their informed consent to your acting in such circumstances; or

.4 there is a real risk that information confidential to another former or existing *client*, or any other person to whom you owe duties of confidence, may be relevant to the matter, such that if, obliged to maintain confidentiality, you could not act in the best interests of the prospective *client*, and the former or existing *client* or person to whom you owe that duty does not give informed consent to disclosure of that confidential information; or

.5 your instructions seek to limit your ordinary authority or discretion in the conduct of proceedings in *court*; or

.6 your instructions require you to act other than in accordance with law or with the provisions of this *Handbook*; or

.7 you are not authorised and/or otherwise accredited to perform the work required by the relevant *instruction*; or

.8 you are not competent to handle the particular matter or otherwise do not have enough experience to handle the matter; or

.9 you do not have enough time to deal with the particular matter, unless the circumstances are such that it would nevertheless be in the *client's* best interests for you to accept; or

.10 there is a real prospect that you are not going to be able to maintain your independence

Bar Council Code of Conduct – extracts

Rules C29–C30 – The cab rank rule

rC29

If you receive *instructions* from a *professional client*, and you are:

.1 a self-employed barrister instructed by a professional client; or

.2 an authorised individual working within a BSB entity; or

.3 a BSB entity and the instructions seek the services of a named authorised individual working for you,

and the *instructions* are appropriate taking into account the experience, seniority and/or field of practice of yourself or (as appropriate) of the named *authorised individual* you must, subject to Rule rC30 below, accept the *instructions* addressed specifically to you, irrespective of:

.a the identity of the *client*;

.b the nature of the case to which the *instructions* relate;

.c whether the *client* is paying privately or is publicly funded; and

.d any belief or opinion which you may have formed as to the character, reputation, cause, conduct, guilt or innocence of the *client*.

rC30

The cab rank Rule rC29 does not apply if:

.1 you are required to refuse to accept the *instructions* pursuant to Rule rC21; or

.2 accepting the *instructions* would require you or the named *authorised individual* to do something other than in the course of their ordinary working time or to cancel a commitment already in their diary; or

.3 the potential liability for professional negligence in respect of the particular matter could exceed the level of professional indemnity insurance which is reasonably available and likely to be available in the market for you to accept; or

.4 you are a Queen's Counsel, and the acceptance of the *instructions* would require you to act without a junior in circumstances where you reasonably consider that the interests of the *client* require that a junior should also be instructed; or

.5 accepting the *instructions* would require you to do any *foreign work*; or

.6 accepting the *instructions* would require you to act for a *foreign lawyer* (other than a *European lawyer*, a lawyer from a country that is a member of EFTA, a *solicitor* or *barrister* of Northern Ireland or a *solicitor* or advocate under the law of Scotland); or

.7 the *professional client*:

.a is not accepting liability for your fees; or

.b represents, in your reasonable opinion, an unacceptable credit risk; or

.c is instructing you as a lay *client* and not in their capacity as a *professional client*; or

Appendix 9

.8 you have not been offered a proper fee for your services (except that you shall not be entitled to refuse to accept *instructions* on this ground if you have not made or responded to any fee proposal within a reasonable time after receiving the *instructions*); or

.9 except where you are to be paid directly by (i) the *Legal Aid Agency* as part of the Community Legal Service or the Criminal Defence Service or (ii) the Crown Prosecution Service:

 .a your fees have not been agreed (except that you shall not be entitled to refuse to accept *instructions* on this ground if you have not taken reasonable steps to agree fees within a reasonable time after receiving the *instructions*);

 .b having required your fees to be paid before you accept the *instructions*, those fees have not been paid;

 .c accepting the *instructions* would require you to act other than on (A) the Standard Contractual Terms for the Supply of Legal Services by Barristers to Authorised Persons 2012 as published on the *Bar Council's* website; or (B) if you publish standard terms of work, on those standard terms of work.

BAR COUNCIL ETHICS COMMITTEE – 'WITNESS PREPARATION' (NOVEMBER 2019)

32 Counsel may also assist in familiarising experts with the process of giving oral evidence, including:

32.1 Explaining the layout of the Court and the procedure of the trial, and

32.2 Providing guidance on giving comprehensive and comprehensible specialist evidence to the Court, and resisting the pressure to go further in evidence than matters covered by his or her specific expertise.

33 However, one must take great care not to do or say anything which could be interpreted as manufacturing or in any way influencing the content of the evidence that the expert is to give in the witness box.

Appendix 10

RTPI Code of Professional Conduct

As last amended by the Board of Trustees
Effective from 10 February 2016

INTRODUCTION

The Royal Town Planning Institute, as constituted by Royal Charter, (the 'Chartered Institute') exists to advance the science and art of planning for the benefit of the public. To achieve this the Chartered Institute requires planning professionals to meet and maintain high standards of competence and conduct themselves in a way that inspires trust and confidence in the profession.

This document is, in accordance with the Chartered Institute's Byelaws, a code of professional conduct and practice setting out the standards, ethics and professional behaviour expected of Members. The Chartered Institute requires its Members to adhere to five core principles, namely:

- Competence, honesty and integrity
- Independent professional judgement
- Due care and diligence
- Equality and respect
- Professional behaviour

The following numbered clauses indicate the required standards, ethics and professional behaviour of these five principles.

These requirements apply regardless of any permission or agreement to the contrary by or with the client or body employing or consulting any Member.

Additional guidance to Members, offering case studies and advice on the behaviours and practices required, may be published by the Chartered Institute.

COMPETENCE, HONESTY AND INTEGRITY

1. Members must take all reasonable steps to maintain their professional competence throughout their career.

2. Members who, as employers or managers, have responsibility for other Members or professionals must take all reasonable steps to encourage and support them in the maintenance of professional competence.

3. Members must act within the scope of their professional competence in undertaking the professional planning services they are employed or commissioned to do.

Appendix 10

4. Members must act with honesty and integrity throughout their career.
5. Members must take all reasonable steps to ensure that their private, personal, political and financial interests do not conflict with their professional duties.
6. Members must disclose to their employer or clients, as appropriate, any potential conflicts of interest.
7. Members must take all reasonable precautions to ensure that no conflict of duty arises between the interests of one employer, client or business associate and the interests of another.
8. Members must not disclose or use to the advantage of themselves, their employers or clients information acquired in confidence in the course of their work.
9. Members must not offer or accept inducements, financial or otherwise, to influence a decision or professional point of view with regards to planning matters.
10. Members must disclose to their employers or clients any offers of inducements, discounts, gifts or commissions received from any third parties in connection with their work.

INDEPENDENT PROFESSIONAL JUDGEMENT

11. Members must exercise fearlessly and impartially their independent professional judgement to the best of their skill and understanding.
12. Members must not make or subscribe to any statements or reports which are contrary to their own bona fide professional opinions, nor knowingly enter into any contract or agreement which requires them to do so.
13. Members must disclose their professional designation where appropriate to their employers, clients, colleagues or others and use their post-nominal letters, where held and where possible, in any professional correspondence as a mark of professional standing.

DUE CARE AND DILIGENCE

14. Members must discharge their duty to their employers, clients, colleagues and others with due care and diligence.
15. Before commencing work on any planning services, Members must:
    (a) ensure that their terms of engagement, which includes a written fee agreement and clear indication as to the likely costs and description of the services proposed, have been given and confirmed in writing to their clients and
    (b) satisfy themselves that these terms have been accepted.
16. Members must honour the terms of engagement provided unless there is written agreement to a variation.
17. Members must notify their clients in writing before undertaking planning work or incurring fees or expenses additional to those previously agreed and satisfy themselves that the necessary instructions have been received.

RTPI Code of Professional Conduct

18. When accepting instructions Members must ensure that the services offered are appropriate to the client's requirements.
19. Members engaging in planning practice must, where applicable, be insured against claims for breach of professional duty.
20. Members who, as employers or managers, have responsibility for the work of an organisation or body engaged in planning work must take all reasonable steps to ensure that planning matters in the organisation or body are conducted in accordance with this Code.

EQUALITY AND RESPECT

21. Members must not discriminate on grounds including but not limited to race, nationality, gender, sexual orientation, religion, disability or age.
22. Members must seek to eliminate discrimination by others and promote equality of opportunity throughout their professional activities.

PROFESSIONAL BEHAVIOUR

23. Members are expected at all times to conduct themselves in such a manner that does not prejudice their professional status or the reputation of the Chartered Institute.
24. The Board of Trustees, acting under Byelaw 19, has power to discipline any Member who:
    (a) in the opinion of a disciplinary committee contravenes any of the provisions of the Code of Professional Conduct, including the supplementary regulations referred to in Annex A to the Code, or of the Royal Charter and Byelaws; or who
    (b) is convicted by a court of a criminal offence which in the opinion of the Panel results in a breach of the provisions of Byelaw 18; or who
    (c) in the opinion of the disciplinary committee is guilty of gross professional misconduct or incompetence or of such conduct as to render him or her unfit to continue to be a member of the Chartered Institute.

GENERAL PROVISIONS

25. The Code applies to all Members, irrespective of their class of membership or territory within which they practise.
26. It is the duty of every Member, subject to any restrictions imposed by law or the courts, to report to the Chartered Institute any alleged breach of this Code of which he or she becomes aware and to assist the Chartered Institute in its investigations.
27. It is the duty of every Member who is the subject of investigation by the Chartered Institute to assist the Chartered Institute in its investigations.
28. Disciplinary action will be taken only when the Chartered Institute believes that the Member is personally responsible for the conduct or action in question.

Appendix 10

29. The Board of Trustees may from time to time publish supplementary regulations and Members must comply with any such regulations.

ANNEXES

A Supplementary regulations

B Relevant byelaws

C Disciplinary action

ANNEX A: SUPPLEMENTARY REGULATIONS

A1: Continuing professional development

Every individual Member except for Affiliates, Student members and Retired members must, subject only to the exercise of the Board of Trustees' discretion in exceptional cases:

(a) at least once a year prepare a professional development plan for the next two years identifying his or her personal professional development needs;

(b) in any two year period undertake a minimum of 50 hours CPD activity related to the undertaking or managing of planning;

(c) maintain a written record of his or her CPD activity;

(d) submit to the Chartered Institute on request and in such form as may be prescribed by the Chartered Institute:

   (i) a copy of his or her current professional development plan and professional development plans covering the previous two years;

   (ii) a written record of his or her CPD activity over the same period of two years, with an assessment of the value to him or her of each activity recorded and an explanation of the relationship between the CPD undertaken and the professional development plan or plans covering the period in question, taking into account any revisions to the plan made during the two year period;

   (iii) where appropriate, an explanation of his or her reasons for not having complied with any part of this regulation.

Notes to Regulation A1

(i) CPD, or continuing professional development, is defined by the Chartered Institute as: 'The systematic maintenance, improvement and broadening of knowledge and skill and the development of personal qualities necessary for the execution of professional and technical duties throughout the practitioner's working life.' Work experience is not in itself CPD, although action-based learning undertaken on a structured basis to fulfil objectives identified in a member's professional development plan would generally be accepted as CPD.

(ii) The Chartered Institute will provide practical advice on how to comply with the CPD regulations, including the prescribed form for the submission of professional development plans and written records of CPD activity.

RTPI Code of Professional Conduct

(iii) Chartered and Non-Chartered members who have retired from practice but who have not transferred to Retired Membership, remain subject to the CPD requirements of the Code.

A2: Advertising

(a) All advertising must be legal, decent, honest and truthful and must avoid exaggeration.

(b) Members must not make derogatory comparisons with the services available from others engaged in planning work and must not misrepresent the services available from their own practices.

(c) When canvassing instructions from a client or private individual, members must:

   (i) indicate that the existing professional adviser (if any) should be consulted;

   (ii) not canvass repeatedly or importunately nor continue canvassing instructions from individuals or clients who have clearly stated that they do not require the services offered.

A3: Use of the RTPI logo

Chartered Members, Legal Associates and practices directly employing two or more Chartered Members may use the Chartered Institute's logo on letter headings and advertising and promotional material in accordance with the following provisions:

(a) For individual members the logo must be accompanied by the words 'Chartered Town Planner', 'Legal Member of the RTPI', 'Legal Associate Member of the RTPI' or 'Legal Associate of the RTPI' (or '… of the Royal Town Planning Chartered Institute') specifically relevant to the class of membership.

(b) For practices directly employing two or more Chartered Members the logo must be accompanied by the words 'Chartered Town Planners'.

(c) Whenever so used by entitled individual Members who are partners or directors of a practice not otherwise entitled to be described as 'Chartered Town Planners' the logo and the accompanying words must clearly refer to the named individual member or members and not to the practice in accordance with the provisions of this regulation.

(d) The logo may not be used by any member, practice or other organisation except in accordance with this regulation and with the most recent guidance issued by the Chartered Institute.

A4: Provision of information to the Chartered Institute

Every Member must, within 28 days of being required to do so or when a subsequent change in circumstances occurs, furnish to the Chartered Institute such particulars in such form as the Board of Trustees will reasonably require:

(a) of his or her firm, if he or she is carrying on professional practice as a sole principal, partner, director or consultant to a firm; and

(b) of his or her employment, if he or she is employed under a contract of service or a contract for services.

Appendix 10

A5: Compulsory professional indemnity insurance regulations

1. Definitions

For the purpose of these Compulsory Professional Indemnity Insurance (CPII) Regulations unless the context otherwise requires:

"Member" means	(a) any individual member of any class of membership of the Chartered Institute (except Retired members) who is or who is held out to the public to be practising as a town planner and who is (i) a sole principal of; or (ii) a partner in; or (iii) a director of; or (iv) a consultant to; a firm offering planning services to the public;
	(b) any individual member of any class of membership of the Chartered Institute who has or was held out to the public to have practised as a town planner in any of those capacities and has within a period of six years ceased to do so;
"Sole principal"	includes a Member who carries on planning practice as a principal whether in addition to other employment or not;
"Consultant"	includes any Member, whether or not expressly described as a consultant, who is employed in any firm offering planning services to the public in which no partner or director is a Member;
"Firm"	includes a sole principal, partnership, body corporate or company incorporated with either limited or unlimited liability;
"Held out to the public"	means described on business stationery or in business communications or material of any nature by words which include 'sole principal', 'partner', 'director' or 'consultant' or otherwise represented to the public as being a town planner or employee to a firm providing planning services. For the avoidance of doubt 'the public' in the context of these CPII Regulations includes professional, corporate and institutional clients;
"Planning services"	covers all work which town planners hold themselves out as being professionally qualified to undertake and includes but is not necessarily limited to:
	development planning, development control or development management;
	site appraisals and development feasibility studies;
	development and design briefs;
	environmental impact assessments;
	master plans and urban design studies;
	policy research;
	government development and urban regeneration strategies;
	coastal and marine planning and waterside development;
	conservation or enhancement of the historic or natural environment;
	contaminated and derelict land;
	economic development;
	minerals planning and the management of waste;
	major housing schemes and new settlements;

RTPI Code of Professional Conduct

	planning for retail, commercial, industrial, healthcare, tourism and leisure uses;
	re-use of surplus land;
	rural planning;
	transportation planning;
	urban regeneration;
	public consultation and community engagement relating to planning practice;
	legal advice and services relating to planning law and procedures;
	climate change;
	energy and infrastructure development
	but excludes teaching and lecturing;
"RTPI Approved Policy"	means the policy wording as last approved by the Board of Trustees;
"Gross Income"	for the purposes of these CPII Regulations means all professional fees, remuneration, commission and income of any sort whatsoever in so far as these have been derived from work undertaken or performed in the United Kingdom (including the Channel Islands and the Isle of Man) and/or within the Republic of Ireland but excluding any sums received for the reimbursement of disbursements, any amounts charged by way of Value Added Tax and any income from judicial or other such offices as the Board of Trustees may from time to time determine;
"Preceding Year"	means the Member's accounting year which ended during the 12 months before the date on which any insurance policy under these CPII Regulations is taken out;
"Uninsured excess"	means the amount of any claim which a Member or his or her firm may be required to pay before any indemnity is granted under the terms of any policy of insurance required under these CPII Regulations.

2. *Scope of cover required*

(a) Members must insure by means of a policy no less comprehensive than the form of the RTPI Approved Policy in force at the time when the policy of insurance is taken out.

(b) Subject to sub-paragraph (c) of this Regulation every Member must ensure that he or she and any firm offering planning services to the public of which he or she is a principal, partner or director should be insured against claims arising from work undertaken or perf\ormed within the United Kingdom (including the Channel Islands and the Isle of Man) and/or within the Republic of Ireland and that each partner or director of or consultant to such firm is also be insured.

(c) If a Member who is practising solely as a consultant to a firm offering planning services to the public can show:

    (i) that the firm to which he or she is a consultant covers the Member under its policy of insurance; and

    (ii) that such policy of insurance gives no less cover to the Member than that required by these CPII Regulations

Appendix 10

then that Member will not be under an obligation to carry any separate insurance cover over and above that carried by the firm concerned.

3. Minimum limits of indemnity

Subject to regulation 4 the minimum amount of cover required under these CPII Regulations must be:

(a) £100,000 for each and every claim where the gross income of the firm in the preceding year did not exceed £40,000; or

(b) for each and every claim two and a half times the gross income of the firm in the preceding year where that income exceeded £40,000 but did not exceed £200,000; or

(c) £500,000 for each and every claim where the gross income of the firm in the preceding year exceeded £200,000.

4. Uninsured excess

The uninsured excess under any policy of insurance must not normally exceed:

(a) in the case of a policy with a limit of indemnity of up to and including £250,000 a maximum sum of £7,500 each and every claim; or

(b) in the case of a policy with a limit of indemnity of more than £250,000 a maximum of 2.5% of the sum insured or £10,000 each and every claim, whichever shall be the greater.

5. Run-off cover

(a) Expert professional advice should always be sought and followed as to whether run off cover is required in all and any relevant circumstances.

(b) In particular, run off cover (and following expert professional advice in respect of the same) is strongly recommended in the following situations:

   (i) any former partner, director, sole principal or consultant be insured on an each and every claim basis against any claim arising from work previous undertaken for a period of six years from the date when such individual ceased to be a partner, director, sole principal or consultant.

   (ii) any former partner, director, sole principal or consultant of a firm that amalgamates, merges, dissolves or is wound up or otherwise ceases to trade be insured for the six-year period following such amalgamation, merger, dissolution or winding up in compliance with the requirements set out in these CPII Regulations.

   (iii) any Member who has formerly practised as a sole principal and has ceased to do so, for a period of at least six years.

6. Monitoring and return of certificates

(a) Every Member must provide to the Chartered Institute within 28 days of being required by the Chartered Institute to do so, such evidence and in such form as the Board of Trustees will from time to time prescribe either that the Member is not subject to these CPII Regulations or that the Member has complied with them.

RTPI Code of Professional Conduct

7. Exclusion of liability

No Member must be insured under a policy of indemnity insurance which contains an exclusion of liability for claims arising from the Member's previous practice activity unless:

(i) it is limited to claims arising as a result of work undertaken more than six years previously; or

(ii) the same liability is covered by a separate policy of indemnity insurance.

8. Territorial application

Although these CPII Regulations do not require Members to insure in respect of work which is undertaken outside the United Kingdom and/or the Republic of Ireland the Chartered Institute advises Members to obtain the best available cover for all work that they undertake wherever it is undertaken and expects them to abide by the spirit of the Regulations in so far as they are compatible with the laws of the countries in which they undertake work.

9. Effective date

These Regulations shall come into force on 10 February 2016.

ANNEX B: RELEVANT BYELAWS

The Byelaws of the Chartered Institute include the following provisions relating to matters of professional conduct and discipline. Last revised and adopted in 2012.

Conduct of membership

17. The Board of Trustees may issue a code or codes of professional conduct and practice setting out the standards, ethics and professional behaviour expected of Members and may from time to time amend any such code or codes or any part or parts thereof.

18. Every Member shall observe the provisions of the Charter and these Bye-laws and shall conduct him or herself in such a manner as shall not prejudice his or her professional status or the reputation of the Chartered Institute and without prejudice to the generality of the foregoing every Member shall, in particular, comply at all times with any code of professional conduct applicable to his or her category of membership prescribed and published by the Board of Trustees under the provisions of the last preceding Bye-law.

19. Procedures for the conduct of disciplinary proceedings in respect of any complaint made against a Member of any action contrary or prejudicial to the aims, objects and interests of the Chartered Institute or of conduct unbecoming to a Member shall be prescribed by Regulations which shall include power to warn, reprimand, suspend or expel a Member and which shall conform to the principles of natural justice and the Board of Trustees may establish a disciplinary committee and such other committees as it sees fit for the conduct of such procedures.

Termination of membership

20. Membership shall cease forthwith:

Appendix 10

20.1 on receipt by the Chief Executive of notice in writing from the Member of his or her intention to resign provided that if a Member has been notified that an investigation into his or her conduct involving any grounds for disciplinary action is to be conducted in accordance with these Bye-laws or that consideration is being given to such an investigation, his or her resignation shall not prevent the Chartered Institute continuing with disciplinary action relating to conduct before the resignation takes effect.

20.2 if a Member is expelled for non-payment of his or her subscription or otherwise in accordance with Regulations made under Bye-law 19.

20.3 the Board of Trustees may reinstate any Member whose membership has been terminated for any reason, and may cause reinstatement to be subject to previous compliance with such conditions as it may determine, including the payment of subscriptions in arrears and a re-registration fee.

ANNEX C: DISCIPLINARY ACTION

C1. The Chartered Institute will not use its disciplinary procedures to review the decisions of local planning authorities nor to investigate allegations of poor administration on the part of local planning authorities or other organisations.

C2. The Chartered Institute will not normally investigate allegations which fall within the competence of a criminal court, civil court, employment tribunal, Local Government Ombudsman or other duly appointed tribunal. In such cases, however, the Conduct and Discipline Panel reserves the right to consider whether any findings of fact or judgement by the relevant tribunal or court constitute a breach of the Code and if they do and if the Panel so determines to take appropriate disciplinary action.

C3. Where there is a remedy that could reasonably be available to the complainant in civil proceedings the Chartered Institute will initiate its own investigation only after the conclusion of any such proceedings.

Appendix 11

RICS Rules of Conduct for Members

Version 7 with effect from 2 March 2020

INTRODUCTION

The Rules of Conduct for Members apply to all members worldwide. They cover those matters for which individual members are responsible and accountable in their professional lives. The rules focus on our regulatory goals and adopt the five principles of better regulation:

(a) Proportionality

(b) Accountability

(c) Consistency

(d) Targeting

(e) Transparency.

For members requiring further guidance, we have prepared a series of help sheets on different aspects of the rules. These can be found at www.rics.org/regulation.

These Rules provide a strong foundation for RICS and its members, helping to protect the public and uphold the reputation of the profession.

These Rules of Conduct for Members of RICS are made by the Standards and Regulation Board of the Royal Institution of Chartered Surveyors (RICS) under Article 18 of the Supplemental Charter 1973 and Bye-Law 5 of RICS Bye-Laws. Version 7 of these Rules shall apply from 02 March 2020.

SCOPE

These Rules set out the standards of professional conduct and practice expected of Members of RICS. These Rules do not repeat obligations placed on Members by the general law, for example in the areas of discrimination and employment.

Not every shortcoming on the part of a Member, nor failure to comply with these Rules, will necessarily give rise to disciplinary proceedings. However, a failure to follow any guidance associated with the Rules is a factor that will be considered should it be necessary to examine the behaviour of a Member. In such circumstances a Member may be asked to justify the steps they took and this may be taken into account. A Member should be guided as much by the spirit of the Rules as by the express terms.

Appendix 11

PART I   GENERAL

1   Interpretation

In these Rules, unless the context otherwise requires, 'Member' means a Chartered Member, non-Chartered Member, Honorary Member or a member of the attached classes.

2   Communication

RICS will communicate with Members by any of the following:

(a)   post

(b)   fax

(c)   email

(d)   telephone

(e)   in person.

PART II   PERSONAL AND PROFESSIONAL STANDARDS

3   Ethical behaviour

Members shall at all times act with integrity and avoid conflicts of interest and avoid any actions or situations that are inconsistent with their professional obligations.

4   Competence

Members shall carry out their professional work with due skill, care and diligence and with proper regard for the technical standards expected of them.

5   Service

Members shall carry out their professional work in a timely manner and with proper regard for standards of service and customer care expected of them.

6   Continuing Professional Development (CPD)

Members shall comply with RICS' requirements in respect of continuing professional development.

7   Solvency

Members shall ensure that their personal and professional finances are managed appropriately.

8   Information to RICS

Members shall submit in a timely manner such information, and in such form, as the Standards and Regulation Board may reasonably require.

9 Cooperation

Members shall cooperate fully with RICS staff and any person appointed by the Standards and Regulation Board.

CONFIDENCE THROUGH PROFESSIONAL STANDARDS

RICS promotes and enforces the highest professional qualifications and standards in the valuation, development and management of land, real estate, construction and infrastructure. Our name promises the consistent delivery of standards – bringing confidence to markets and effecting positive change in the built and natural environments.

Index

[all references are to paragraph number]

A

Adjournment
  hearings procedure, 6.30
  inquiries procedure, 5.110
Appealable decisions
  generally, 1.07–1.13
Appeals
  See **Planning appeals**
Appellants
  applications and appeals against decisions of Secretary of State, 9.12
  generally, 1.14–1.17
  hearings procedure, 6.07
  inquiries procedure, 5.11
Appearances
  hearings procedure, 6.07
  inquiries procedure, 5.11–5.14
Applications and appeals against decisions of Secretary of State
  appellants, 9.12
  costs, 9.15
  introduction, 9.01
  judicial review
    general right, 9.02–9.03
    permission, 9.05
    time limits, 9.06
  listed buildings orders, 9.04
  local planning authorities, 9.12–9.13
  parties, 9.11–9.14
  permission, 9.05
  persons aggrieved, 9.14
  Planning Court, 9.07–9.10
  right to challenge decisions, 9.02–9.06
  statutory review
    general right, 9.02–9.03
    permission, 9.05
    time limits, 9.06
  time limits, 9.06
  timescales, 9.09
  Transport and Works Act orders, 9.04
  validation provisions, 9.05
  venue, 9.07–9.10

C

'Caborn criteria'
  call-in, and 1.25

Called-in applications
  costs, 8.37
  generally, 1.23–1.26
  inquiries procedure, 5.03–5.06
  introduction, 1.18–1.19
Case management conferences (CMC)
  generally, 4.24–4.33
Closing submissions
  hearings procedure, 6.24
  inquiries procedure, 5.24
Codes of Professional Conduct
  Bar Standards Board, 5.64
  expert evidence, and, 3.34–3.45
  RICS, 3.36
  RTPI, 3.35
Commencement of appeals
  art 37 DMPO 2015, under
    generally, 2.03
    identification of case, 2.06
    requirements, 2.07–2.08
    time limits, 2.03–2.05
  case of parties, 2.06
  'enforcement' appeals, 2.22
  ground of appeal, 2.06
  hearing statements
    generally, 2.51–2.64
    interaction with statements of case, 2.52–2.54
    meaning, 2.55
  infrastructure project inquiries procedure, 2.27
  introduction, 2.01
  mode of appeal, 2.28–2.31
  PINS form, 2.07
  'planning' appeals, 2.21
  practice, in, 2.28–2.31
  procedure rules
    'enforcement' appeals, 2.22
    generally, 2.20–2.27
    'planning' appeals, 2.21
    Wales, 2.24
  reasons for refusal, 2.06
  section 78 TCPA 1990, under
    generally, 2.02
    identification of case, 2.06
    procedure time limits, 2.03–2.05

260

Commencement of appeals – *contd*
  section 78 TCPA 1990, under – *contd*
    time limits, 2.03–2.05
    statements of case
      content, 2.58–2.60
      'enforcement' appeals, 2.65–2.66
      further information, 2.61
      generally, 2.51–2.64
      grounds of appeal, 2.65–2.66
      interaction with hearing statements, 2.52–2.54
      introduction, 2.06
      meaning, 2.56
      mode of appeal, and, 2.30
      practical pointers, 2.67–2.71
    statements of common ground, 2.41–2.50
    statutory basis, 2.02–2.03
    time limits, 2.03–2.05
    timescales, 2.32–2.40
    validation appeals, 2.11–2.19
    Wales, in
      procedure rules, 2.24
      statutory basis, 2.03–2.04
      validation appeals, 2.12

Compulsory purchase order (CPO) appeals
  costs, 8.15–8.17
  inquiries procedure, 5.10

Conditions sessions
  hearings procedure, 6.26–6.29
  inquiries procedure, 5.83–5.85

Core documents
  digital documents, 7.08
  generally, 3.75–3.78
  SoCG Pro Forma, 7.15

Costs
  aims, 8.07–8.09
  amount of award, 8.39–8.40
  analogous Planning Acts orders, 8.18
  applications, 8.23–8.24
  applications and appeals against decisions of Secretary of State, 9.15
  called-in applications, 8.37
  challenges to decisions, 8.05
  compulsory purchase appeals, 8.15–8.17
  default position, 8.06
  detailed assessment, 8.40
  discretion to award, 8.03–8.04
  examples of decisions, 8.29–8.36
  guidance, 8.25–8.28
  highways appeals, 8.19
  interested parties, 8.38
  jurisdiction, 8.11–8.21
  lawfulness of decisions, 8.05
  legal basis, 8.01–8.06
  listed buildings appeals, 8.18
  nature, 8.11–8.21

Costs – *contd*
  NPPG, 8.25–8.28
  objectives, 8.07–8.09
  'planning' appeals, 8.12–8.14
  power to award
    procedure, 8.22
    statutory basis, 8.01–8.02
  procedure, 8.22–8.24
  purpose, 8.10
  quantum, 8.39–8.40
  scope, 8.11–8.21
  unreasonable behaviour, 8.20–8.21

Covid-19 pandemic
  generally, 7.02
  issues and objectives, 7.05
  Written Ministerial Statement, 7.03–7.04

Cross examination
  BSB Handbook, 5.64
  conduct, 5.53–5.64
  generally, 5.41–5.44
  Inspector's questions, and, 5.73
  parameters, 5.65–5.72
  purpose, 5.45–5.52
  refusal to permit, 5.42
  right, 5.41
  third party questions, and, 5.74

D

Deadlines
  hearings procedure, 4.13–4.15
  written representations, 4.10–4.12

Detailed assessment
  costs, 8.40

Digital documents
  generally, 7.06–7.16
  summary, 7.05
  use, 10.02–10.05
  Written Ministerial Statement, 7.03

Discretion
  costs, 8.03–8.04

E

Enforcement appeals
  hearings procedure, 6.02–6.04
  inquiries procedure, 5.07
  meaning, 2.22
  procedure rules, 2.20
  timescales 2.32

Evidence in writing
  See also **Oral evidence**
  achieving objectives
    effectiveness of evidence, 3.49–3.71
    introduction, 3.03
    permissible evidence, 3.34–3.45
    usability of evidence, 3.72–3.83
  audience, 3.27–3.33

Index

Evidence in writing – *contd*
balance of planning considerations, 3.08–3.11
brevity, 3.49–3.50
case example, 3.15–3.23
Codes of Professional Conduct, 3.34–3.45
core documents, 3.75–3.78
documentation in support, 3.24–3.26
drafting documentation
  brevity, 3.49–3.50
  facts, assessment and opinions, 3.58–3.65
  issues within issues, 3.65–3.71
  structure, 3.51–3.57
effectiveness of evidence, 3.49–3.71
facts, assessment and opinions, 3.58–3.65
factual features of proposal, 3.08
fee agreements, 3.46–3.48
format of evidence
  core documents, 3.75–3.78
  generally, 3.72–3.73
  summary proofs, 3.79–3.83
identification of issues
  case example, 3.15–3.23
  main issues, 3.04–3.07
  positive case by appellant, 3.08–3.11
  other issues, 3.12–3.14
introduction, 3.01–3.03
issues within issues, 3.65–3.71
opinions, 3.58–3.65
other issues, 3.12–3.14
permissible evidence, 3.34–3.45
policy features of proposal, 3.08
positive case by appellant, 3.08–3.11
practicality of evidence
  core documents, 3.75–3.78
  format, 3.72–3.73
  summary proofs, 3.79–3.83
professional duties of experts, 3.34–3.45
RISC Rules, 3.35–3.36
RTPI Rules, 3.35–3.36
scope and objective
  audience, 3.27–3.33
  identification of issues, 3.04–3.07
  introduction, 3.02
  supporting documentation, 3.24–3.26
specialist topics, 3.27–3.28
structure, 3.51–3.57
summary proofs, 3.79–3.83
supporting documentation, 3.24–3.26
third party evidence
  Codes of Professional Conduct, 3.34–3.45
  fee agreements, 3.46–3.48
utility of evidence
  core documents, 3.75–3.78

Evidence in writing – *contd*
utility of evidence – *contd*
  format, 3.72–3.73
  summary proofs, 3.79–3.83
Evidence in chief
inquiries procedure, 5.29–5.40
Exchange of evidence
hearings procedure, 6.17

F

Fee agreements
expert evidence, and, 3.46–3.48
Franks Committee
Administrative Tribunals and Inquiries, 5.90–5.91

G

Ground of appeal
enforcement notices, and, 2.06

H

Hearing statements
generally, 2.51–2.64
interaction with statements of case, 2.52–2.54
meaning, 2.55
Hearings procedure
See also **Written evidence**
adjournment, 6.30
agenda, 6.20
appearances, 6.07
closing submissions, 6.24
conditions 'sessions', 6.26–6.29
conduct of proceedings
  duty of inspector, 6.11–6.16
  features, 6.09
  inquisitorial nature, 6.10
  introduction, 6.08
  late evidence, 6.17
dates, 6.05–6.06
deadlines, 4.13–4.15
duty of inspector, 6.11–6.16
'enforcement' appeals, 6.02
exchange of evidence, 6.17
format, 6.19–6.25
inquiries, and, 6.01
inquisitorial nature, 6.10
introduction, 6.01
late evidence, 6.17–6.18
listed buildings appeals, 6.02
notifications, 6.05–6.06
opening procedure, 6.19
'planning' appeals, 6.02
planning conditions, 6.26–6.29
procedure rules
  generally, 6.02–6.03
  introduction, 2.20

Index

Hearings procedure – *contd*
procedure rules – *contd*
Wales, 6.04
right to be heard, 6.11–6.15
section 78 TCPA 1990 appeals, 6.02
site view, 6.27–6.32
summary of cases by Inspector, 6.19
telephone hearings procedure, 6.22
video hearings procedure, 6.22
Highways appeals
costs, 8.19
inquiries procedure, 5.08

I

Infrastructure project inquiries procedure
commencement, 2.27
Inquiries procedure
See also **Written evidence**
adjournment, 5.110
appellants, 5.11
appearances, 5.11–5.14
call-ins, for, 5.03–5.06
closing submissions, 5.24
compulsory purchase orders, 5.10
conduct of inquiry, 5.15–5.24
costs
aims, 8.07–8.09
amount of award, 8.39–8.40
analogous Planning Acts orders, 8.18
applications, 8.23–8.24
called-in applications, 8.37
compulsory purchase appeals, 8.15–8.17
detailed assessment, 8.40
examples of decisions, 8.29–8.36
guidance, 8.25–8.28
highways appeals, 8.19
interested parties, 8.38
jurisdiction, 8.11–8.21
legal basis, 8.01–8.06
listed buildings appeals, 8.18
nature, 8.11–8.21
NPPG, 8.25–8.28
'planning' appeals, 8.12–8.14
power to award, 8.22
procedure, 8.22–8.24
purpose, 8.10
quantum, 8.39–8.40
scope, 8.11–8.21
unreasonable behaviour, 8.20–8.21
cross examination
BSB Handbook, 5.64
conduct, 5.53–5.64
generally, 5.41–5.44
Inspector's questions, and, 5.73
parameters, 5.65–5.72

Inquiries procedure – *contd*
cross examination – *contd*
purpose, 5.45–5.52
refusal to permit, 5.42
right, 5.41
third party questions, and, 5.74
'enforcement' appeals, 5.07
evidence in chief, 5.29–5.40
hearings, and, 6.01
highways, 5.08
inquiry room, 5.105–5.106
interested persons, 5.102–5.104
introduction, 5.01–5.02
local planning authorities, 5.11
opening statements, 5.15–5.19
oral evidence
chief, in, 5.29–5.40
cross-examination, 5.41–5.72
generally, 5.25–5.27
Inspector's questions, 5.73
re-examination, 5.75–5.82
third party questions, 5.74
persons entitled to appear, 5.11–5.14
'planning' appeals, for, 5.03–5.06
planning conditions 'session', 5.83–5.85
planning obligations, 5.84, 5.86
practice
inquiry room, 5.105–5.106
interested persons, 5.102–5.104
language, 5.107–5.109
procedural fairness, 5.90–5.101
procedure rules, 2.20
purpose, 5.01
re-examination, 5.75–5.82
Rule 6 status, 5.11
section 78 TCPA 1990, under, 5.03–5.06
section 106 TCPA 1990 deeds, 5.84, 5.86
site visits, 5.87–5.89
statutory parties, 5.11
structure, 5.15–5.24
timescales 2.32
Transport and Works Act 1992, under, 5.08–5.09
types, 5.03–5.10
venue, 5.105–5.106
Welsh language, 5.107–5.109
Inquisitorial proceedings
hearings procedure, 6.10
Inspectors
audience, 3.27–3.28
discretion, 1.06
Interest in land
appellants, and 1.14–1.16
Interested persons
costs, 8.38
inquiries procedure, 5.102–5.104

Index

J

Judicial review
general right, 9.02–9.03
introduction, 1.04
permission, 9.05
time limits, 9.06

L

Late evidence
hearings procedure, 6.17–6.18
Listed buildings orders
applications and appeals against decisions of Secretary of State, 9.04
costs, 8.18
hearings procedure, 6.02
Local inquiries procedure
See also **Inquiries procedure**
generally, 1.10–1.13
Local planning authorities
applications and appeals against decisions of Secretary of State, 9.12–9.13
hearings procedure, 6.07
inquiries procedure, 5.11

M

Management of appeals
See also **Case management**
case management conferences, 4.24–4.33
deadlines
  hearings procedure, 4.13–4.15
  written representations, 4.10–4.12
effective and efficient conduct, 4.34–4.41
introduction, 4.01–4.05
Planning Inspectorate role, 4.04
pre-inquiry engagement, 4.22
Rosewell Review, and
  case management conferences, 4.24–4.33
  considerations, 4.17
  effective and efficient conduct, 4.34–4.41
  introduction, 4.02
  recommendations, 4.18–4.23
  scope, 4.16
  timetable, 4.08
telephone hearings procedure, 4.23
timetable, 4.06–4.08
Mode of appeal
See also **Rosewell Review**
criteria, 2.37
generally, 2.28–2.31
variation, 2.34, 6.10

N

National Planning Practice Guidance (NPPG)
costs, 8.25–8.28

National Planning Practice Guidance (NPPG) – *contd*
purpose of appeals, and, 1.01
transparency, 10.11
Notifications
hearings procedure, 6.05–6.06

O

Opening statements
hearings procedure, 6.19
inquiries procedure, 5.15–5.19
Oral evidence
chief, in, 5.29–5.40
cross-examination
  BSB Handbook, 5.64
  conduct, 5.53–5.64
  generally, 5.41–5.44
  Inspector's questions, and, 5.73
  parameters, 5.65–5.72
  purpose, 5.45–5.52
  refusal to permit, 5.42
  right, 5.41
  third party questions, and, 5.74
generally, 5.25–5.27
Inspector's questions, 5.73
re-examination, 5.75–5.82
third party questions, 5.74

P

Parties
applicants, 1.14–1.17
applications and appeals against decisions of Secretary of State, 9.11–9.14
hearings procedure, 6.07
inquiries procedure, 5.11–5.
recovery by Secretary of State
  generally, 1.20–1.22
  introduction, 1.18–1.19
Permission
applications and appeals against decisions of Secretary of State, 9.05
Persons aggrieved
applications and appeals against decisions of Secretary of State, 9.14
applications and appeals against decisions of Secretary of State, 9.12
costs, 9.15
judicial review
  general right, 9.02–9.03
  permission, 9.05
  time limits, 9.06
listed buildings orders, 9.04
local planning authorities, 9.12–9.13
parties, 9.11–9.14
permission, 9.05
persons aggrieved, 9.14
Planning Court, 9.07–9.10

264

Persons aggrieved – *contd*
  statutory review
    general right, 9.02–9.03
    permission, 9.05
    time limits, 9.06
  time limits, 9.06
  timescales, 9.09
  Transport and Works Act orders, 9.04
  validation provisions, 9.05
  venue, 9.07–9.10

Planning appeals
  appealable decisions, 1.07–1.13
  appellants, 1.14–1.17
  call-in, and
    generally, 1.23–1.26
    introduction, 1.18–1.19
  commencement, 2.01–2.71
  management, 4.01–4.41
  meaning, 1.02–1.06
  parties
    applicants, 1.14–1.17
    Secretary of State, 1.18–1.22
  purpose, 1.01
  recovery by Secretary of State
    generally, 1.20–1.22
    introduction, 1.18–1.19
  relevant decisions and determinations, 1.07–1.13
  rights, 1.08–1.09
  scope, 1.01–1.26
  source, 1.07–1.13
  use, 1.02–1.06
  written evidence, 3.01–3.83

Planning conditions
  hearings procedure, 6.26–6.29
  inquiries procedure, 5.83–5.85

Planning Court
  applications and appeals against decisions of Secretary of State, 9.07–9.10

Planning obligations
  inquiries procedure, 5.84, 5.86

Procedural fairness
  inquiries procedure, 5.90–5.101

Re-examination
  inquiries procedure, 5.75–5.82

Pre-inquiry engagement
  generally, 4.22

Professional teams
  generally, 10.21–10.25

Publicity and community engagement
  remote events, 7.03

Procedure rules
  'enforcement' appeals, 2.22
  generally, 2.20–2.27
  'planning' appeals, 2.21
  Wales, 2.24

R

Recovery by Secretary of State
  generally, 1.20–1.22
  introduction, 1.18–1.19

Remote events
  Covid-19 pandemic, and
    generally, 7.02
    issues and objectives, 7.05
    Written Ministerial Statement, 7.03–7.04
  digital documents, 7.06–7.16
  introduction, 7.01
  issues 7.01–7.05
  publicity and community engagement, 7.03
  Rosewell Review, 7.04
  site visits, 7.23–7.24
  virtual events, 7.17–7.22
  Written Ministerial Statement, 7.03

RICS Rules
  expert evidence, and, 3.35–3.36

Right to be heard
  hearings procedure, 6.11–6.15

Rights of appeal
  generally, 1.08–1.09

Rosewell Review
  case management conferences, 4.24–4.33
  considerations, 4.17
  effective and efficient conduct, 4.34–4.41
  introduction, 4.02
  recommendations, 4.18–4.23
  remote events, 7.04
  scope, 4.16
  timetable, 4.08

RTPI Rules
  expert evidence, and, 3.35–3.36

Rule 6 status
  comparison to third parties generally, 5.74
  costs, 8.38
  definition, 2.64
  inquiries procedure, 5.11

S

Secretary of State
  applications and appeals against decisions
    costs, 9.15
    introduction, 9.01
    parties, 9.11–9.14
    right to challenge decisions, 9.02–9.06
    timescales, 9.09
    venue, 9.07–9.10
  called-in applications
    generally, 1.23–1.26
    introduction, 1.18–1.19
  recovery by
    generally, 1.20–1.22
    introduction, 1.18–1.19

Index

Secretary of State – *contd*
  statutory powers 1.05
Section 78 TCPA 1990 appeals
  commencement
    generally, 2.02
    identification of case, 2.06
    procedure time limits, 2.03–2.05
    time limits, 2.03–2.05
  costs, 8.12–8.14
  hearings procedure, 6.02
  inquiries procedure, 5.03–5.06
Section 106 TCPA 1990 agreements
  inquiries procedure, 5.84, 5.86
Section 288 TCPA 1990 appeals
  generally, 9.03
Site visits
  generally, 7.23–7.24
  hearings procedure, 6.27–6.32
  inquiries procedure, 5.87–5.89
  summary, 7.05
  Written Ministerial Statement and social distancing, 7.03
Statements of case
  content, 2.58–2.60
  'enforcement' appeals, 2.65–2.66
  further information, 2.61
  generally, 2.51–2.64
  grounds of appeal, 2.65–2.66
  interaction with hearing statements, 2.52–2.54
  introduction, 2.06
  meaning, 2.56
  mode of appeal, and, 2.30
  practical pointers, 2.67–2.71
Statements of common ground
  generally, 2.41–2.50
Statutory parties
  inquiries procedure, 5.11
Statutory review
  general right, 9.02–9.03
  permission, 9.05
  time limits, 9.06
Summary proofs
  written evidence, and, 3.79–3.83

T

Telephone hearings
  generally, 4.23
  hearings procedure, 6.22
  use, 10.06–10.09
Third party evidence
  Codes of Professional Conduct, 3.34–3.45
  fee agreements, 3.46–3.48
Time limits
  applications and appeals against decisions of Secretary of State, 9.06

Time limits – *contd*
  commencement, 2.03–2.05
Timescales
  applications and appeals against decisions of Secretary of State, 9.09
  commencement, 2.32–2.40
Timetable
  generally, 4.06–4.08
Transparency
  generally, 10.10–10.20
Transport and Works Act 1992 orders
  applications and appeals against decisions of Secretary of State, 9.04
  inquiries procedure, 5.08–5.09

U

Unreasonable behaviour
  costs, 8.20–8.21

V

Validation
  applications and appeals against decisions of Secretary of State, 9.05
  commencement, 2.11–2.19
Venue
  applications and appeals against decisions of Secretary of State, 9.07–9.10
  inquiries procedure, 5.105–5.106
Video hearings
  hearings procedure, 6.22
  use, 10.06–10.09
Virtual events
  generally, 7.17–7.22
  summary, 7.05
  Written Ministerial Statement, 7.03

W

Wales
  commencement
    procedure rules, 2.24
    statutory basis, 2.03–2.04
    validation appeals, 2.12
Welsh language
  inquiries procedure, 5.107–5.109
Written evidence
  achieving objectives
    effectiveness of evidence, 3.49–3.71
    introduction, 3.03
    permissible evidence, 3.34–3.45
    usability of evidence, 3.72–3.83
  audience, 3.27–3.33
  balance of planning considerations, 3.08–3.11
  brevity, 3.49–3.50
  case example, 3.15–3.23
  Codes of Professional Conduct, 3.34–3.45

Written evidence – *contd*
  core documents, 3.75–3.78
  documentation in support, 3.24–3.26
  drafting documentation
    brevity, 3.49–3.50
    facts, assessment and opinions, 3.58–3.65
    issues within issues, 3.65–3.71
    structure, 3.51–3.57
  effectiveness of evidence, 3.49–3.71
  facts, assessment and opinions, 3.58–3.65
  factual features of proposal, 3.08
  fee agreements, 3.46–3.48
  format of evidence
    core documents, 3.75–3.78
    generally, 3.72–3.73
    summary proofs, 3.79–3.83
  identification of issues
    case example, 3.15–3.23
    main issues, 3.04–3.07
    positive case by appellant, 3.08–3.11
    other issues, 3.12–3.14
  introduction, 3.01–3.03
  issues within issues, 3.65–3.71
  opinions, 3.58–3.65
  other issues, 3.12–3.14
  permissible evidence, 3.34–3.45
  policy features of proposal, 3.08
  positive case by appellant, 3.08–3.11

Written evidence – *contd*
  practicality of evidence
    core documents, 3.75–3.78
    format, 3.72–3.73
    summary proofs, 3.79–3.83
  professional duties of experts, 3.34–3.45
  RISC Rules, 3.35–3.36
  RTPI Rules, 3.35–3.36
  scope and objective
    audience, 3.27–3.33
    identification of issues, 3.04–3.07
    introduction, 3.02
    supporting documentation, 3.24–3.26
  specialist topics, 3.27–3.28
  structure, 3.51–3.57
  summary proofs, 3.79–3.83
  supporting documentation, 3.24–3.26
  third party evidence
    Codes of Professional Conduct, 3.34–3.45
    fee agreements, 3.46–3.48
  utility of evidence
    core documents, 3.75–3.78
    format, 3.72–3.73
    summary proofs, 3.79–3.83
Written representations
  See also **Written evidence**
  deadlines, 4.10–4.12
  procedure rules, 2.20
  timescales 2.32